# A Strange and
# Unquenchable Race

## CORNWALL AND THE CORNISH
## IN QUOTATIONS

compiled by
DEREK R. WILLIAMS

ISBN 978 185022 205 7

Published by Truran, Croft Prince, Mount Hawke,
Truro, Cornwall TR4 8EE
www.truranbooks.co.uk

Truran is an imprint of Truran Books Ltd

Compilation © Derek R. Williams 2007
Cover photograph © Phil Monckton CLoSP

Printed and bound in Cornwall by R. Booth Ltd,
Antron Hill, Mabe, Penryn, TR10 9HH

### Acknowledgements

The author thanks Donald Rawe for reading the manuscript and for making useful suggestions.

The author and publishers thank the following for giving permission to quote: Bert Biscoe, Sarah Foot, Michael Tangye, David St John Thomas, Bernard Deacon, Ken George, Donald Rawe, Roger Burt, Annette Egerton (David Penhaligon), Howard Curnow, Brendon McMahon, Alan M. Kent, Mark Stoyle, Simon Parker, Graham Sandercock, Wella Brown, Charles Thomas, Frank Ruhrmund, Ann Trevenen Jenkin, James Whetter, Richard Gendall, Philip Payton, Audrey Randle Pool, Mrs R. G. Clemo (Jack Clemo), Carcanet Press Ltd (Hugh MacDiarmid), Joan Douch (HL Douch), Tangye Estate (Derek Tangye), Society of Authors (Quentin Bell, Virginia Woolf), Julia Berlin (Sven Berlin), Curtis Brown Group Ltd, London on behalf of the Estate of Elizabeth Bowen, David Highham Associates Ltd (Charles Causley, John Heath-Stubbs, Jill Paton Walsh), Harper Collins Publishers Ltd (Nick Danziger), Robin Ilbert (H. A. L. Fisher), Sebastian Halliday (F. E. Halliday), Mrs S. M. Lanyon (Peter Lanyon), David Mudd, R. Morton Nance Estate, Yale University Press (Nikolaus Pevsner), Mrs G. F. Symondson (Quiller-Couch), Johnson and Alcock Ltd (A. L. Rowse), Nicholas Dowler (Malcolm Saville), Martin Val Baker (Denys Val Baker), Cecil W. T. Gray Testamentary Trust (Cecil Gray/Peter Warlock), Michael Williams, Random House Group Ltd (Virginia Woolf), Curtis Brown Group Ltd, London (Angela and Daphne du Maurier).

Every effort has been made to contact copyright holders and we apolgise for any omissions.

# CONTENTS

# PREFACE

Thirty years ago the late Len Truran, publisher and Cornish patriot, wrote: 'Cornwall was a Country, it is a Country and will be a Country as long as there are Cornish people who assert their historic nationhood.' Just over seventy years earlier Henry Jenner and others had been instrumental in kick-starting the movement to rouse Cornish people from a perceived indifference to their own past and culture, only for the attempt to stall, largely as a result of the homogenization engendered by two world wars. In the 1950s the Cornish Movement gathered momentum again until, at the beginning of the 21st century, widespread support for the campaign to establish a Cornish Assembly and the decision by the British government to include Cornish in the European Charter for Regional or Minority Languages seemed between them to suggest a breakthrough. As can be seen from many of the quotations in this book, Cornwall was a nation and is still a nation for many Cornish patriots. Whether or not she will continue to be a nation in an increasingly homogenized world and whether she will enjoy a wider recognition of her 'special' status is, as Len Truran maintained, in the hands of loyal Cornish folk in Cornwall, beyond the Tamar and across the globe.

Two factors have been instrumental in the compiling of A Strange and Unquenchable Race, the title of which is taken from R. Thurstan Hopkins' Cornwall (quotation 712). First and foremost, in November 1988, the first batch of Tom Tucker's 'Tyscasow Kernewek' ('Cornish Gleanings') appeared in An Baner Kernewek/The Cornish Banner. Heading that initial selection was, appropriately enough, Leslie Rowse's sparkling statement: 'Cornwall has a quite exceptional capacity to draw and retain the hearts of its children, wherever they may be.' Although his paternal grandfather, William T. Tucker, left the homeland for Canada in the early 1900s, Tom has retained an abiding awareness of his Cornishness and can trace his ancestors back to the Grampound area nearly three hundred years earlier. His 'gleanings' still appear regularly in An Baner Kernewek and continue to be a source of inspiration.

The second factor in the gestation of this collection was my discovery of Meic Stephens' A Most Peculiar People: quotations about Wales and the Welsh, in which nationality and nationhood figure prominently. "Why not make Cornwall and the Cornish the subject of a similar collection, itself underpinned by our own sense of difference and identity?" I asked myself.

Since then I have been amassing quotations from a wide variety of sources, sometimes conscientiously, sometimes not – hence my inability in a few instances to provide a source. Whilst the chronological arrangement – from Diodorus Siculus, c. 44BC through to the Simpsons at the end of 2004 – reveals at a glance important events in Cornwall's history, the accompanying subject index allows the reader to search for specific themes – from the Cornish character to the Cornish chough and from Wesleyan Methodists to wreckers. As I have already indicated, many of the quotations are concerned with how others see Cornwall and the Cornish and with how we see ourselves, hence the large number of entries under such headings as "territorial status", "difference" and "national identity". Cornwall's ties with the other Celtic nations have also proved a rich seam.

Given his ability to express himself in a forthright and succinct manner, it is not surprising that there are more quotations from A. L. Rowse than from anyone else. For him Cornwall was, as it is for me, "the obsession that awaits ... around the corner".

# NOTES FOR THE READER

The numbered quotations – 1,267 in all – are arranged in chronological order. An asterisk indicates that the quotation has been translated from another language, usually Latin, French or, occasionally, Cornish. Within each year there is a further chronological arrangement by date where this is known. The date given is usually that of the first published appearance, although in instances where the quotation is taken from traditional sources, the years during which the events were said to have taken place are preferred. Where known, a source is specified; where I have not seen the primary source, a secondary one is , in nearly all circumstnces, given in square brackets. Authors quoted are listed in a separate index on page 197. Where the author is unknown, as is sometimes the case with quotations from newspapers or from an anonymous book, the newspaper or book title is listed in the author index. A detailed subject index can be found on page 205. I have standardized the spelling used in early quotations, except for placenames, which I have retained in their original form out of historical interest.

# CORNWALL AND THE CORNISH IN QUOTATIONS

## c. 44 BC

1 The people of that promontory of Britain called Belerion [Penwith] are friendly to strangers and, from their contact with foreign merchants, are civilised in their way of life. They carefully work the ground from which they extract the tin. *

> **Diodorus Siculus**, Bibliotheke Historike, c. 44 BC [Craig Weatherhill, Belerion: ancient sites of Land's End, 1981]

## 813AD

2 This year ... King Egbert spread devastation in Cornwall from east to west. *

> Entry for 813, **Anglo-Saxon Chronicle** [Britannia's online version of Everyman edition, 1912]

## 825

3 This year a battle was fought between the Welsh in Cornwall and the people of Devonshire, at Camelford ... *

> Entry for 825, **Anglo-Saxon Chronicle** [Britannia's online version of Everyman edition, 1912]

## 838

4 This year came a great naval armament into West-Wales [Cornwall], where they were joined by the people, who commenced war against Egbert, the West-Saxon king. When he heard this, he proceeded with his army against them and fought with them at Hengeston where he put to flight both the Welsh [Cornish] and the Danes. *

> Entry for 838, **Anglo-Saxon Chronicle** [Britannia's online version of Everyman edition, 1912]

## c. 850–870

5 I, Kenstec, bishop-elect to the nation of Cornwall in the monastery which

in the British language is called Dinurrin [Bodmin] ... *

**Part of Bishop Kenstec's submission to the see of Canterbury,**
c.850–870 [H. Miles Brown, *The Church in Cornwall*, 1964]

## c. 850

6 ... the power of the Irish over Britain was great, and they divided Britain
between them into estates ... and the Irish lived as much east of the sea as they
did in Ireland and their dwellings and their royal fortresses were made there ...
[including] Dind map Lethain, that is Dun maic Liathain, in the lands of the
Cornish Britons. *

**Cormac of Cashel,** *Glossary*, c. 850 [Susan M. Pearce, *The Kingdom of
Dumnonia*, 1978]

## 875

7 Dungarth king of Cernyw (that is of the Cornish) was drowned. *

***Annales Cambriae***, 875 [Medieval Source Book online version of
Everyman edition, 1912]

## 909

8 [The three estates of Pawton, Caellwic and Lanwithan established by King
Egbert were transferred to Eadulf, Bishop of Crediton] that he might visit the
Cornish people to extirpate their errors. For in times past, as far as possible,
they resisted the truth and were not obedient to the apostolical decrees [of the
Roman Church]. *

**Decree of Edward "the Elder",** 909 [Brown, 1964]

## 926

9 ... King Athelstan took to the kingdom of Northumbria, and governed all
the kings that were in this island ... First, Howel, King of West-Wales
[Cornwall] ... And with covenants and oaths they ratified their agreement ...
on the fourth day before the ides of July, and renounced all idolatry, and
afterwards returned in peace. *

Entry for 926, ***Anglo-Saxon Chronicle***

## c. 930

10      Hosts will come.
        We shall possess riches
        Prosperity and peace;
        Generous rulers, benevolent lords;
        And, after disruption, the region settled.

Fierce men, wrathful, mighty
Bold in combat, angry, powerful,
As far as Caer Weir will rout their foes.
Celebration follows devastation,
Agreement between Prydein and Dublin;
Ireland, Mon, Scotland, Cornwall
At one in their endeavour.

**Armes Prydein** ('Prophecy of Britain'), c. 930 [ms. c. 1275] [*The Celtic Seers' Source Book*, ed. John Matthews, 1999]

## 981

11 In this year was St. Petroc's-stow plundered; and in the same year was much harm done everywhere by the sea-coast, both upon Devonshire and Wales [Cornwall]. *

Entry for 981, **Anglo-Saxon Chronicle**

## 994

12 ... the province of Cornwall. *
**Ethelred's Charter**, 994

## 1125

13 [Athelstan] attacked them [the Cornish] with great energy, compelling them to withdraw from Exeter which until that time they had inhabited on a footing of legal equality with the English. He then fixed the left bank of the Tamar as the shore boundary... Having cleansed the city if its defilement by wiping out that filthy race, he fortified it with towers and surrounded it with a wall of square-hewn stone. *

**Wiliam of Malmesbury**, *Gesta Regum Anglorum*, 1125 [Pearce, 1978]

## 12th century

14 He [Heilyn son of Gwynn] opened the door and looked out at the Bristol Channel and Cornwall, and as he did so they all became as conscious of every loss they had suffered, of every friend and relative they had lost, of every ill that had befallen them, as if it had all just happened ...

**The Mabinogion**, 12th century, translated by Jeffrey Gantz, 1976

15 ... [for the qualities of ignorance and boorishness] always look on Cornish men as we in France consider our Flemings ...

**Richard of Devizes**, 12th century [Mark Stoyle, *West Britons*, 2002]

# c. 1136

16 Corineus ... called the region of the kingdom [Britain] which had fallen to his share Cornwall, after the manner of his own name, and the people who lived there he called Cornishmen. Although he might have chosen his own estates before all the others who had come there, he preferred the region which is now called Cornwall, either for its being the *cornu* or horn of Britain, or through a corruption of his own name. *

> **Geoffrey of Monmouth**, *The History of the Kings of Britain*, c.1136 [1966]

17 They [the Saxons] landed in parts of Northumbria and occupied the waste lands from Albany [Scotland] to Cornwall. *

> **Geoffrey of Monmouth**, *The History of the Kings of Britain*, c.1136 [1966]

18 The race that is oppressed shall prevail in the end, for it will resist the savagery of the invaders. The Boar of Cornwall [Arthur] shall bring relief from these invaders, for it will trample their necks beneath its feet. *

> **Geoffrey of Monmouth**, 'The Prophecies of Merlin', in *The History of the Kings of Britain*

19 The mountains of Armorica shall erupt and Armorica itself shall be crowned with Brutus' diadem. Kambria shall be filled with joy and the Cornish oaks shall flourish. *

> **Geoffrey of Monmouth**, 'The Prophecies of Merlin', in *The History of the Kings of Britain*

20 The Daneian Forest shall be wakened from its sleep and, bursting into human speech, it shall shout: "Kambria, come here! Bring Cornwall at your side!" *

> **Geoffrey of Monmouth**, 'The Prophecies of Merlin', in *The History of the Kings of Britain*

21 A wolf will act as standard-bearer and lead the troops, and it will coil its tail around Cornwall. A soldier in a chariot will resist the wolf and transform the Cornish people into a Boar. As a result the Boar will devastate the provinces, but it will hide its head in the depths of the Severn. *

> **Geoffrey of Monmouth**, 'The Prophecies of Merlin', in *The History of the Kings of Britain*

# 1133–89

22 [Cornwall is] the fagg end [backside] of the world.

> **A versifier at the court of Henry II**, 1133–89 [Stoyle, 2002]

## c. 1148

23 ... it is the will of the highest Judge that the Britons shall through weakness lose their noble kingdom for a long time, until Conan shall come in his chariot from Brittany, and Cadwalader the venerated leader of the Welsh, who shall join together Scots and Cumbrians, Cornishmen and men of Brittany in a firm league, and shall return to their people their lost crown, expelling the enemy and renewing the times of Brutus ...

**Geoffrey of Monmouth**, *Vita Merlini*, c.1148 [Matthews, 1999]

## c. 1173

24 Reginald son of the King, Earl of Cornwall to all the Barons of Cornwall and to all knights and to all freeholders and to all men both Cornish and English, greeting. *

**Earl Reginald**, in a charter granted to the Burgesses of Truro, c1173

## c. 1188

25 On his return from Ireland, on the first Saturday after Easter [1172], Henry II, king of the English, spent the night in this same town of Cardiff. He heard Mass on the Sunday morning. When the service was over, all those present left Saint Piran's chapel, except the King himself, who stayed behind at his devotions longer than usual. *

**Gerald of Wales**, *The Journey through Wales*, c.1188

26 In both Cornwall and Brittany they speak almost the same language as in Wales. It comes from the same root and is intelligible to the Welsh in many instances, and almost in all. *

**Gerald of Wales**, *The Journey through Wales*, c.1188

27 Those [Britons] who retreated to the southern corner of the island could not continue their resistance, for their territory has no natural protection. It is called Cornwall after their leader Corineus. *

**Gerald of Wales**, *The Journey through Wales*, c.1188

## 1201

28 ... we have granted that all our tinners in Cornwall and Devon shall be free, and quit of pleas of natives (bondmen), whilst they work to the advantage of our farm, or for the increase of our new rent of marks, because the stannaries are our demesnes ... We have granted also that the chief custos (warden) of the stannaries, and his bailiffs for him, shall have over the aforesaid tinners full power to judge ... *

King John, *Charter of Liberties to the Tinners of Cornwall and Devon,* 1201 [J. A. Buckley, *Medieval Cornish Stannary Charters,* 2001]

## mid 13th century

29    'Tis not worth while her [Cornwall's] worth here to recount
Her quick relief of the poor to great amount
In fish and tin she knows no rival coast. *
**Michael Blakenpayne,** mid 13th century

## 14th century

30 Cornewayle is in Engelonde and is departed in hundreds, and is ruled by the law of Engelonde, and holds shire and shire days as other shires do.
**John Trevisa,** 14th century [Stoyle, 2002]

## 1305

31 We will, moreover, and firmly command that all the tin, as well white as black, wheresoever it shall be found and wrought in the county aforesaid, shall be weighed at Lostwythiel, Bodmynyan, Liskeret, Trevern (Truro), or Helleston, by our weights for this ordered and signed, upon forfeiture of all the tin aforesaid …
**Edward I,** *Charter of Liberties to the Tinners of Cornwall,* 1305 [Buckley, 2001]

## 1327

32 [Cornwall is] … not only the ends of the earth, but the very ends of the ends thereof. *
**John de Grandisson, Bishop of Exeter,** *Register,* 1327 [Philip Payton, *The Making of Modern Cornwall,* 1993]

## 1328–9

33 … moreover, the language found in the extreme part of Cornwall is not English, but British. *
**John de Grandisson, Bishop of Exeter,** *Register,* 1328/9 [Crysten Fudge, *The Life of Cornish,* 1982]

## 1336

34 … most of the said parishioners gave their promise in English or French, but others who only knew the Cornish language, in Cornish, which the said interpreter translated to the said father. *
**John de Grandisson, Bishop of Exeter,** *Register,* 1336

## 1337

35 [We are advancing] ... our most dear first begotten Edward ... to be Duke of Cornwall, over which awhile ago Dukes for a long time successively presided as chief rulers.

**Edward III**, 1337 [Payton, 1993]

## 1339

36 [Under the terms of a licence granted to J. Polmarke, he was] to expound the word of God in the said church [St. Merryn] in the Cornish language. *

**John de Grandisson, Bishop of Exeter**, *Register*, 1339

## c. 1342

37 ... though Alfred of Beverley has said previously that Cornwall is not classified amongst the shires of England, it is quite proper to classify it amongst them, because it belongs neither to Wales nor to Scotland, but is in England, adjoining Devonshire. *

**Ralph/Ranulph Higden**, *Polychronicon*, c.1342 [English translation by John Trevisa, printed by Caxton as *The Description of Britain* in 1482]

## 1342

38 ... the folk of these parts are quite extraordinary, being of a rebellious temper and obdurate in the face of attempts to teach and correct.

**Adam de Carleton, Archdeacon of Cornwall**, 1342 [Stoyle, 2002]

## 1352

39 [Ascertain which of the lands under your jurisdiction are] held by the men of Cornewaille and England.

**Edward the Black Prince**, in a letter to the Sheriff of Cornwall in 1352 [Stoyle, 2002]

## 1422

40 ... the County of Cornwall should always remain as a Duchy to the eldest sons of the King of England ...

**Parliament of Henry V**, 1422 [Payton, 1993]

## 1478

41 [The River Tamar marks the boundary] of the County and Province of Cornwall.

**William Worcestre**, *Itineraries*, 1478, ed. J. H. Harvey, 1967

# 1497

**42** [I shall have] ... a name perpetual, and a fame permanent and immortal.
   **Michael Joseph 'An Gof', 1497**

**43** [Henry refused to permit any elaborate celebration of his victory at Blackheath] saying that he had not gained a worthy victory, having been against such a base crew as those Cornish men.
   **Henry VII** on his return to London, 1497 [Stoyle, 2002]

**44** The Cornish men never gave over to the last, and certainly, had they been well armed, and their cause answerable to their stomachs, they had gone near to have endangered the day, but in the end were overcome and put to flight, leaving two thousand and upwards of their companions dead on the field.
   **The "Short View"**, c.1497 [George Borrow, *Celtic Bards, Chiefs and Kings*, 1928]

# 1504

**45**    Of all Cornwall, Duke am I
         As was also my Father.
         A great lord in the country,
         From the Land's End to the Tamar. *
   ***Beunans Meriasek/The Life of St. Meriasek*, 1504**

# c. 1506

**46** We are in a very wild place [West Cornwall] which no human being ever visits, in the midst of a most barbarous race, so different in language and customs from the Londoners and the rest of England that they are as unintelligible to these last as to the Venetians.
   **Vincenzo Quirini, Venetian Ambassador to Castille**, c1506 [Stoyle, 2002]

# 1509

**47** ... the nine children of honour, upon great coursers [horses], apparelled on their bodies in blue velvet, powdered with fleur de lys of gold, and chains of goldsmith's work, every one of their horses trapped with a trapper of the king's title, as of England, and France, Gascony, Guienne, Normandy, Anjou, Cornwall, Wales, Ireland, wrought upon velvets with embroidery and goldsmith's worth (sic).
   **Coronation procession of Henry VIII**, 1509 [Philip Payton, *Cornwall*, 1996]

# 1515

48 ... one man [should] be sent from every parish of England, Cornwall and Wales to inhabit Ulster.

**An English official**, 1515 [Stoyle, 2002]

# 1531

49 The language of the English, Welsh and Cornish men is so different that they do not understand each other ... the Welshman is sturdy, poor, adapted to war and sociable; the Cornishman is poor, rough and boorish; and the Englishman mercantile, rich, affable and generous.

**Lodovico Falier**, in a dispatch to the Venetian Senate, 1531 [Stoyle 2002]

# 1535

50 Englonde, being the chief part of Britaine ... is limited ... on the West part with the bounds of Cornewall and Wall[e]s ...

**Polydore Vergil**, *Anglica Historia*, 1535 [Stoyle, 2002]

51 ... the whole Country of Britain ... is divided into iiii parts; whereof the one is inhabited of Englishmen, the other of Scottes, the third of Wallshemen, [and] the fourth of Cornishe people, which all differ among themselves, either in tongue, either in manners, or else in laws and ordinances.

**Polydore Vergil**, *Anglica Historia*, 1535 [Stoyle, 2002]

# 1538

52 [The Kingdom also] contains Wales and Cornwall, natural enemies of the rest of England, and speaking a [different] language.

**Gaspard de Coligny**, French ambassador to the court of Henry VIII, 1538 [Stoyle 2002]

# 1542

53 The shire hall of Cornwall is at Lostwithiel, and there is also the Coinage Hall for tin.

**John Leland**, *Itinerary*, 1542 [*John Leland's Itinerary*, 1993]

54 In Cornwall is two speeches: the one is naughty Englyshe, and the other is Cornyshe speech. And there be many men and women the which cannot speak one word of Englyshe, but all Cornyshe.

**Andrew Boorde**, *The First Book of the Introduction of Knowledge*, c.1542

55    I am a Cornishman, I can brew;
It will make you shit, also spew;
It is thick and smoky, and also it is thin;
It is like water that pigs have wallowed in.
**Andrew Boorde**, *The First Book of the Introduction of Knowledge*, c.1542

56 Cornwall is a poor and very barren country of all manner [of] thing[s], except Tin and Fish.
**Andrew Boorde**, *The First Book of the Introduction of Knowledge*, c.1542

57 A Cornishman will try the law, for the wagging of a straw.
**Andrew Boorde**, *The First Book of the Introduction of Knowledge*, c.1542

58 In Englande, and under the dominion of England, be many sundry speeches beside Englyshe ... the Walshe tongue is in Wales, the Cornyshe tongue in Cornewall, and Iryshe in Irlande ...
**Andrew Boorde**, *The First Book of the Introduction of Knowledge*, c.1542

## c. 1544

59 So many depraved, brutish soldiers from all nations under the sun – Welsh, English, Cornish, Irish, Manx, Scots, Spaniards, Gascons, Portingals [Portuguese], Italians, Albanians, Greeks, Turks, Tartars, Almains, Germans, Burgundians, Flemings, who had come there ... to have a good time under the king of England, who by nature was too hospitable to foreigners.
**Contemporary comment on the army assembled for Henry VIII's adventure on the continent, c.1544 [Payton, 1996]**

## 1549

60 Item we will not receive the new service because it is but like a Christmas game, but we will have our old service of Matins, Mass, Evensong and procession in Latin as it was before. And so we the Cornyshe men (whereof certain of us understand no Englysh) utterly refuse this new Englysh.
Extract from the articles of the **Prayer Book rebels**, 1549

## 1550s

61 ... the lands [of Leighdurrant in S. E. Cornwall] are very fineable, by reason there is such utterance and sale of all manner of victuals to the town of Plymouth, and the people more civil than in the west part of Cornwall and better disposed to plant and set and furnish their habitations with orchards ...
**William Humberstone**, 1550s [A. L. Rowse, *Tudor Cornwall*, 1941]

# 1560

62 ... it may be lawful for such Welch or Cornish children as can speak no English to learn the Praemises in the Welsh tongue or Cornish language.

**Resolution of a conference of the new Anglican Church**, 1560 [Fudge, 1982]

# 1568

63 ... the Cornishmen, being remnants of the old Britons, as they are the stoutest of all the British nations, so they are accounted to this day the most valiant in warlike affairs.

**Humphry Lluyd**, *A Breviary of Britain*, 1568 [Philip Payton, *A. L. Rowse and Cornwall*, 2005]

# 1572

64 [U]pon DEW WHALLAN GWA METTEN IN EGLOS DE LALANT, viz. upon all hallow day just past about the middle of the service in the parish church of Lalant Moryshe David's wife and Cicely James came into the church of Lalant together and in chiding with words together Cycely called Agnes Davy (———) and (———) in English not in *Cornowok*.

1572, from the **Consistory Depositions**, 1569–1572 [*Old Cornwall* vol. 2, no. 11, Summer 1936]

# c. 1584

65 The inhabitants call it 'Kernow', the English 'Cornwall' and the Latinists 'Cornubia'.

**John Norden**, *Speculi Britanniae Pars: A Topographical and Historical Description of Cornwall*, c.1584

66 And as they [the baser sort of the Cornish population] are among themselves litigious, so seem they yet to retain a kind of concealed envy against the English, whom they yet affect with a desire of revenge for their fathers' sakes, by whom their fathers received the repulse.

**John Norden**, *Speculi Britanniae Pars: A Topographical and Historical Description of Cornwall*, c.1584

67 But of late the Cornishe men have much conformed themselves to the use of the Englishe tongue, and their Englishe is equal to the best, especially in the eastern parts; even from *Truro eastward* it is in manner wholly Englishe. In the west part of the Country, as in the hundreds of *Penwith* and *Kerrier*, the Cornishe tongue is most in use amongst the inhabitants, and yet (which is to be marvelled) though the husband and wife, parents and children, Master and servants, do mutually communiate in their native language, yet there is none

of them in a manner but is able to converse with a *Stranger* in the Englishe tongue, unless it be some obscure people, that seldom confer with the better sort. But it seems that in a few years the Cornishe Language will be by little and little abandoned.

**John Norden**, *Speculi Britanniae Pars: A Topographical and Historical Description of Cornwall*, c.1584

68 ... a stranger traveller in those parts [Cornwall] can hardly find contentment in ordinary inns in lodging or diet, by reason (as I take it) for that there is no great haunt into those parts, unless sometimes merchants repair thither about their tin, or in the time of pilchard fishing; and therefore the ordinary provisions in these places are very meagre.

**John Norden**, *Speculi Britanniae Pars: A Topographical and Historical Description of Cornwall*, c.1584

## 1587

69 The Cornish and Devonshire men, whose country the Britons call Cernyw, have a speech in like sort of their own, and such as hath indeed more affinity with the Armorican tongue than I can well discuss of ... Thus ... in the south parts of the realm we have three several tongues, that is to say, English, British, and Cornish ...

**William Harrison**, *The Description of Britain*, 1587

## 1589

70 [Cornwall ...] that disordered county.
**Privy Council Report**, 1589 [Stoyle 2002]

## 1591

71 If the men do not continue their fishing the country round will miss their best relief. The country is poor, and there is little flesh and less butter or cheese.
**Thomas Celey**, *Calendar of State Papers Domestic (1591–4)*, 1591

## 1599

72 Le Roy! A Cornish name: art thou of Cornish crew?
**William Shakespeare**, Pistol to King Henry, *Henry V*, 1599

## 1602

73 ... nature hath shouldered out Cornwall into the farthest part of the realm, and so besieged it with the ocean, that [it is] as a demi-island in an island ...
**Richard Carew**, *The Survey of Cornwall*, 1602

74 ... Cornwall being cast out into the sea, with the shape of a horn, borrowed the one part of her name from her fashion ... and the other from her inhabitants, both which conjoined make Cornuwalliae, and contrived, Cornwall: in which sense the Cornish people call it Kernow, derived from Kerne, a horn.
     **Richard Carew**, *The Survey of Cornwall*, 1602

75 ... the English speech doth still encroach upon it [the Cornish language] and hath driven the same into the uttermost skirts of the shire. Most of the inhabitants can speak no word of Cornish, but very few are ignorant of the English; and yet some so affect their own as to a stranger they will not speak it, for if meeting them by chance you inquire the way or any such matter, your answer shall be, *Meea Navidna Cowzasawzneck* ... [I *will* not speak English].
     **Richard Carew**, *The Survey of Cornwall*, 1602

76 Why seek we in corners for petty commodities when as the only mineral of Cornish Tin openeth so large a field to the country's benefit?
     **Richard Carew**, *The Survey of Cornwall*, 1602

77 One point of their former roughness some of the western people do yet retain ... namely, how fostering a fresh memory of their expulsion long ago by the English, they second the same with a bitter repining at their fellowship ...
     **Richard Carew**, *The Survey of Cornwall*, 1602

78 All Cornish gentlemen are cousins.
     **Richard Carew**, *The Survey of Cornwall*, 1602

79 Cornwall, as an entire state, hath at divers times enjoyed sundry titles: of a kingdom, principality, duchy, and earldom ...
     **Richard Carew**, *The Survey of Cornwall*, 1602

80 Meanwhile, while the miners thus play the Moldwarps, unsavoury Damps do here and there distemper their heads, though not with so much danger in consequence as annoyance for the present.
     **Richard Carew**, *The Survey of Cornwall*, 1602

# 1603

81 [Elizabeth] possessed nine languages so thoroughly that each appeared to be her native tongue ... five of these were the languages of peoples governed by her: English, Welsh, Cornish, Scottish ... and Irish.
     Letter from the **Venetian ambassador** in London, 1603 [Stoyle 2002]

82    For courage no whit second to the best,
      The Cornishmen most active bold and light.
      **Michael Drayton**, *The Barons' Wars*, 1603


83 ... it is no great marvel if we understand them [animals] not: no more do we the Cornish, Welch, or Irish.
      John Florio's translation of **Montaigne**, c.1603 [Stoyle, 2002]

## c. 1606

84 The Cornishmen two wrestlers had for theirs [banner].
      **Michael Drayton**, 'Ballad of Agincourt' in *Poems, Lyric and Heroic*, c.1606

## 1607–8

85 ... in our silver mines lately discovered in our Realm of Scotland, We think fit to use the service of some of the Miners of our Duchy of Cornwall who are held to be the best experienced and most exercised in such works of all other our People.
      **James I**, Warrant to the Warden of the Duchy of Cornwall, 1607–8

## c. 1610

86 All persons within Devon or Cornwall may fetch sea-sand for the manuring of their land ... It shall and may be lawful to and for all persons whatsoever ... to fetch and take sea-sand at all places under the full water mark, where the same is or shall be cast by the sea, for the bettering of their land and for the increase of corn and tillage, at their will and pleasures.
      **Law passed in the 7th year of James I's reign**, c. 1610 [*The Times*, 17 July 1937]

## 1614

87    I love thee, Cornwall, and will ever,
      And hope to see thee once again!
      For why? – thine equal knew I never
      For honest minds and active men.
      **Thomas Freeman**, *Encomion Cornubiae*, 1614

## 1616

88 England is ... divided into 3 great Provinces, or Countries ... every of them speaking a several and different Language, as English, Welsh, and Cornish, and their language (which is strange) alters upon the sudden, even as the Provinces part; for in this Town they speak English and do not understand Cornish, and in the next Town Cornish and not understanding English.
      **Arthur Hopton**, *A Concordancy of Yeares*, 1616

# 1619

89 [When they tell me] that I take away God's Grace from them [by erecting a lighthouse at the Lizard], their English meaning is that they now shall have nor receive no benefit from shipwreck. They have been so long used to real purchase by the calamity of the ruin of shipping, as they claim it hereditary.

> **Sir John Killigrew**, in a letter to Trinity House, 1619 [Richard and Bridget Larn, *Shipwreck Index of the British Isles* vol. 5, 2000]

# 1621–22

90 The Cornish being a race of men stout of stomach, mighty of body and limb, and that lives hardly in a barren country, and many of them could for a need live underground that were Tinners.

> **Francis Bacon**, *Life of Henry VII*, 1621–22

# 1628

91 ... the ignorance of these Cornish parts, almost as much divided from reason and intelligence as their island [is] from the world ...

> **Sir John Eliot MP**, in letter to Sir Robert Cotton, July 1628 [Stoyle 2002]

# 1630

92 ... that viper ... [of rebellion] was ... hatched ... in Cornwall.

> **Thomas Westcote**, *A View of Devonshire in 1630* [Stoyle 2002]

# 1632

93 Never credit me but I will spout some Cornish at him.

> **Richard Brome**, *The Northern Lasse*, 1632 [Henry Jenner, *A Handbook of the Cornish Language*, 1904]

# 1634

94 10,000 Cornish, grudging to pay your [Henry VII's] subsidies, have gathered a head.

> **John Ford**, *Perkin Warbeck*, 1634 [Stoyle, 2002]

# 1635

95 [I have] no desire [to pass] over Tamar, to [visit] the horned-nockhole Land's-end, nor ... the rough, hard-bred and brawny strong-limbed wrastling inhabitants thereof.

> **East Anglian traveller**, 1635 [Stoyle, 2002]

# 1641

96 Arthur, the son of Uter-pendragon and Igerna, succeeded his father in the principality; therefore, called the 'Boar of Cornwall', because begot and born in that country, and of a Cornish duchess.

> **Thomas Heywood**, *The Life of Merlin …*, 1641 [R. J. Stewart & John Matthews, (eds.), *Merlin through the Ages*, 1995]

# 1643

97    To the inhabitants of the county of Cornwall.

We are so highly sensible of the merit of our county of Cornwall, and of their great zeal for the defence of our person and the just rights of our crown in a time when not only no reward appeared, but great probable dangers were threatened to obedience and loyalty, of their great and eminent courage and patience, in their indefatigable prosecution of their great work against so potent an enemy, backed with so strong, rich, and populous cities, and so plentifully furnished and supplied with men, arms, money, ammunition, and provisions of all kinds, and of the wonderful success with which it pleased Almighty God (though with the loss of some eminent persons, who shall never be forgotten by us), to reward their loyalty and patience by many strange victories over their and our enemies, in despite of all human probability, and all imaginable disadvantages, that as we cannot be forgetful of so great desert, so we cannot but desire to publish it to all the world, and perpetuate to all time the memory of their merits and of our acceptance of the same, and to that end we do hereby render our royal thanks to that county in the most public and lasting manner we can devise, commanding copies hereof to be printed and published, and one of them to be read in every church and chapel therein, and to be kept for ever as a record in the same, that as long as the history of these times and of this nation shall continue, the memory of how much that county hath merited from us and our crown, may be derived with it to posterity.

> **Charles I**, Letter to the Inhabitants of Cornwall, 10 September 1643

# 1644

98 The King and army march presently for Plymouth. Jesus give the King it and all. The King in the hearing of thousands, as soon as he saw me in the morning, cried to me – 'Dear Mr. Sheriff, I leave Cornwall to you safe and sound.'

> **Sir Francis Basset**, Letter to his wife, September 1644

99 This language [Cornish] is spoken altogether at Goonhilly and about Pendennis, and at Land's End they speak no English. All beyond Truro they

speak the Cornish language.

**Richard Symonds**, *Diary*, 1644

**100** This part of Cornwall [Menheniot] which we have seen they account barren. The people speak good and plain English here hitherto.

**Richard Symonds**, *Diary*, 1644

**101** We are amongst a people as far removed from humanity as they are from sanctity, they serve neither God nor man but after the old fashion of their forefathers.

An **English soldier**, 1644 [Mary Coate, *Cornwall in the Great Civil War*, 1933]

**102** ... the cursed Cornish ... are as very heathen as the ignorant Welsh that knew no religion nor God, but the King is more than God in that country and Wales.

**Besieged Parliamentarian garrison** in Plymouth, 1644 [Coate, 1933]

**103** ... [the] gallant Cornish ... are all resolved to spend their lives for his Sacred Majesty.

**Sir John Berkenhead** in *Mercurius Aulicus*, July 1644 [Stoyle, 2002]

**104** ... the Cornish men will not bring victuals ... [to Essex's army] but hide it.

**The Parliament's Scout**, 8–15 August 1644 [Stoyle, 2002]

**105** ... [the] heathenish Cornish ... pillaged our fort, yea and commanders too ... and stripped many to their shirts, and pulled off their boots, shoos and stockings ... and made them go barefoot.

**The Parliament's Scout**, 5–13 September 1644 [Stoyle, 2002]

**106** [The King's commanders] have French to ravish, Welsh to thieve [and] Cornish to ... plunder.

**Mercurius Britanicus**, [Parliamentarian pamphlet] 7–14 October 1644 [Stoyle, 2002]

**107** ... heathenish, I had almost said Hellish, Cornwall.

**John Vicars** in *Mercurius Britanicus*, 4–11 November 1644 [Stoyle, 2002]

**108** ... no Prince in Christendom hath better subjects [than the Cornish] ...

[who] still value their honour and their consciences above their blood.
**Sir John Berkenhead** in *Mercurius Aulicus*, 4–10 August

109 ... the men of Cornwall are very heathens, a corner of ignorants and atheists, drained from the mines.
**Parliamentarian pamphleteer**, 1644 [Stoyle, 2002]

# 1644–45

110 ... [the Cavaliers at Oxford] exclaim against Cornwall as much as your forces do, and it is believed that now the King has armed them they will neither suffer his Majesty's nor ... [Parliament's] forces to come amongst them.
**Sir Samuel Luke**, *Letter Books* ... 1644–45 [Stoyle, 2002]

# 1645

111 ... the Cornish blood-hounds have had their bellies full.
*Mercurius Britanicus*, 13–20 January 1645 [Stoyle, 2002]

112 [The common people of Wales are] more unreducible [to the Parliament's cause] than any other parts of the kingdom ... except Cornwall, where the people are swayed by the like principles.
**Sir Thomas Myddleton**, in a letter, March 1645 [Mark Stoyle, *Soldiers and Strangers*, 2005]

113 ... the Old Cornish slip away daily, and tomorrow morning some have appointed a rendezvous of their own accord where I have sent for horse to meet them. I shall deal freely with it.
**Lord George Goring**, in letter to Prince of Wales' Council, 28 July 1645 [Stoyle, 2002]

114 This [Cornwall] I told you would be ... [the Royalists'] last refuge and here now they take up station, as if (when all else failed) they meant to make a petty kingdom of it, and erect a new monarchy ... At Pendennis or St. Michael's Mount it's but imagining a man were at Whitehall and St. James Park. The tin-mines may serve for silver ... and a Crown too [be] made ... And all this may be done with a strong phantasy.
*Mercurius Britanicus*, 1–8 December 1645 [Stoyle, 2002]

# 1646

115 It is acknowledged to your eternal honour, O ye noble Cornwallians that you of this County, both Gentry and Commonalty, have in all these unnatural wars hitherto behaved yourselves gallantly and bravely, like stout men, loyal

subjects and good Christians.

**Lionel Gatford**, in sermon delivered to Cornish troops, January 1646, [Stoyle 2002]

**116** [T]he prince himself ... is come to Tavistock, with whom the Cornish ... are resolved to live and die, and to manifest their engagement and more particular interest in him ... they call him not the prince, but altogether the Duke of Cornwall.

**Parliamentarian report** , in *The City's Weekly Post* [Stoyle, 2005]

**117** ... there is ... much danger in a Cornish hug ...

**Mercurius Academicus** [Royalist pamphlet], 2–7 March 1646 [Stoyle 2002]

**118** I answered a common murmuring amongst them [the Cornish], that their country was never conquered.

**Hugh Peters**, 21 March 1646 [**P. Q. Karkeek**, 'Fairfax of the West 1645–46', *Transactions of the Devon Association*, 8, 1876]

## 1647

**119** [Cornwall is] enrapt with the sea on all sides, except toward Devonshire, and there bounded by the River Tamar, which ... runs almost from sea to sea.

**J. Sprigg**, *Anglia Rediviva: England's Recovery*, 1647

## 1647–52

**120** ... the people of Wales and Cornwall are rising in favour of the King.

**Venetian Ambassador**, Calendar of State Papers Venetian 1647–52 [Stoyle 2002]

## 1648

**121** ... the spirit it seems of malignancy is so prevalent with them [the people of the far west of Cornwall], that it will not suffer their disaffected spirits to be at quiet, although their stirring is irrational and tend [s only] to their own confusion.

**Buller Papers**, ed. R. N. Worth, 1895 [Stoyle 2002]

## 1649

**122** Cornwall is the Cornucopia, the complete and replete horn of abundance for churlish hills and affable courteous people: they are loving to requite a kindness, placable to remit a wrong and tardy to retort injuries ...

**John Taylor**, *Wandering to see the Wonders of the West*, 1649 [1967 edition]

# 1652

123 … we have Indians* … in Cornwall, Indians in Wales, Indians in Ireland.
[* a term applied by inhabitants of Stuart England to groups that they felt to
be 'un-English']

**Roger Williams**, English Puritan preacher, 1652 [Stoyle 2002]

# c. 1654

124      The Cornish hurling of the silver ball,
But Hyde Park a man might truly say
Had in it much the glory of that day.
Stout Cornwall, always loyal to their kings,
A hundred brave resolved persons brings
Of their own country to the park that day,
One of their country's exercise to play;
Where, being come, themselves they do divide
To east and west, their manhood to decide.
I' th' midst O' th' park's thrown up a silver ball,
Which being done, stoutly to it they fall.
Heels were tript up and bodies came to ground,
The Cornish hug always good play was found.
Long time it lasted, and now east, then west,
At several times had each of them the best.
Thousand spectators stood with greedy eyes,
To see them at this manly exercise;
His Highness York's great duke beheld the same,
With other persons of renowned fame.
Brave Cornishmen you are to be commended
And will be so until the world is ended.

**Ballad-monger in the reign of Charles II**, c.1654. [Louis T. Stanley,
*Journey through Cornwall*, 1958]

# c. 1657

125 The next [commodity] is our tin or pewter, which is so excellent in
Cornewell that it's only not silver.

**Henry Belasyse**, *An English Traveller's First Curiosity, or the Knowledge
of his Own Country*, c.1657

# 1659

126 While I was in Cornwall there were great shipwrecks about the Land's

End. It was the custom of that country at such a time, both rich and poor went out to get as much of the wreck as they could, not caring to save the people's lives; and in some parts of the country they called shipwrecks God's grace.

**George Fox**, *Journal*, 1659

## c. 1660–70

127 Do not leave the old road for the new road. *

**Nicholas Boson**, *Jowan Chy-an-Horth*, c. 1660–1670

## 1662

128 When Cornishmen went ... to go to London, it was usual with them to make their wills as if they took their voyage into a foreign country.

**Thomas Fuller**, *The History of the Worthies of England*, 1662 [Stoyle, 2002]

129 ... it must be pitied that these people [the Cornish] ... have so often abused their valour in rebellions ... however, the[y] ... have since plentifully repaired their credit by their exemplary ... loyalty in our late civil Wars.

**Thomas Fuller**, *The History of the Worthies of England*, 1662 [Stoyle, 2002]

130 Mr. Dicken Gwyn [Dick Angwyn] lives not far off, in St. Just's parish, who is the only man we could hear of that can now write the Cornish language. We met with none here but what could speak English; few of the children could speak Cornish; so that language is like, in a short time, to be quite lost.

**John Ray**, *Itinerary*, 1662 [*Memorials of John Ray*, 1846]

## 1668

131  Belgia [Belgium] me birth, Britane [Britain] me breeding gave,
    Cornwall a wife, ten children, and a grave.

**Inscription on the table-tomb of Alexander Danial** in Madron churchyard, 1668

## 1669

132 The Cornish foot ... were the very best foot that ever I saw, for marching and fighting.

**Capt. Richard Atkyns**, 1669 [Stoyle 2002]

## c. 1680

133 ... the Cornish people had wont to call any stranger whom they liked not Size (i.e. Sax or Saxon, whom they had no cause to love).

**William Scawen**, *Antiquities Cornu-Brittanic*, c.1680 [Stoyle, 2002]

**134** ... our people, as I have heard in Q[ueen]Elizabeth's time, desired that the common Liturgy should be in the English Tongue to which they were then for novelty's sake affected.

**William Scawen**, *Antiquities Cornu-Brittanic*, c.1680 [Stoyle, 2002]

**135** For we have some among these few [old folks] that do speak Cornish, who do not understand a word of English ... and those may be many in some of the western parts, to whom Mr. Francis Robinson, parson of Landawednack told me, he had preached a sermon not long since, in the Cornish tongue, only well understood by his auditory.

**William Scawen**, *Antiquities Cornu-Brittanic*, c.1680 [Stoyle, 2002]

**136** ... the poor speak Cornish, but are laughed at by the rich that speak it not.

**William Scawen**, *Antiquities Cornu-Brittanic*, c.1680 [Stoyle, 2002]

**137** ... in the ... Civil War, we began to make some use of ... [the Cornish language] upon the Runnagates [Cornish Royalist deserters] that went from us to the contrary part, from our opposite works: and more we should have done, if the enemy had not been Jealous [suspicious] of them, and prevented us.

**William Scawen**, *Antiquities Cornu-Brittanic*, c.1680 [Stoyle, 2002]

**138** It may, I confess, be lamented, and heavily laid to the charge of us and our ancestors ... to have been much wanting to ourselves in the loss of the Cornish speech.

**William Scawen**, *Antiquities Cornu-Brittanic*, c.1680 [Stoyle, 2002]

**139** Tho' [Cornwall] were heretofore honoured with the title of one of 4 dinasties, yet it is but a small county in respect to others next conjoined.

**William Scawen**, *Antiquities Cornu-Brittanic*, c.1680 [Stoyle, 2002]

## 1695

**140** The old Cornish is almost quite driven out of the Country, being spoken only by the vulgar in two or three Parishes at the Lands-end; and they too understand the English. In other parts, the inhabitants know little or nothing of it; so that in all likelihood, a short time will destroy the small remains that are left of it.

**Edmund Gibson** in his edition of William Camden's *Britannia or Remaines Concerning Britane*, 1695

# 1697

**141** … their ordinary food [is] potatoes and barley bread (as coarse as horse bread), with gruel thickened oftener with barley meal than oat meal … [B]y reason of the cold and hunger their youth suffer, having not rags enough to cover them, [and] men are so reduced from well-grown persons as to be now (comparatively) mere pigmies in stature and strength, which is lamentable to behold.

> **Cornish gentleman**, *Tinners' Grievance*, 1697 [A. K. Hamilton Jenkin, *The Cornish Miner*, 3rd edn., 1962]

# 1698

**142** I saw not a windmill all over Cornwall or Devonshire tho' they have wind and hills enough.

> **Celia Fiennes**, *Journies …*, 1698 [1957]

**143** … my relation … would have engaged my stay with them a few days or weeks to have given me the diversion of the country and to have heard the Cornish Nightingales, as they call them (the Cornish Cough [sic] a sort of Jackdaw if I mistake not), a little black bird which makes them a visit about Michaelmas …

> **Celia Fiennes**, *Journies …*, 1698 [1957]

# 1700

**144** … where we have no acquaintance, we find the people more suspicious and jealous … than in any country we have travelled … we have been strictly examined in several places; and I am told the people, notwithstanding our long continuance here, have not yet removed their jealousy.

> **Edward Lhuyd**, in letter to Thomas Tonkin from St. Ives, 15 October1700 [R. T. Gunther, *Early Science in Oxford vol. xiv: Life and Letters of Edward Lhwyd*, 1945]

**145**     The old saying is a true saying,
          A tongue too long never did good:
          But the man with no tongue lost his land. *
     **Anonymous**, c.1700

**146** … I do remember that being about half a dozen years of age, I could neither speak nor understand it [Cornish], the reason I conceive to be a nicety of my mother's forbidding the servants and neighbours to talk to me otherwise than in English. *

> **Nicholas Boson**, *Nebbaz Gerriau dro tho Carnoack* [A Few Words about Cornish], c1700

**147** Our Cornish tongue hath been so long in the Wane that we can hardly hope to see it increase again, for as the English confined it into this narrow Country first, so it presseth on still, leaving it no Place but about the Cliff and Sea, it being almost only spoken from the Land's-End to the Mount and towards St. Ives and Redruth, and again from the Lizard to Helston, and towards Falmouth, … within which little Extent also there is more of English spoken than of Cornish, for here may be found some that can hardly speak or understand Cornish, but scarce any but both understand and speak English; therefore it seems difficult to stay and recover it again, for the old Men dying away, We find the young Men to speak it less and less, and worse and worse, and so it is like to decay from Time to Time.

> **Nicholas Boson**, *Nebbaz Gerriau dro tho Carnoack* [A Few Words about Cornish], c1700

## Early 1700s

**148** The "Hurlian" is that Cornish custom of playing with a ball which was so much the favourite among our ancestors; that it has generated this proverbial kind of speech amongst them "Hurlian yu ghen guare nyi", "Hurling is our sport". Of this the long-settled Ruanites talk much; and seem to glory in the prowess of their ancestors at this work.

> **Rev. John Whitaker**, based on reminiscences of the early 1700s in 'History of Ruan Lanihorne', *JRIC* NSvii 2 (1974)[H. L. Douch, *Old Cornish Inns*, 1966; P. A. S. Pool, *The Death of Cornish*, 1975]

## 1701

**149**    [Gone] the four wheels of Charles' Wain,
     Grenville, Godolphin, Trevanion, Slanning slain.

> **John Prince**, *Damnonii Orientales Illustres, or The Worthies of Devon*, 1701

**150** The Cornish is much more corruptly spoken than the Armorican, as being confin'd to half a score of parishes towards the Land's End …

> **Edward Lhuyd**, in letter to Henry Rowlands 10 March 1701 [Gunther, 1945]

## 1705

**151** William Trevarthen buried in Camborne Church, August 13th, being destroyed to a hurling with Redruth men at the high downs the 10th day of August, AD 1705.

> **Camborne Parish Register**, 1705

# 1707

152 The places in Cornwal that at this day retain the Ancient Language, are the Parishes of St. Just, St. Paul, Burrian, Sunnin, St. Lavan, St. Krad, Marva, Maddern, Sunner, Trewednok, St. Ives, Lelant, Leigian, Kynwal or (as now pronounced) Gyval; And all along the sea shore from the Land's End to St. Kevern's near the Lizard point. But a great many of the Inhabitants of those Parishes, especially the Gentry, do not understand it; there being no necessity thereof, in regard there's no Cornish Man but speaks good English.

**Edward Lhuyd**, *Archaeologia Britannica*, 1707

# 1711

153     At building Babel's Tower as books do tell
    Did Gomar grandson unto Noah dwell
    To whom the ancient Cornish language fell.

    Cornwall now mourns thy tongue just lost and gone
    Jenkins our Cornish bard is fled among
    the saints to sing his everlasting song.

**John Boson**, an elegy on the death of James Jenkins, 1711 [P. Berresford Ellis, *The Cornish Language and its Literature*, 1974]

# 1720

154 ... they write from Cornwall that upon the first notice of this misfortune [the running aground at The Lizard of the *Royal Anne*], the people on the sea coast ran out of the churches, armed with their hatchets etc, to the sea side, in quest of plunder.

**The London Journal**, 25 November 1720 [John Vivian, *Tales of the Cornish Wreckers*, 1969]

# 1724

155 Quitting Falmouth Haven from Penryn west, we came to Helstone, about 7 miles, and stands upon the little river Cober, which however admits the sea so into its bosom as to make a tolerable good harbour for ships a little below the town. It is the fifth town, allowed for the coining TIN, and several of the ships called 'tin' ships are loaded here.

**Daniel Defoe**, *A tour through the whole island of Great Britain*, vol. 1, 1724

# 1725

156 The game called the Hurlers, is a thing the Cornish men value themselves

much upon; I confess, I see nothing in it, but that it is a rude violent play among the boors, or country people; brutish and furious, and a sort of an evidence that they were, once, a kind of barbarians.

**Defoe**, *A tour through the whole island of Great Britain*, vol. 2, 1725

157 The wrestling in Cornwall is, indeed, a much more manly and generous exercise [than hurling], and that closure, which they call the Cornish Hug, has made them eminent in the wrestling rings all over England ...

**Defoe**, *A tour through the whole island of Great Britain*, vol. 2, 1725

## 1727

158 As it's natural and full of honour to love one's Country so it's as natural (and why not as praise-worthy?) to love its language. And I hear of a Gentleman in Cornwall (in Antique Age Renowned for Love to Saints and Shipwrecks!) who has taken noble mighty pains in translating the Bible into Cornish or Cornubian Welch.

**Andrew Brice**, *Weekly Journal*, no. 52, 2 June 1727 [Ellis, 1974]

## 1731

159    John Udy of Luxillion
His tin was so fine
It gilderd this punch bowl
And made it to shine.
Pray fill it with punch,
Lett the tinners sit round –
They never will budge
Till the bottom they sound.

**Rhyme on a punch bowl in the Victoria and Albert Museum**, 1731

## 1732

160 The ship came on shore [on the north coast of Cornwall] entire, with all the hands on board, and she might and would have been preserved, together with her whole cargo, but for the Natives and Inhabitants of the country adjoining, who in a Barbarous and Tumultuous manner came down in vast numbers and not only plundered and forcibly carried off and destroyed their cargo and lading belonging to the owner and master, but ripped and cut the ship to pieces and carried off the materials ...

**Anonymous**, 1732 [Vivian, 1969]

# 1736

**161** As for the vulgar Cornish now spoken ... it is reduced to such a small nook of the county, and those ancient persons that still speak it, are even there so few, the language itself so corrupted, and they too for the most part such illiterate people, that I cannot sufficiently commend your great industry in gathering together so much of it, and that so correct, as you have now enabled me to set forth; since what it has been my fortune to collect myself has been so little in comparison, as not to deserve the naming separately.

> **Thomas Tonkin**, in letter to William Gwavas 19 July 1736 [P. A. S. Pool, *The Death of Cornish*, 1975]

**162** ... I had often read Mr. Carew's Survey of Cornwall which I looked upon as a very imperfect and lame account of our county and being from my earliest youth much delighted in the study of antiquities, had always entertained a design of attempting a more perfect and large description of it ...

> **Thomas Tonkin**, 'An Alphabetical Account of all the Parishes in Cornwall', 1736 [H. L. Douch, 'Thomas Tonkin: an appreciation of a Neglected Historian', *JRIC* vol. 4, pt. 2, 1962]

# 1739

**163** Ludgvan is like a buxom girl of eighteen, always laughing and playing, and affording plentifully all the superficial pleasures of mirth and jollity; but St. Just is an old haggard philosopher, whose ruthful appearance would deter the soft and the luxurious from having anything to do with him; but ... is full of riches within ...

> **William Oliver**, in letter to William Borlase, 13 August 1739, [P. A. S. Pool, *William Borlase*, 1986]

**164** ... I have been informed by several old men, particularly the late Mr. Udey West, of Redruth, that all the rocky ground under Carn Bray Castle, the Rocky Hill, and from there to Port Treth were covered with stout trees in their remembrance so that squirrels (of which there were many) could leap from one to the other all the way.

> **Thomas Tonkin** ms., 1739

# 1743

**165** I saw a strange sight, the sun shining in Cornwall.

> **Charles Wesley**, 1743, in *The Wesleys in Cornwall: extracts from the Journals of John and Charles Wesley* ... , ed. J. Pearce, 1964

**166** Charles Wesley is come to town
To try if he can pull the churches down.
**Gentlewoman of St. Ives** to John Wesley, 31 August 1743 [Pearce, 1964]

## 1744

**167** I took a view of the ruins of the house [at St. Ives] which the mob had pulled down a little before, for joy that Admiral Matthews had beat the Spaniards. Such is the Cornish method of thanksgiving.
**John Wesley**, 5 April 1744 [Pearce, 1964]

## 1745

**168** The rabble roared with all their throats, 'Bring out the Canorum! Where is the Canorum?' (an unmeaning word which the Cornish generally use instead of Methodist).
**John Wesley**, 4 July 1745 [Pearce, 1964]

**169** They [the Cornish militiamen raised in response to the Jacobite scare] all express great readiness to defend their country, but they mean their county.
**Anonymous**, 1745 [Linda Colley, *Briton: Forging the Nation 1707–1837*, 1992]

## 1746

**170** I rode to Sithney, where the word begins to take root. The rebels of Helston threaten hard. All manner of evil they say of us. Papists we are that is certain; and are for bringing in the Pretender. Nay, the vulgar are persuaded I have brought him with me …
**Charles Wesley**, 19 July 1746 [Pearce, 1964]

## 1747

**171** How strangely has one year changed the scene in Cornwall! This is now a peaceable, nay, honourable station.
**John Wesley**, 30 June 1747 [Pearce, 1964]

**172** On the other [sic] hand stands the Mount, a stupendous pile, a most romantic piece of rock work, on the other a town most charmingly situated in the centre of the Bay, gently descending to a stately pier filled with trading vessels, and sea covered over with boats, the shores resound with huzzas from eager fishermen, answering their signals from their Hewers, who with their bushes from the adjacent hills point out the courses of the scaly tribe, till captiv'd in the fatal nets, they struggle for their liberty in vain.
**Walter Borlase**, in letter to Peggy Borlase, 1 August 1747

# 1749

**173** As he [Edward Lhuyd] … was conversant in all dialects of British, and a very good critic in general, every language he has touched upon has received light and improvement from him; but our county in particular is so much indebted to him for his Cornish Grammar, that … without … the help of Mr. Lhuyd, I think it would have been impossible at this time to attempt a language so near its last gasp, with any prospect of success.

**William Borlase**, in letter to Charles Lyttleton 15 April 1749 [Pool, 1986]

# 1750

**174** A ship has just been thrown on the rocks near Looe; seven men and a boy, being all the hands on board, perished. 'Tis said that all the horses in the neighbourhood are taken up about the plunder.

**Anonymous** writer from Liskeard, April 1750 [A. K. Hamilton Jenkin, *Cornwall and its people*, 1945]

**175** The people of Cornwall are very hospitable and exceedingly civil to strangers, and the common people are much polished and ready to do all kind offices, which I observed more especially among the tinners.

**Dr. Richard Pococke**, *Travels through England*, 1750

**176** In Cornwall and Devonshire they have few wheel carriages by reason of the steep hills but every thing is carried either on hooks on each side of the horses, which are long or short according to the nature of the burden …

**Dr. Richard Pococke**, *Travels through England*, 1750

**177** Mr. William Jackman, the then vicar, and chaplain also of Pendennis Castle at the siege thereof by the parliament army, was forced for divers years to administer the sacrament to the communicants [of the parish of Feock] in the Cornish tongue, because the aged people did not well understand English, as he himself often told me.

**William Hals**, *The Compleat History of Cornwall* Vol. 1, 1750

# 1751

**178** They [those gathered on the shore near Looe on the occasion of a wreck] are so used to night-work [smuggling], so habituated to a defiance of authority, and contempt of the laws, and generally more or less so inflamed with spirituous liquors, that they are ever ready to perpetuate any villainy that their violent temper or love of lucre shall prompt them to.

**Letter from a clergyman in Cornwall** to *General Evening Post* (London), January 1751 [Vivian, 1969]

# 1752

**179** Nothing would have carried me thither, but the prospect of finding a *sweet* bed to sleep in, which is seldom to be found at the inns in Cornwall, for both the houses and the beds stink worse than a pigsty.

**Charles Lyttelton**, 1752

# 1753

**180** The riches of the land and sea is in full gallop to France and the countenance given to the smugglers by those whose business it is to restrain these pernicious practices hath brought them so bold and daring that nobody can venture to come near them with safety whilst they are at their work.

**George Borlase**, in letter, 1 February 1753 [Hamilton Jenkin, 1945]

**181** The coasts here swarm with smugglers from the Land's End to the Lizard ...

**George Borlase**, in letter, 1 February 1753 [Hamilton Jenkin, 1945]

**182** The people who make it their business to attend these wrecks are generally tinners, and as soon as they observe a ship on the coast, they first arm themselves with sharp axes and hatchets, and leave their tin works to follow these ships ... They'll cut a large trading vessel to pieces in one tide, and cut down everybody that offers to oppose them.

**George Borlase**, in letter, 1 February 1753 [Hamilton Jenkin, 1945]

**183** ... A dear friend of ours brought up an evil report of this land. It flows with milk and honey. I scarce believe it to be Cornwall, the accommodations everywhere are so good, and the people so cleanly ...

**Charles Wesley**, 4 October 1753 [Pearce, 1964]

**184** On Wednesday the 25th [July] the stewards met at St. Ives from the western part of Cornwall. The next day I began examining the society, but I was soon obliged to stop short. I found an accursed thing among them: wellnigh one and all bought or sold uncustomed goods.

**John Wesley**, 1753 [Pearce, 1964]

# 1754

**185** Cornwall, I believe, at present has the worst roads in all England, a great part of which are intolerable, remaining just in the same situation in which the deluge left them, and most of those which have been improved, are still so extremely narrow and uneven, that they are almost inaccessible to all kinds of wheeled vehicles.

**Gentleman's Magazine** 1754 [Hamilton Jenkin, 1945]

# 1756

**186** Cornwall has not in the memory of the oldest person now living been known to be so very dear so soon after so good and plentiful a harvest; if some course be not speedily taken the Poor must be either hanged or starved.

**The Sherborne Mercury**, December 1756 [Douch, 1966]

**187** ... in these days of discontent, all are pleased with *him* [Edward Boscawen], and I assure you it will discredit any new administration if he is excluded his share in it. No! that cannot, shall not be; it would put the very ocean in a storm, and the large continent of Cornwall into a rebellion.

**Elizabeth Montagu**, in letter to Frances Boscawen, 6 November 1756 [Payton, 1996]

**188** P[upil]. What language is spoken by the inhabitants of this county [Cornwall]? T[utor]. In some few parishes, indeed, near the Land's-end, there is a corrupt dialect of the Cornish tongue even still retained; but the gentry, and other people of fashion, talk as pure English as the natives of London.

**Youth's Philosophical Entertainer, or the Natural Beauties of Cornwall, Devonshire, Dorsetshire and Somersetshire** ..., 1756

# 1757

**189** As we rode through Gwithian parish Mr. Harris pointed out the place where his father and many of his ancestors lived. It is now only a mountain of sand. Within a few years this so increased as to bury both the church and the whole town.

**John Wesley**, 8 September 1757 [Pearce, 1964]

**190** At six I preached at St. Austell, a neat little town on the side of a fruitful hill.

**John Wesley**, 24 September 1757 [Pearce, 1964]

# 1758

**191** ... when the liturgy at the reformation was appointed by authority to take the place of the mass, the Cornish desired that it should be in the English language, being apprehensive that it might be injoined them in their mother tongue, as it was with regard to the Welsh. By this means and the gentry mixing gradually with the English, the Cornish language lost ground in proportion as it lay nearer to Devon.

**William Borlase**, *Natural History of Cornwall*, 1758

192 The corruption of our boroughs at the electing members for Parliament begins with intemperance and riot; these dissipate every generous sentiment of freedom, love of country, and inclination to industry.

**William Borlase**, *Natural History of Cornwall*, 1758

193 Large numbers of the inhabitants have their attention so much engrossed by tin and copper that agriculture and all other employments are neglected in the greedy quest of metals.

**William Borlase**, *Natural History of Cornwall*, 1758

194 A second reason of litigiousness in Cornwall is that we have as many sorts of law-courts here as in any part of England.

**William Borlase**, *Natural History of Cornwall*, 1758

195 That we may attend it to the grave: this language is now altogether ceased, so as not to be spoken anywhere in conversation.

**William Borlase**, *Natural History of Cornwall*, 1758

## 1759

196 ... they [Cornish choughs] have the character of a thievish Bird, as they will carry from a Person's House whatever they can find to suit their Humour, even Coals, or anything on fire, they will carry away, and thereby endanger Houses, which are generally thatched in those parts; hence they become very obnoxious in the Neighbourhood where they much abound.

**Benjamin Martin**, *The Natural History of England*, 1759

## 1762

197 I rode to Week St. Mary. It was a kind of fair day, and the people were come far and near for wrestling and other diversions; but they found a better way of employing their time, for young and old flocked to church from all quarters.

**John Wesley**, 27 September 1762 [Pearce, 1964]

198     O Cornwall, barren wretched spot of ground,
       Where nought but rocks and stones are to be found,
       Thy barren hills won't find thy pigmy sons with bread,
       Or wood to make 'em coffins when they're dead.

**Samuel Johnson**, 1762 [*Cornish Magazine*, vol. 10, no. 2, June 1967]

# 1765

**199** ... this place [Penzance] is said to be the Emporium for Smuggling in the West of England.

*The Exeter Mercury or West Country Advertizer*, October 1765

# 1766

**200** ... the natural amphi-theatre at Gwennap [is] ... the finest I know in the kingdom. It is a round, green hollow, gently shelving down, about fifty feet deep; but I suppose it is two hundred across one way, and near three hundred the other. I believe there were full twenty thousand people; and, the evening being calm, all could hear.

**John Wesley**, 14 September 1766 [Pearce, 1964]

# 1770

**201** I took a walk to the top of that celebrated hill, Carn Brea. Here are many monuments of remote antiquity scarce to be found in any other part of Europe: Druid altars of enormous size, being only huge rocks, suspended one upon the other; and rock-basins, hollowed on the surface of the rock, it is supposed, to contain the holy water.

**John Wesley**, 1 September 1770 [Pearce, 1964]

# 1773

**202** She [Dolly Pentreath] does indeed talk Cornish as readily as others do English, being bred up from a child to know no other language; nor could she (if we may believe her) talk a word of English before she was past twenty years of age ...

**Daines Barrington**, in letter to John Lloyd 31 March 1773 [Fred W. P. Jago, *The Ancient Language, and the Dialect of Cornwall* ..., 1882]

**203** How changed is this town [Helston] since a Methodist preacher could not ride through it without hazard of his life.

**John Wesley**, 16 August 1773 [Pearce, 1964]

# 1775

**204** I think this [the amphitheatre at Gwennap] is the most magnificent spectacle which is to be seen on this side of heaven.

**John Wesley**, 3 September 1775 [Pearce]

**205** The Natives [of West Cornwall] ... seem to be very happy when they can sit down to a furze blaze, wringing their shirts and pouring the mud and water out of their boots. But the common people here are very strange kind of beings, half savages at the best. Many thousands of them live entirely underground, where they burrow and breed like rabbits. They are rough as bears, selfish as swine, obstinate as mules, and hard as the native iron.

**Anonymous Londoner**, 1775 [Hamilton Jenkin, 1962]

# 1776

206 Cornwall presents a wild and strange appearance.

**St. James's Chronicle**, 1776 [Hamilton Jenkin, 1945]

207 The labourers in general bring up their families with only potatoes or turnips, or leeks or pepper grass, rolled up in black barley crust, and baked under the ashes, with now and then a little milk.

**St. James's Chronicle**, 1776 [Hamilton Jenkin, 1945]

208 My age is three score and five. I am a poor fisherman. I learnt Cornish when I was a boy. I have been to sea with my father and 5 other men in the boat, and have not heard one word of English spoke in the boat for a week together. I never saw a Cornish book. I learnt Cornish going to sea with old men. There is not more than 4 or 5 in our town can talk Cornish now, old people four score years old. Cornish is all forgot with young people.

**William Bodinar**, in letter to Daines Barrington, 3 July 1776 [Pool, 1975]

# 1778

209 In the western part of this county smuggling, since the soldiers have been drawn off, has been carried on almost without control.

**Edward Giddy**, in letter to chief customs officer, 1778 [Hamilton Jenkin, 1945]

210 ... it would be mere pedantry to attempt to describe ... the shocking effects, the moral and political consequences of smuggling carried to such a daring height, but I cannot help saying that perjury, drunkenness, idleness, poverty, contempt of the law and an universal corruption of manners are in this neighbourhood too plainly seen to accompany it.

**Edward Giddy** 1778, [Douch, 1966]

211 A tinner is never broke until his neck is broke.

**William Pryce**, *Mineralogia Cornubiensis*, 1778

# 1780

212 Near to this rock basin I perceived a stone of vast size which struck me as having the appearance of a rocking stone ... It proved however to be one, as I

soon found by putting it easily in motion with one of my hands.

**Rev. John Swete**, 'A Tour in Cornwall in 1780', in *JRIC* vol. 6, pt. 3, 1971

## 1782

213    God gives the word, the preachers throng around,
Live from his lips, and spread the glorious sound:
That sound bespeaks salvation on her way,
The trumpet of a life-restoring day;
'Tis heard where England's eastern glory shines,
And in the gulfs of her Cornubian mines.

**William Cowper**, *Hope*, 1782

## 1785

214 This [St. Ives] was the first place in Cornwall where we preached and where Satan fought fiercely for his kingdom; but now all is peace.

**John Wesley**, 26 August 1785 [Pearce, 1964]

215    Hail Mousehole! birth place of old Doll Pentreath
The last who gabber'd Cornish…

**Peter Pindar** (Dr. John Wolcot), in *Universal Magazine*, 1785

## 1789

216 I am sorry to learn the disposition for mobbing prevails in Cornwall on account of Flower [sic], and though I wish to contribute to their relief, yet I dare not send any Flower from London to them lest they should talk again of Arsenick.

**Matthew Boulton**, in letter to Thomas Wilson, 5 September 1789 [Hamilton Jenkin, 1962]

217 Tuesday the 29th of September was the day appointed for the Tinners Grand Sweepstakes, over Redruth Course. The horses to be the Cornish breed and rode by their owners.

**The Times**, 7 October 1789

218 I am lately returned from the mining parishes of Cornwall, where I have been witness to the greatest imaginable poverty and distress, insomuch that I have seen women gathering snails to make broth for the support of their families!

**Nicholas Donnithorne**, in letter to the Directors of the East India Company, 1789 [Hamilton Jenkin, 1962]

# 1790

**219** This [the similarity between Cornish and Breton] is evidenced by the colloquial resemblance to this day subsisting betwixt the Cornish on the south-western margin of the County, and their opposite neighbours at Morlaix, and other parts of Bas Bretagne, where the low French and the Cornish seem almost one and the same dialect.

**William Pryce**, *Archaeologia Cornu-Britannica*, 1790

# 1791

**220** William the Conqueror and his descendants parcelled out the country and bribed some parts of it by what they called Charters, to hold the other parts of it the better subjected to their will. This is the reason why so many of these Charters abound in Cornwall; the people were averse to the government establishment at the conquest, the towns were garrisoned and bribed to enslave the Country. All the old Charters are badges of this conquest.

**Thomas Paine**, *Rights of Man*, 1791

**221** This [the drowning of three passengers at Restronget] should caution boatmen against the imprudence of overcrowding their boats; a practice too frequent in Cornwall.

**Exeter Flying Post**, September 1791

# 1792

**222** Cornwall hath long been infamous to a proverb, for the inhospitality of the inhabitants, on occasions of shipwreck; but the truth is, the charge against Cornwall is founded more on local circumstances, than on any peculiar depravity in the people ...

**Committee appointed by Summer Assizes**, Bodmin, 1792

# 1794

**223** [Under Methodism] wayside chapels again became a feature of the Cornish landscape and the people were gathered once more into intimate devotional groups, now called bands or classes.

**James Forbes**, *Tour in Cornwall to the Land's End in Letters ... in 1794* [JRIC, 9, 1983]

**224** It requires a strong stomach and a large degree of curiosity to go through all this [dressing up in order to go underground] – for besides the fatigue and toil in the mine, the clothes they give you are greasy and filthy to a degree, smell abominably and are often stocked with a republic of creepers.

James Forbes, *Tour in Cornwall to the Land's End in letters ... in1794* [Hamilton Jenkin, 1962]

# 1795

225 A multitude of ancient stones or crosses are still standing in all the roads and in many fields all over the county of Cornwall – many of them have the upper part of the stone defaced or broken – but several I have seen are perfect.
**Unknown diarist, 1795**

# 1797

226 It is natural to love those whom you have had opportunities of serving, and I confess I have real affection for St. Ives and its inhabitants, in whose memory I have an ardent desire to continue a little longer than the usual time of those do of whom there is no ostensible memorial. To that end my vanity prompted me to erect a mausoleum and to institute certain periodical returns of a ceremony ...
**John Knill**, Trust Deed, 1797 [Beryl James, 'John Knill 1734–1811', *Old Cornwall*, vol. 9, no. 6, Spring 1982]

# 1798

227 The Tinners of Sithney offer themselves to be led by the now Lord Warden (he being a native of the Stannaries) to any part of the Kingdom against the French. And tho' Tinners have not been called to Arms for these two hundred years, doubt not but we will prove ourselves loyal and good subjects, Hardy Soldiers and show that we are the true descendants of the Ancient Britons who never have been, and we never will be, Slaves.
***One and All***, 1798 [Douch, 1966]

# 1801

228 In the mining districts ... large bodies of tinners have assembled, particularly in the neighbourhood of St. Austle, where they went round to the farmers, carrying a written paper in one hand and a rope in the other. If the farmers hesitated to sign this paper, which pledged them to sell their corn at a reduced price, the rope was fastened about their necks, and they were terrified into compliance.
***Royal Cornwall Gazette***, 4 April 1801

229 Riot and disorder during the last and present week have so generally prevailed throughout the county that we might fill our paper with all the detail

of their particulars.

**Royal Cornwall Gazette**, 18 April 1801

230 The three chief courts of Arthur: Caerllion upon Usk in Cambria; Celliwig [Callington] in Cornwall; and Edinburgh in the North. These are the three at which he kept the three chief festivals; that is to say, Christmas, Easter and Whitsuntide.

**Iolo Morganwg** (compiler), *The Triads of Britain*, 1801 [1977]

231 The three powerful swineherds of the Isle of Britain ... The second was Coll son of Collvrewi, who kept the sow of Dallwaran Dalben that came burrowing as far as Penrhyn Penwedig [Land's End] ...

**Iolo Morganwg** (compiler), *The Triads of Britain*, 1801 [1977]

## 1802

232 Walking on the cliff [at The Lizard] in the afternoon saw a smuggler land his goods, but in consequence of this we had very few hearers.

**Richard Treffry**, *Journal*, 5 May 1802

233 The only political trust to which your St. Mawes electors will bind you is the belief that the Pilchard is the best of all possible fish which, as long as you are not obliged to taste it, you may undertake for their sakes to believe.

**The Marquis of Buckingham**, in letter to the Rt. Hon. Richard Wyndham, July 1802 [F. Audrey Hosier, 'St Just and St. Mawes', *Old Cornwall* vol. 6, no. 11, Autumn 1966]

234 'Till within a few years Cornishmen were famous as wrestlers; nor is this gymnastic sport entirely discontinued now. But every old inhabitant of this county can tell you how very much it has declined.

**Royal Cornwall Gazette**, 18 September 1802

## 1803

235 ... Penzance is a very different place from the commonly received opinion. We have cards for the sedentary, books for the lounger, balls for the light-heeled, clubs for the convivial, picnics for the gay and thoughtless. Turbot and red mullet swim almost to our very doors, our bay is inferior only to the bay of Naples.

**'A Penzance Man, but no Smuggler, Miner, Wreck-Ravager, Cannibal, nor Hottentot'**, in *Royal Cornwall Gazette*, 19 November 1803

# 1804

**236** These parishioners of St. Piran have given the tone to all the tinners in the County, and exalted him into the patronage of them all. They all keep his feast upon the 5th March ...

John Whitaker, *Ancient Cathedral of Cornwall Historically Surveyed*, 1804

**237** ... English too was not *desirea* by the Cornish as vulgar history says, and as Dr. Borlase avers; but, as the case shows itself plainly to be, *forced* upon the Cornish by the tyranny of England, at a time when the English language was yet unknown in Cornwall. This act of tyranny was at once gross barbarity to the Cornish people, and a death-blow to the Cornish language.

John Whitaker, *Ancient Cathedral of Cornwall Historically Surveyed*, 1804

**238** I have heard in my visit to the west [August 1779] of two persons still alive that could speak the Cornish language. On my offer of English money for Cornish words to the men at Land's End they referred me to an old man living about three miles off towards the south at St. Levan ... and intimated that I might have as many words as I would choose to purchase.

John Whitaker, *Ancient Cathedral of Cornwall Historically Surveyed*, 1804

# 1806

**239** It is in contemplation to run a mail coach from Plymouth through to Falmouth. It is high time, indeed, to do something to quicken the mails on this line of road, on the eastern part of which their delay has become proverbial.

*Royal Cornwall Gazette*, 29 November 1806

# 1807

**240** I cannot relish their food; they [the Cornish] eat their meat half raw; the vegetables are never boiled enough to be soft; and everything is insipid except the bread, which is salt, and disagreeable.

Manuel Alvarez Espriella [Robert Southey], *Letters from England*, 1807

# 1808

**241** Each cottager on an average is wont to lay in about a thousand fish for winter use. The quantity of salt necessary is about seven pounds to a hundred fish ... [S]alt is now increased to 4d per lb, and a thousand fish cannot be cured under £1 3s 4d, a sum of unattainable magnitude to a poor man who gets only 6s or, at most, 7s per week for his labour.

Rev. Richard Warner, *A Tour Through Cornwall ... in 1808*, [1809]

242 Rank as the pilchard may be esteemed by those who are unaccustomed to eat it, yet, throughout Cornwall, it is considered the greatest delicacy.

**Rev. Richard Warner**, A *Tour Through Cornwall … in 1808*, [1809]

243 The customs which, some years ago, brutalised the miners of Cornwall and kept them in a state little better than savages, are now in great measure, exploded … You will naturally enquire *who* have been the immediate instruments of so much good, in a district so unlikely to exhibit such gratifying appearances, and I feel that I am but doing justice to a class of people much, though undeservedly calummated, when I answer, the Wesleyan Methodists …

**Rev. Richard Warner**, A *Tour Through Cornwall … in 1808*, [1809]

## 1809

244 The small remnant of corn that remained standing soon yielded to the sickle, when a blooming daughter of Ceres advanced in front of the party … She displayed, in seeming triumph, a small bunch of wheat-ears, intermingled with flowers and bound together with ribbons. In a moment all was silence. She waved the trophy over her head – an honest rustic caught the sight, and instantly exclaimed in seeming rapture "Anneck! Anneck! hurrow!" "I have it! I have it!" rejoined the damsel, upon which the whole company burst forth in a grand chorus of "Anneck! Anneck! hurrow!" And this they repeated three several times. In vain were all my enquiries for the meaning of this singular custom.

**Royal Cornwall Gazette**, 9 September 1809 [Michael Tangye, 'Customs Remembered', *Old Cornwall* vol. 9, no. 6, Spring 1982]

## 1810

245 The tinners of Cornwall may be divided into two classes, the streamers and miners. They are men who are occupied in two distinct departments of the same general branch, but whose habits, manners, customs, genius and understanding bear little or no resemblance to each other.

**The Tradesman**, v, 249, 1810 [Hamilton Jenkin, 1962]

246 I observed that the impression on the minds of those who inhabit other parts of the kingdom is that the Cornish miner has something of the savage character, but that I, on the other hand, found them civil and obliging and not at all of the description supposed.

**Joseph Farrington**, *Diary*, 1810 [Hamilton Jenkin, 1962]

# 1811

**247** No county affords a greater variety of wheel and other carriages than Cornwall.

> **G. B. Worgan**, *A General View of the Agriculture of the County of Cornwall*, 1811

**248** A large white, long-sided, razor-backed pig was the true Cornish breed.

> **G. B. Worgan**, *A General View of the Agriculture of the County of Cornwall*, 1811

# 1816

**249** The Methodists in Western Cornwall are very numerous, and of a respectable description; the changes which they have effected in the morals of the miners is really incredible …

> [J. A. Paris], **A Guide to Mounts Bay and the Land's End**, 1816

# 1816–17

**250** I have scarcely a doubt but the Stannary Parliaments were a continuation, even to our own times, of the old British courts before the times of Julius Caesar.

> **Richard Polwhele**, *The History of Cornwall*, 1816/1817

**251** Not many years ago were seen on the hospitable board … the fresh-boiled buttock of cow-beef with sippets and onions, the squab pye, the leek and pork pie – on which clotted cream was profusely poured – the goose and parsnip, and the fish and apple pie. At some houses in West Cornwall the *dash-an-darras* or stirrup cup is scarcely even now out of fashion.

> **Richard Polwhele**, *The History of Cornwall*, 1816/1817

**252** The ardent spirits to which the vulgar Cornish are habituated, are unquestionably prejudicial to health.

> **Richard Polwhele**, *The History of Cornwall*, 1816/1817

# 1816

**253** The extent to which smuggling is carried on among us, by all ranks and both sexes, forms a curious comment on our boasted patriotism and humanity in these distressing times … Descending thro' the middle to the lower classes, you find all tributary to France; from those who use French articles of dress, down to such as import to drink French brandy; and, consequently, all contributing to the public distress, which all so loudly complain of.

> **West Briton**, April 1816

254 The Midsummer Eve bonfires have long been a source of danger to the town and I give notice that they must be held on the Western Green.

**Henry Boase**, *Diary*, 26 May 1816 [J. E. Hooper, 'The Mayor's Diary: Penzance in 1816', *Old Cornwall* vol. 3, no. 9, Summer 1941]

## 1817

255 Desperate wrestling matches, inhuman cock-fights, pitched battles, and riotous revellings, are now happily of much rarer occurrence than heretofore.

**C. S. Gilbert**, *An Historical Survey of the County of Cornwall*, 1817 [–1838]

256 [It is] the custom in Cornwall to ascribe everything that is great and whose use is unknown to that immortal hero [Arthur].

**C. S. Gilbert**, *An Historical Survey of the County of Cornwall*, 1817 [–1838]

## 1819

257 Thousands of acres of downs, commons, and wastes have been enclosed and are continually being enclosed by the miners and others on a small scale, generally from three to six acres in a tenement, on each of which one or two cottages are erected.

**Richard Thomas**, *Report on Mining Area*, 1819

## 1820

258 ... in general the roads of Cornwall are narrow, intricate, and worn into deep ruts; some of them are mere gullies formed by torrents.

**The History and Topography of Cornwall**, 1820

259 Grampound was not a mixed scene of good and evil; it did not present a medley of voters, of whom some were corrupt and others incorrupt, it was one mass of notorious corruption; all the electors received money, all received it without shame.

**Lord John Russell**, *Annual Register*, 1820

## 1821

260 The mines of Cornwall occupy the attention of the principal inhabitants. As you advance to the west, so you hear them more and more talked about till you arrive at Truro; there their whole ideas are immersed in the value of the shares of such and such a mine; if you go to Redruth, then it is the weight of a piece of ore or the quality of what was raised or dug up yesterday.

**Diary of Thomas Preston covering his tour through the West of England and Wales**, 1821 [*Old Cornwall*, vol. 7, no. 11, Autumn 1972]

261 I went per coach to Redruth, this being the centre of the mines ... in

fact Redruth is nothing but the residence of the people who manage the mines, for the night, and in the morning they ride off again to their respective places.

**Diary of Thomas Preston covering his tour through the West of England and Wales,** 1821 [*Old Cornwall*, vol. 7, no. 11, Autumn 1972]

262 "Tressilian?" answered my host of the Bear, "a worthy name; and, as I think, of Cornish lineage; for what says the south proverb –

By Pol, Tre, and Pen,

You may know the Cornish men.

Shall I say the worthy Mr. Tressilian of Cornwall?"

"Say no more than I have given you warrant for, mine host, and so shall you be sure you speak no more than is true. A man may have one of these honourable prefixes to his name, yet be born far from Saint Michael's Mount."

**Walter Scott,** *Kenilworth,* 1821

# 1822

263    Now pleasure fills the sparkling glass,
Of Cornwall's sons we'll sing;
For they are worthy kindness yet,
And praise my lays shall bring:

*For 'tis our watchword still,*
*Rise, one and all!*
*And where's the heart that will not warm*
*At "One and All!"*

1st verse and chorus of **The Watchword of Cornwall**, 9 April 1822 [*Old Cornwall* no. 11, Summer 1930]

# 1824

264 Pengwinion, you Cornish Chough, has the good wind blown you north?

**Walter Scott,** *Redgauntlet,* 1824

265 At present we hold its [the Cornish language] mighty shadow in the pages of our history, and even this is gradually disappearing. The only scattered remnants which have survived its oral existence, may be found in those provincial phrases, and local names, for which Cornwall is so peculiarly remarkable.

**Fortescue Hitchens & Samuel Drew,** *The History of Cornwall,* 1824

266 It is much to be doubted if in any walks of life similar to theirs a race of men more hospitable, polite, communicative, and intelligent than the

captains of the Cornish mines are, can be found in England.

**Fortescue Hitchens & Samuel Drew**, *The History of Cornwall*, 1824

267 "One and All" accompanied by three huzzas will infallibly reanimate their [the Cornish] spirits, in the midst of a doubtful exploit.

**Fortescue Hitchens & Samuel Drew**, *The History of Cornwall*, 1824

## 1825

268 [The inhabitants of the county] are taught from infancy to old age to look upon the fatalities of the sea as the most fortunate occurrence that they can possibly witness ...

John Robeson, 'Tales of the Cornish Wreckers', in *English Chronicle*, 1825 [Vivian, 1969]

269     A good sword and a trusty hand!
        A merry heart and true!
        King James's men shall understand
        What Cornish lads can do!

**Robert Stephen Hawker**, *The Song of the Western Men*, 1825

## 1826

270 To Cornish People residing in London – James Philp, Bookseller, Falmouth, respectfully informs his friends and Cornish people in general residing in town, that he has commenced a monthly publication, entitled *The Selector, or Cornish Magazine* ...

**John Bull**, 5 February 1826

271 The effects of Methodism in making the drunkard sober, the idle industrious, the profligate moral, and in inducing men to provide decently and comfortably for their families, and to give a suitable education to their children, can be attested to by thousands of witnesses.

[John William Gilbert], *Letters from West Cornwall written in the year 1826* [1861]

272 In no county does the ox stand in higher estimation for all kinds of work than in Cornwall.

[John William Gilbert], *Letters from West Cornwall written in the year 1826* [1861]

273 ... even the young female Methodists dress gayer now, though still they

have not become so worldly as to wear bows of ribbons in their bonnets.

[John William Gilbert], *Letters from West Cornwall written in the year 1826* [1861

274 There is a vast number more shops in this place [Hayle] than there was twenty years ago.

[John William Gilbert], *Letters from West Cornwall written in the year 1826* [1861]

275 No one more sincerely rejoices than does the editor of this ancient mystery [The Passion Poem] that the Cornish dialect of the Celtic or Gaelic languages has ceased altogether from being used by the inhabitants of Cornwall ...

Davies Gilbert, *Mount Calvery* ..., 1826

## 1827

276 The amount of milk eked out to them [the poor] after the farmer's family and pigs and calves have been fed, is too sparing to be worth mentioning. By far the greater part of them do not taste milk, because they cannot procure it, from one end of the year to another.

Dr. Clement Carlyon, *Observations on the Endemic Typhus Fever of Cornwall*, 1827

277 ... two shoals, by colour, passed out, but no 'Hevva', it being Sunday.

Old Diary, 12 August 1827 [Hamilton Jenkin, 1945]

278 Cornishmen are intractable if put the least out of their way. They harmonize together 'one and all', but not with strangers ...

Capt. Andrews, *Journey from Beunos Ayres...undertaken on behalf of the Chilian and Peruvian Mining Association, 1825–26*, [1827]

279 Annually, on Midsummer Eve, fires are lighted on the heights of Cornwall.

Thomas Hogg, *Fabulous History of the Ancient Kingdom of Cornwall*, 1827

## 1831

280 Wesleyanism is the established religion of Cornwall.

Bishop Henry Phillpotts, 1831 [Keith Austin, *A History of Methodism and the Penzance Wesleyan Society*, http://iriss.co.uk/Chapel_Street/methodist-history-3.html]

# 1832

**281** The rage for emigration that now prevails in the north of this county is wholly unprecedented in Cornwall ...
   **West Briton**, 6 April 1832

**282** Surely the tin mines are not to be sacrificed in order to supply a revenue for the Heir Apparent.
   **West Briton**, 7 September 1832

# 1834

**283** One of the great defects of Cornish Methodism [is that] while the number of members is increased sevenfold there are only three times the number of preachers.
   **Richard Treffry Jnr.**, *Memoirs of Mr. John Edwards Trezise of St. Just*, 1834 [1837]

# 1835

**284** Miners in Cornwall never appeared to be so deficient in education as in most other counties.
   **Mr. Taylor**, manager of the Consolidated Mines, *Parliamentary Papers*, 1835

# 1837

**285** If it is thought that the first born son of the Crown receives any additional dignity by being born Duke of Cornwall, by all means let that dignity be kept up, and a provision suitable be made; but let us not keep up an ineligible sort of property, an oppressive tax, and a knot of sinecurists, merely for the sake of that dignity.
   **West Briton**, 1 December 1837

# 1838

**286** A white cross on a black ground was formerly the banner of St. Perran, and the standard of Cornwall; probably with some allusion to the black ore and the white metal of tin.
   **Davies Gilbert**, *Parochial History of Cornwall*, 1838

**287** I found the beach [between Sennen and Priest Cove] covered, for the space of a mile, with the ship's cargo, which the coastguards of the adjoining stations were doing their utmost to protect ... There were four or five thousand people of all classes present, who were engaged in staving in the casks, drinking the liquor and wine, and plundering the property of every description ...

**Alexander Shairp**, in letter to the comptroller-general of coastguards, 4 October 1838 [Hamilton Jenkin, 1945]

## 1839

**288** ... The population on the coast of Cornwall has long been addicted to this species of plunder ... Whilst on other parts of the English coast, persons may assemble by hundreds for plunder on the occasion of a wreck, on the Cornish coast they assemble ... in thousands.

**First Report of the Constabulary Force Commissioners**, 1839 [Hamilton Jenkin, 1945; Bella Bathurst, *The Wreckers*, 2005]

**289** Great as are the advantages which this nation in general enjoys from the invention of the steam engine, and the successive improvements which it has received; there is, perhaps, no place in particular, where these advantages have been greater, or more evident, than in Cornwall.

**Thomas Lean**, *On the Steam Engines in Cornwall*, 1839 [Payton, 1993]

## 1840

**290** The mines [of the St. Day district] are situated in bleak desert, rendered all the more doleful by the unhealthy appearance of its inhabitants... Several woeful figures in tattered garments, with pick-axes on their shoulders, crawled out of a dark fissure and repaired to an hovel, which I learned was a gin-shop. There they pass the few hours allotted to them above ground and drink, it is to be hoped, an oblivion of their subterraneous existence.

**West Briton**, 24 January 1840

**291** On Monday last, the ceremony of dispelling the supposed evil influence of witchcraft took place at Newlyn. It appears that a mackerel seine, called the 'Broom', had the ill-luck of invariably missing whatever fish she shot at, and the cause was attributed to the evil wishes of a simple young woman of the place. The mode adopted to counteract it was burning a portion of the article under the influence of the supposed witch, amid the cheers and huzzas of the assembly.

**Penzance Gazette**, 20 May 1840

**292**    Barley bread's upon the board,
Wheaten bread we can't afford.
Wheaten bread must pay the rent,
Else to Bodmin we'll be sent.

[Before the repeal of the Corn Laws in 1846 wheat flour was very expensive]
**Anonymous**, c.1840 [William Paynter, *Old St Ives*, 1927]

## 1842

293 The working miner is attached to his calling because it gives him more leisure time than a day labourer enjoys.
**John Buller**, A *Statistical Account of the Parish of St. Just-in-Penwith*, 1842

294 We, this great English nation, whose race and language are now overrunning the earth from one end of it to the other, we were born when the white horse of the Saxons had established his dominion from the Tweed to the Tamar …
**Thomas Arnold**, *Introductory Lecture on Modern History*, 1842

295 There is an inn [in Boscastle] called 'The Robin', homely, but clean and neat, and as everywhere in Cornwall, right hospitable to the stranger.
**Cyrus Redding**, An *Illustrated Itinerary of Cornwall*, 1842

296 The attraction of the Pit [Gwennap Pit] never, within our remembrance, appeared to be greater, and no one could have gazed on that amphitheatre, crowded as it was in every part, and to its very brim, with so many thousands of people in cheerful holiday dresses, and have participated in the happy holiday proceedings which evidently pervaded the assembly, without considering himself well repaid for the journey he may have made to get there.
***Royal Cornwall Gazette***, 20 May 1842

297 The Devil will not venture among the Cornish, for fear of being sainted or put in a pie; the variety of sainted churches as of pies being pretty nearly equal, and some of them both excellent in their way.
**England in the 19th Century – Illustrated Itinerary of the County of Cornwall**, How & Parsons, 1842

## 1843

298 The Carriages on the Hayle Railway commenced carrying passengers to day, for the first time, when some hundreds were carried down and up, it being free for the first time.
**Thomas Nicoll**, 'A Redruth Journal … ' 1843, in *Old Cornwall*, vol. 5, no. 7, 1956

## 1844

299 [Mr. Tregaskis of the Temperance Society] alluded to an old custom which had long been kept up in Padstow at the first of May, called the Hobby Horse

– a remnant of the May games of former times, and which has now become a scene of riot, debauchery and general licentiousness – a perfect nuisance to all the respectable inhabitants of the place.

**West Briton**, June 1844 [Douch, 1966]

# 1845

300 To the Proprietors of the Hobby Horse of Padstow.

This is to give you notice that on or about the end of the month I shall offer you the Bullock according to promise. It is for you to consult against that time, whether you will give up your vain practice of the Hobby for the more rational amusement of eating Roast Beef.

**Thomas Tregaskis**, on poster erected in Padstow dated 10 April 1845

301 Fellow Townsmen

We have read the proposal Mr. Tregaskis made to the 'Proprietors of the Hobbyhorse', which we decidedly reject ... The bones of every Padstow Boy are fired by the Hobbyhorse. As soon as a child is able to lisp its parent's name it will chant the glorious strains of our ancient Festival Song ... And shall we allow aliens and strangers to usurp our pleasures, and rob us of our birth-right, that we have inherited from Mother to Daughter, from Father to Son? No we will not: and poor Sir Tommy shall not be crowned King of the Hobbyhorse.

**The Mayers**, on poster printed by them [Donald R. Rawe, *Padstow's Obby Oss and May Day Festivities*, 1971]

302 Of those who bore the honour of sanctity, St. Piran may be ranked the most venerated. A native of Ireland, a nave at Exeter Cathedral contained an altar to his name. An ancient catalogue of relics of Exeter confirms 'brachium Sancti Pirani confessoris', an arm of St. Piran.

**G. Oliver**, *Monasticon Dioecesis Exoniensis*, 1845

# 1846

303 The first part of this little collection contains specimens of the present Cornish provincial dialect, which is but little known out of the county; and even there is gradually wearing away in the towns; and is scarcely to be heard in its full richness except in the mining districts, or in the parts most remote from traffic and intercourse with strangers.

**Uncle Jan Trenoodle** [William Sandys], *Specimens of Cornish Provincial Dialect*, 1846

304 We last week adventured on a journey into Cornwall – a matter which

many of our readers who are personally unacquainted with the district … will think very easy of accomplishment. We assure them, however, that they would find themselves very much mistaken if they attempted it themselves. They would learn that a journey by the Telegraph as the Cornish coach is misnomered, has anything but the velocity of that ingenious contrivance to recommend it.

**The Times**, 3 January 1846

305 Whenever a wreck takes place, plunder generally ensues, be the locality where it may – and 'the people of the neighbourhood' are spoken of as 'having very improperly conducted themselves in carrying off the property,' etc, etc; but if it happens on the coast of *our* county, they are at once held up to execration as 'Cornish Wreckers'.

**Penzance Gazette** 2 December 1846 [Vivian, 1969]

# 1847

306 Cornwall should be treated as an Island. *One and All* is our motto.
**Rev. John Wallis**, *The Cornwall Register*, 1847

307 For 800 years we have been deprived of our ancient See.
**Rev. John Wallis**, *The Cornwall Register*, 1847

308 Miners of Cornwall! Be true to yourselves and maintain your character for order and submission to the laws. Trust your employers to guard you and then you will find every disposition to alleviate the distress which now prevails – but persist in riot and tumult, and you will bitterly feel the power of the law, and ere have to lament Husbands, Fathers, Sons and Brothers suffering the punishment which inevitably awaits the evil doer.
**West Briton**, 11 June 1847

309 Burnard, our Cornish sculptor, dined with us. He is a great, powerful, pugilistic-looking fellow at twenty-nine; a great deal of face, with all the features massed in the centre; mouth open, and all sorts of simplicities flowing out of it.
**Caroline Fox**, *Memories of Old Friends*, 4 October 1847

# 1848

310 A gentleman wished to have in his possession a living specimen of the chough, or Cornish crow, a bird which is now becoming rare …
**Rev. C. A. Johns**, *A Week at the Lizard*, 1848

# 1849

311 He was a tributer, and tributers look with as great a contempt upon the tutmen, as the latter do upon the surface labourers.

**Anonymous**, *Morning Chronicle*, 24 November 1849

# 1851

312 The Cornish are essentially a cheerful, contented race. The views of the working men are remarkably moderate and sensible – I never met with so few grumbles anywhere.

**Wilkie Collins**, *Rambles Beyond Railways*, 1851

313 A Cornishman's national pride is in his pilchards …

**Wilkie Collins**, *Rambles Beyond Railways*, 1851

314 … the difficulty of comprehending it [Cornish talk] is still further increased by the manner in which the people speak. They pronounce rapidly and indistinctly, often running separate syllables into one another through a sentence, until the whole sounds like one long fragmentary word.

**Wilkie Collins**, *Rambles Beyond Railways*, 1851

315 … Cornwall – a county where, it must be remembered, a stranger is doubly a stranger, in relation to provincial sympathies; where the national feeling is almost entirely merged in the local feeling; where a man speaks of himself as *Cornish* in much the same spirit as a Welshman speaks of himself as Welsh.

**Wilkie Collins**, *Rambles Beyond Railways*, 1851

316 … by my father's side I am of Cornish blood … the best blood in the world

**George Borrow**, *Lavengro*, 1851

# 1851–4

317 Cornish revivals were things by themselves … Every year, in one part or another, a revival would spring up, during which believers were refreshed and sinners awakened … [I]t is well-known that revivals begin and continue for a time and that then they cease as mysteriously as they began.

**Rev. William Haslam**, *From Death into Life*, [1851–4], 1880

# 1854

318 This amphitheatre [Gwennap Pit] is regarded by the lord of the manor as in the possession of the Methodists, and for their exclusive use.

**Rev. Joseph Entwisle**, *Memoir*, 1854

319 ... more mines have been discontinued from want of management than from want of mineral, jealousy and petty squabblings being fertile sources of failure.
**George Henwood**, *Lectures on Mining and Geology*, 1854

320 You can only see Cornwall or know anything about it by walking through it. It is romantic to a degree, though probably one would not like to live in it.
**George Borrow**, 1854 [Ida Proctor, *Visitors to Cornwall*, 1982]

321 O Cornwall, happy blessed spot of ground,
   Where richest ores of every kind abound,
   Thy very hills are brass, thy rocks are tin,
   Thy wealth is not exposed without, but hid within.
**Mining Journal**, 1854 [*Cornish Magazine* vol. 10, no. 2, June 1967]

## 1855

322 The keen Cornish miners have a kind of proverb amongst them, which they keep pretty closely to their own companies, and which is to this effect:- That the county is divided into two classes, Cornish men and 'Lun'oners', and that it is the privilege of the former to live – not by the mines, but by the latter; in other words, by the speculation of strangers. There is much truth in this.
**J. R. Leifchild**, *Cornwall's Mines and Miners*, 1855

323 In the mining districts of the west, about Camborne and Redruth, the ground is literally sown with cottages, and out of each cottage issues a whole crop of children at the sound of any passing vehicle.
**J. R. Leifchild**, *Cornwall's Mines and Miners*, 1855

324 ... the three Duchy Charters are sufficient in themselves to vest in the Dukes of Cornwall, not only the government of Cornwall, but the entire territorial dominion in and over the county which had previously been invested in the Crown ... not only all the territorial possessions of the Crown in Cornwall, but every prerogative right and source of revenue ...
**Duchy of Cornwall**, *Preliminary statement ...* , 1855 [Payton, 1993]

325 ... from earliest times Cornwall was distinct from the Kingdom of England, and under separate government ... Cornwall, like Wales, was at the time of the Conquest, and was subsequently treated in many respects, as distinct from England.
**Duchy of Cornwall**, *Preliminary statement ...* , 1855 [Payton, 1993]

# 1857

326 The portion of Britain assigned to Troenius was the Western Keryn or promontory, extending from Torbay to the Land's End, part of which is now known as Cornwall. From the Keryn, Troenius changed his name into Keryn that is, the duke within it exercised the same prerogatives as the kings of Lloegria, Cambria and Albyn did within their territories. Next to these crowns, it is the oldest title in Britain.

**R. W. Morgan**, *The British Kymry*, 1857

327 The thorough Cornish man's respect for his own shrewdness and that of his clan is unbounded, or only equalled by his profound contempt for 'foreigners' from the east …

**Herman Merivale**, 'Cornwall', in *The Quarterly Review* 102, 1857

## c. 1857–60

328 The Cornish are a race partly Celtic, partly Saxon, but more Celtic than Saxon. They are incomparably the strongest men in Britain; they make the best soldiers and perhaps sailors …

**George Borrow**, *Celtic Bards, Chiefs and Kings*, c. 1857–60 [1928]

329 … though portions of the Welsh mysteries exist, no entire piece has been preserved, so that not much can be said about them, not a tenth part of what can be said of the mysteries in another dialect of the Cimbric tongue, the beautiful Cornish, the speech of the writer's own forefathers.

**George Borrow**, *Celtic Bards, Chiefs and Kings*, c. 1857–60 [1928]

330 The Cornishmen, a poor, but strong, brave, and high-spirited race…

**George Borrow**, *Celtic Bards, Chiefs and Kings*, c. 1857–60 [1928]

## 1858

331 The active life of a miner, supposing it to commence at ten years of age, terminates in eighteen years, at the very early age of twenty-eight, when, in most other occupations, he would be in the prime of manhood and vigour.

**Dr. Richard Couch**, *Proceedings of Royal Cornwall Polytechnic Society*, 1858

## 1859

332 This extraordinary viaduct [Royal Albert Bridge] … for novelty and ingenuity of construction stands unrivalled in the world …

**Murray**, *Handbook for Travellers in Devon and Cornwall*, 1859

333 The Cornish are remarkable for their sanguine temperament, their indomitable perseverance, their ardent hope in adventure, and their desire for discovery and novelty; hence their wide distribution all over the world, in the most remote corners of which they are to be found amongst the pioneers; and to this very cause has science to boast of so many brilliant ornaments who claim Cornwall as their birthplace.

**George Henwood**, 1859 [Payton, 1993]

## c. 1860

334 Natural depravity and the custom of centuries have inspired the inhabitants of the coast with a rapacity for plundering those wrecks ... the name 'Wrecker', therefore, applies to vast numbers inhabit the various parishes along the coast; and unfortunately such has been the frequency of wrecks every winter, that the people look as naturally for them at that season, as the sharks for the devotees who perish in the waters of the Ganges.

**Rev. G. C. Smith**, c. 1860 [Hamilton Jenkin, 1945]

## 1861

335 In the Cornish tongue, Midsummer is called Goluan, which means light and rejoicing. At that season, the natives make a procession through the towns or villages with lighted torches.

**W. Winwood Reade**, *The Veil of Isis, or, the Mysteries of the Druids*, 1861

336 On May Eve the Cornish erect stumps of trees before their doors. On the first of the month the famous May-pole is raised, adorned with flowers and encircled by the pretty country lasses who little know of what this pole ... is an emblem.

**W. Winwood Reade**, *The Veil of Isis, or, the Mysteries of the Druids*, 1861

337 The provincial language of the Cornish of the present day is hardly a dialect, but rather, for the country, a singularly pure English, spoken in a kind of recitative twang that it would not be easy to describe.

**J. O. Halliwell**, *Rambles in West Cornwall*, 1861

338 [Cornwall is] one of the most un-English of English counties ...

**Chambers Journal**, 17 February 1861

339 The ancient Cornish language lies like a buried city under our feet – we pass to and fro above it, but heed it not in the hustle of everyday life.

**John Bellow**, 'On the Cornish Language', in *Royal Cornwall Polytechnic Society Annual Report*, 1861

340 The Cornish Celt is migratory, seafaring, commercial, self-reliant … in fact, everything the Welshman and Breton are not.
> *Journal of the Royal Institution of Cornwall*, 43.2, 1861 [Bernard Deacon, 'On being a Cornish 'Celt' … : Lecture to International Celtic Congress, Dublin, July 2003]

## 1862

341 "Now, sir," said John Jones, "the way straight forward is the ffordd newydd and the one on our right hand is the hen ffordd. Which shall we follow, the new or the old?"
"There is a proverb in the Gerniweg [Cornish]", said I, "which was the language of my forefathers, saying, 'ne'er leave the old way for the new,' we will therefore go by the hen ffordd."
> **George Borrow**, *Wild Wales*, 1862

## 1863

342 It is … highly gratifying to learn that wherever the Cornish miner goes, he is generally well received, and rarely fails not only to benefit himself, but those of his friends remaining at home, by the welcome remittances which arrive by almost every mail.
> **West Briton**, 23 October 1863

## 1864

343 We have four mine establishments with an oven in each of them, large enough to contain two hundred pasties or hoggans. We have benches round a long room where they can sit down, and hot water is always prepared for dinner-time.
> **Mine Manager**, *Report of the Royal Commissioners Appointed to Inquire into the Condition of All Mines in Britain* … , 1864

344 I have stood upon the hill, just where we cross North and South Crofty, many times, to look at the faces of the miners as they come up, and you will see very few old men.
> **Mine Captain**, *Report of the Royal Commissioners Appointed to Inquire into the Condition of All Mines in Britain* … , 1864

345 Mistletoe has recently been introduced into West Cornwall from Devon

and Somerset. At Redruth, the Druids' town, many of the inhabitants did not know the nature or modern use of mistletoe ...

**Illustrated London News**, 2 January 1864

346 The Cornish seine owners and fishermen are more than ever of opinion that the present season will prove to be the most productive one on record. The catches [of mackerel] for the week ending Saturday last were enormous, and many of the local markets were overstocked.

**The Times**, 17 May 1864

# 1865

347 Lamorna, formerly one of the most romantic spots on the coast of West Penwith, is now being selected for the site of some granite works, little better than a mason's yard.

**Murray**, *Handbook for Travellers in Devon and Cornwall*, 1865

348 Examples of longevity must not be sought among the miners. On an average, they do not live beyond forty years.

**Visitor to Cornwall**, 1865 [Hamilton Jenkin, 1962]

349 We have few turbulent demagogues in Cornwall. A miner who has any rhetorical powers and strong lungs prefers the pulpit to the platform.

**Western Morning News**, 10 January 1865

350 Cornwall is proud, and justly so, of her miners. Who can say what England owes to these men? They produce riches and scarcely enjoy common necessaries themselves.

**Henri A. Esquiros**, *Cornwall and its Coasts*, 1865

351 It has been said of the Cornish miners that they possess the mathematics of the mole. Endowed with a species of instinct and an admirable judgment, they find means, practically of solving certain problems which seem to demand all the calculations of geometry.

**Henri A. Esquiros**, *Cornwall and its Coasts*, 1865

352 I admit that neither of these two Cornish gentlemen [Thomas Tonkin and William Gwavas] had any pretensions to a knowledge of Welsh; but for the Cornish of the 18th century, I am satisfied that they were the very best authorities of their time, and ought not to be despised by Welsh linguists, over whom they had certainly an immense advantage of a practical knowledge of their mother-tongue, although they may have been inferior in general linguistic attainments.

**Prince L. L. Bonaparte**, *Some Observations on the Rev. R. Williams's Preface to his 'Lexicon Cornu-Britannicum'*, 1865

353 Those wild dreams which swayed with irresistible force the skin-clad Briton of the Cornish hills, have not yet entirely lost their power where even the National and British Schools are busy with the people, and the Mechanics' Institutions are diffusing the truth of science.
**Robert Hunt**, *Popular Romances of the West of England*, 2nd series, 1865

# 1866

354 The merchants, it seemed, were well known to the Cornishmen on shore, and Hereward went up with them unopposed; past the ugly dykes and muddy leats, where Alef's slaves were streaming the gravel for tin ore; through rich alluvial pastures spotted with red cattle; and up to Alef's town [Gweek].
**Charles Kingsley**, *Hereward the Wake*, 1866

355 If we should permit the Cornish miners to emigrate, let us for a moment consider the people whom we should lose. Every one who knows them must be ready to affirm that England has no labourers who possess more industrial virtues. Their hazardous and difficult emplyment has made them brave, enduring, and intelligent; and their sobriety and religious devotion still bear testimony to the fact that amongst this population Wesley achieved his greatest and most lasting triumph.
**Henry Fawcett**, in letter to *The Times*, 23 August 1866

# 1867

356 It may cause a moment's distress to one's imagination when one hears that the last Cornish peasant who spoke the old tongue of Cornwall is dead, but, no doubt, Cornwall is the better for adopting English, for becoming more thoroughly one with the rest of the country.
**Matthew Arnold**, *On the Study of Celtic Literature*, 1867

357 The year now ended is one of the most disastrous for the mining interests of Cornwall during the present century ...
**West Briton**, 4 January 1867

358 The various committees appointed to carry out the extensive system of relief to the poor now organised at Redruth, have for the last fourteen days been unceasing in their labour ...
**West Briton**, 1 February 1867

359 Hurrahing at the neck cutting, and the pitching up of the crow sheaf are less frequent than formerly, what is termed cutting the neck is well known throughout the county but catching the crow sheaf only in the eastern part. It was the sheaf that was placed to complete the mow at one end; when the sheaf was thrown up, the person making the mow would call out, 'I have it! I have it!' The person throwing up the sheaf enquiring 'What have you? What have you?' The reply would be 'A crow! A crow!' Then all being assembled in the mowhay, a hearty hurrah would be given which was frequently heard at a considerable distance.

**West Briton**, 28 June 1867 [Tangye, 1982]

360 A Cornish revival is a very stormy thing, and would astound and alarm you frigid Northerners.

**Rev. William Mills**, in S. Mills, *Memoir of the Rev. William Mills*, 1867 [Michael S. Edwards, *The Divisions of Cornish Methodism*, 1964]

# 1868

361    We shall see the rolling ocean,
We shall breathe the fresh sea air,
See, the country comes to greet us,
And the swallows can't outfly,
Houses, trees and hedges greet us,
Running by, and running by.
Happy Camborne!
Where the railway is so nigh.

**Rev. Samuel Coley**, *Life of the Rev. Thomas Collins*, 1868

362 Within easy memory every boat in Newlyn always set aside a portion of the catch, and left it in a collected heap on the beach to propitiate 'Bucka'

**One and All**, June 1868

# 1869

363 … under the elevating influence of sobriety and true religion, the Cornish are rapidly rising above their former degrading credulousness.

**Rev. C. G. Honor**, 1869 [Hamilton Jenkin, 1945]

364 I congratulate you on the possession of a treasure, which you are not aware of. The Ordinale of St. Meriadoc … is a genuine Cornish mystery, the existence of which has hitherto been unknown.

**Rev. Robert Williams**, in letter to W. W. E. Wynne, 1869 [Ellis, 1974]

365 Her [Gwenny Carfax's] father [Simon] seems to have been a miner, a Cornishman (as she declares) of more than average excellence, and better than any two men to be found in Devonshire, or any four in Somerset.

**R. D. Blackmore**, *Lorna Doone*, 1869

## 1870

366 The Cornish seem fine tall folk, especially the women, much taller larger people than the Welsh, and most of them appear to be dark-haired.

**Francis Kilvert**, *Diary*, 1870–1 [*Kilvert's Cornish Diary*, 1989]

367 A bitter moment it was when the Tamar was crossed and Cornwall left behind, perhaps forever. I seemed to linger once more over the last fond look at the Cornish sea.

**Francis Kilvert**, *Diary*, 1870–1[*Kilvert's Diary: selections* ..., 1960]

368 ... persons living west of Penzance were regarded as great travellers if they had "crossed over Hayle", which, at that time [c.1800], was a dangerous undertaking, on account of its shifting quicksands; and people living further east were looked on as foreigners by the west-country folks.

**William Bottrell**, *Traditions and Hearthside Stories of West Cornwall*, 1870

369 This primitive race of the hills knew next to nothing of any occurrences beyond their immediate neighbourhood, and being, like all the Celtic race, of a loquacious turn and sociable disposition, their chief resource for passing the eventide, and other times of rest, was the relation of traditional stories, or, as they say "drolling away the time" in public-house or chimney-corner ...

**William Bottrell**, *Traditions and Hearthside Stories of West Cornwall*, 1870

370 Distance frightens us; but steam and the telegraph have abolished distance. A Cornish miner and his family can now emigrate to the Burra Burra with greater ease, and at less expense, than a hundred years ago they would make their way to a Lancashire coal-pit.

**J. F. Froude**, 'England and Her Colonies', in *Fraser's Magazine*, January 1870 [Eric Richard, *Britannia's Children...*, 2004]

371 It is said to be a common custom among Cornish miners to marry and emigrate within a week of the performance of the solemn contract.

**The Times**, 10 February 1870

## 1871

372 Although there is the utmost activity at the Cornish tin mines ... large

numbers of working miners continue to leave the county for the north of England, and for other countries, chiefly America and Australia.

*The Times*, 25 October 1871

373 There is intense excitement in Cornwall concerning tin mining and speculation is going on at a dangerous rate.

*The Times*, 8 December 1871

## 1872

374 Two matters of vast importance to Cornish mining – the serious and still increasing price of coal and the scarcity of working miners – are occupying the earnest attention of managers, pursers, and other officials.

*The Times*, 30 August 1872

## 1873

375 ... so many of the miners were Cornishmen as to give Moonta and Wallaroo the air of Cornish towns.

**Anthony Trollope**, *Australia*, 1873

376 The usually quiet and orderly Cornish miners broke out into open riot at Camborne on Tuesday; but considering they had the town ... completely at their mercy for several hours, the amount of damage done is not great.

*The Times*, 9 October 1873

377 The place [the North Cornish cliffs] is pre-eminently (for one person at least) the region of dream and mystery. The ghostly birds, the pall-like sea, the frothy wind, the eternal soliloquy of the waters, the bloom of dark purple cast that seems to exhale from the shore-ward precipices, in themselves lend to the scene an atmosphere like the twilight of a night vision.

**Thomas Hardy**, *A Pair of Blue Eyes*, 1873

## 1874

378 Tin mining in Cornwall is now in a most critical position.

*The Times*, 24 February 1874

379 Many a Cornish man may thank the accident of his birthplace for an immortality he can scarcely have hoped for when he sees the writings he must have had some difficulty in recollecting blazoned over pages of this handsome volume [*Bibliotheca Cornubiensis*].

'Cornish Literature and Litterateurs', in **The Times,** 10 March 1874

380 There is quite a panic in the West Cornish mines.
   **West Briton**, 13 April 1874

# 1875

381 In the history of mining in Cornwall it has known no such disastrous year as that of 1874.
   **West Briton**, 7 January 1875

382 The memory of the Cornish language as a past tradition lingers to a greater degree in certain families than is commonly suspected. I have found some half dozen persons (mostly, I own, belonging in one family) who can recite the Cornish numerals up to 20.
   **Rev. W. S. Lach-Szyrma**, 'The numerals in Old Cornish', in *Academy*, 20 March 1875

# 1876

383 The gloom which surrounds the mining industry of Cornwall is relieved by an occasional glimpse of sunshine.
   **The Times**, 12 January 1876

# 1877

384 Of Gelli Wic (or, as it is generally written, Gelliwig), in Cornwall, frequent mention is made in the Triads, where it is named as one of the three national thrones of the Island of Britain, and one of King Arthur's chief seats of empire, in which he was used to celebrate the high festivals of Christmas, Easter, and Whitsuntide.
   **Lady Charlotte Guest**, *The Mabinogion – English translation and notes*, 1877

385 The Cornish fishermen suspend work on Sundays, but the east country fishermen, who come to St. Ives in the season have no such scruples.
   **West Briton**, 14 May 1877

386 I am the son of a King …
   **Billy Bray**, in F. W. Bourne, *The King's Son; or A Memoir of Billy Bray*, 1877

# 1878

387 The rain was coming down with a thoroughness characteristic of the county – there was a Cornish 'one-and-all'-ness about it that was unmistakable.
   **Mark Guy Pearse**, 'Christmas Eve in the 'Vivid'', in *Cornish & Devon Post*, 21 December 1878

# 1879

**388** The Cornish Bank (Messrs. Tweedy, Williams & Co.) ... stopped payment on Saturday. Not since the failure of Messrs. Hawkey, Whitford, & Co., Falmouth, bankers, in 1866, has there been such a calamity in Cornwall as this failure.

*The Times*, 6 January 1879

# 1880

**389** By his sanctified wit, Christian simplicity, fervid faith and many self-denying labours he commended himself to a wide circle of friends while living, and the published records since his death of his memorable sayings and doings has made his name familiar as a household word in our own and other lands.

**Inscription on the obelisk in memory of Billy Bray** in Baldhu churchyard, 1880

**390** Baldhu Church, like a city set upon a hill which cannot be hid, is visible for miles around; and from the burial ground where the ashes of Billy [Bray] rest, the visitor can see near and afar off the valleys that echoed to his words of ejaculatory praise, and the bleak hills scored with rough roads over which he travelled with light step and gladsome heart to declare to multitudes the tidings of salvation ...

**J. H. Blatt**, in letter dated 10 February in *Bible Christian Magazine*, 1880

**391** With the introduction of the railways and the increased means of communication that has brought and brings every year more strangers to West Cornwall, the peculiar dialect is fast dying out ...

**M. A. Courtney**, *Glossary of words in use in Cornwall – West Cornwall*, 1880

# 1882

**392** Rude as the *patois* of Cornwall may appear to strangers, yet no Cornishman familiar with it, listens to it other than with fondness. Whether at home, or in the distant colonies, the sound of the homely Cornish dialect falls pleasantly on the ear, and revives a host of kindly thoughts and feelings.

**Fred W. P. Jago**, *The Ancient Language and the Dialect of Cornwall*, 1882

**393** The Cornish dialect may be called the shadow, or penumbra of the ancient language; the link between the old and the new tongue; between Celtic and English.

**Fred W. P. Jago**, *The Ancient Language and the Dialect of Cornwall*, 1882

## c. 1883

394    One and All at duty's call,
       Shoulder to shoulder we stand or fall,
       On land and sea, where'er we be,
       We Cornish are ready, aye, One and All.
       Chorus to **E. H. Moore**'s 'The Cornish Motto Song', first sung in public
       c1883 [*Cornish Magazine*, vol. 4, no. 1, May 1961]

## 1884

395 Many ministers who labour in Cornwall have an eye on the Pit [Gwennap
Pit], where they may display their sacred oratory on the spot where John Wesley
stood ... but it is reserved for only a few. Mental vigour, apart from physical
strength, does not qualify a man for displaying his gladiatorship in that arena.
       **Royal Cornwall Gazette**, 30 May 1884

396 There is in the older Cornish church an indefinable something which
makes them seem more identified with the local surroundings than is the case
with church architecture in other parts of England.
       **John Dando Sedding**, 1884

397 Cornish art is wild, rustic, Moorish; it is unique; its strong salt flavour
unsuits it for other markets, just as other markets will not suit Cornwall.
       **John Dando Sedding**, 1884

## 1885

398 ... for a strong grasp of the leading questions of the day, and for close,
shrewd reasoning upon them, Cornish miners' meetings may be backed against
any corresponding assembly in London or Birmingham.
       **Daily News**, 1885

399 It may be worth consideration that the high physical and intellectual
average of the Cornish people may not be partly due to their having in their
veins a double portion of the blood of the old Romano-British chiefs and
military class ...
       **John Beddoe**, *Races of Britain*, 1885

400 The Cornish are generally dark in hair and often in eye: they are
decidedly the darkest people in England proper; they resemble the Scottish
Highlanders in their warmth of colouring ...
       **John Beddoe**, *Races of Britain*, 1885

**401** We wish this happy venture [*The Cornish Magazine and Devon Miscellany*] every success. We have long felt that there was room in the West of England for a popular periodical, quite outside and beyond the scope of our own Journal, and in The Cornish Magazine we have the realisation of our desires.

**The Western Antiquary**, 1885

# 1887

**402** The Cornishman is, and always has been, sui generis.

**W. H. Tregellas**, 'County characteristics – Cornwall', in *The Nineteenth Century*, November 1887

**403** Uther is still used as a Christian name in Cornwall.

**M. A. Courtney**, *Cornish Feasts and Folk-lore*, 1887 [1973]

**404** All men are boys in Cornwall.

**M. A. Courtney**, *Cornish Feasts and Folk-lore*, 1887 [1973]

**405** Cornish people possess in a marked degree all the characteristics of the Celts. They are imaginative, good speakers and story-tellers, describing persons and things in a style racy and idiomatic, often with appropriate gestures.

**M. A. Courtney**, *Cornish Feasts and Folk-lore*, 1887 [1973]

**406** Every stream in Cornwall however small is called a river ...

**M. A. Courtney**, *Cornish Feasts and Folk-lore*, 1887 [1973]

# 1888

**407** It is not too much to say that between the census of 1871–81 a third of the mining population of Cornwall left the county.

**L. L. Price**, Royal Statistical Society, 1888

**408** The Newlyners are the most significant body of painters now in England.

**Alice Meynell**, Review of a Royal Academy exhibition, 1888 [John Branfield, *A Breath of Fresh Air*, 2001]

**409** The Cornish miner is simply the most ill-paid, patient, hard-working mortal on the face of the earth.

**Edward Bosanketh**, *Tin*, 1888

## 1890–1

410 No ... bird with which I am acquainted ... unites the perfection of tameness with the limitless impetuosity of unreclaimed nature [like the chough].

    **A. H. Malan**, 'Cornish Choughs', in *JRIC*, 10, 1890–1

## 1891

411 A Cornishman is the easiest-going creature in existence if you only let him have his own way. Give him his head, and let him feel that he is going of his own accord, and he will do anything that you insinuate. Once try to coerce him, and no more unreasonable, hot-headed, fanatical man is to be met with anywhere.

    **Katharine Lee** (Mrs. Henry Jenner), *Love or Money: A Novel*, 1891

412 The great gale, with snow, the like of which had never before been heard of in these quarters. Lots of wrecks and damage ... All stayed up till about 2, while the slates, windows and launders blew off.

    **Henry Scott Tuke**, *Diary*, 9 March 1891

413 [W]e are awfully conceited people ... Nobody thinks so much of his country as a Cornishman. People are born elsewhere ... but they don't seem to make half so much fuss about it as Cornishmen.

    **Rev. Mark Guy Pearse**, 'Some Old Folks at Home', lecture given in Gawler, March 1891 [*The Bunyip*, Gawler, 27 March]

## 1892

414 Lady Hester Stanhope believed she could make something great of the Cornish; for my part, I can make nothing of them at all. A division of races, older and more original than that of Babel, keeps this close, esoteric family apart from neighbouring Englishmen.

    **R. L. Stevenson**, *Across the Plains*, 1892

## 1893

415 The Delectable Duchy
    **Title of book**, 1893

416 O my country, if I keep your secrets, keep for me your heart!
    **'Q'**, *The Delectable Duchy*, 1893

417 England beyond the Tamar ... [was] considered to be almost a foreign country.

S. R. Gardiner, *History of the Great Civil War 1642–49*, vol. 1, 1893
[Stoyle, 2005]

**418** Amongst the several causes which contributed to the high death rate [amongst Cornish miners] the principal were, undoubtedly, the accumulation of particles of carbon in the lungs, the result of the use of the miner's candle for lighting purposes, and of powder for blasting. But another important cause was the state of exhaustion daily produced by climbing to and from work on the ladders.

**J. C. Burrow and W. Thomas**, *'Mongst Mines and Miners*, 1893

**419** Dolcoath is the deepest mine in Cornwall, its neighbour Cook's Kitchen being the second deepest.

**J. C. Burrow and W. Thomas**, *'Mongst Mines and Miners*, 1893

**420** ... the Cornish miners have mostly emigrated.

**Charles G. Harper**, *From Paddington to Penzance*, 1893

**421** The people are very warm and kindly, quick-witted, and keen. Their faults are characteristically Celtic: they are not very 'straight', and are exceedingly suspicious; they fall out easily among themselves, but do not make up again easily; feuds go on from year to year, and last out lifetimes. They have a very curious habit of giving, by preference, any reason for their action except the one that has really determined it ... The Cornish Celt is prolific and exceedingly prone to sexual irregularity.

'Ethnographic Survey of the United Kingdom. First Report of the Committee', in ***Report of the British Association for the Advancement of Science***, 1893 [1894]

# 1895

**422** Though somewhat funereal, the cross of St. Piran is a grand symbol, and specially appropriate to Cornwall (the land of tin); and I wonder why, with the revival of so many old things, it has not been restored.

**W. S. Lach-Szyrma**, *A Church History of Cornwall* ... , 1895

**423** Twenty years' work in Cornwall has taught me, as it has taught others, that only by lay aid can the Cornish be re-won to the Church.

**W. S. Lach-Szyrma**, *A Church History of Cornwall* ... , 1895

**424** My "first visit" to Cornwall was on the occasion of my birth, and I have known it for 40 years since, and, as far as I am capable of giving an opinion, I should say that a musical intonation is characteristic of almost all the shades of Cornish dialect ...

**Rev. John Isabell**, in letter to *The Times*, 30 August 1895

# 1896

**425** When we arrived at the Park Station a perfect mob of people appeared to be waiting for us ... Indeed, it seemed as if every Rand man who had hailed from the rocky moorland, every Jack from Camborne or Redruth, every fisherman from Mount's Bay, and every reefman who claims the Duchy as his native heath, had made it his business to be on the platform that morning.

**Fanny Moody-Manners**, *Diary*, 1896 [David Mudd, *Cornishmen and True*, 1971]

**426** It seems hardly to be known that the conditions of climate which are essential to the invalid exist in our islands, and yet it is so; for the south coast of Cornwall presents them in a marked degree.

**Sir Joseph Fayrer**, in paper read at the AGM of the British Medical Association, 1896

**427** The "tea-wreck", in particular, was a wonderful piece of good fortune for folks, very few of whom could ever indulge in such an expensive luxury. There was also the "coffee-wreck", when many tasted that delicious stimulant for the first time.

**Mrs. Bonham**, *A Corner of Old Cornwall*, 1896

**428** A scene of great disorder occurred yesterday at Newlyn, near Penzance, in consequence of a violation of local fishing customs. Cornish fishermen make a practice of refraining from Sunday fishing, and rarely go to sea on Friday or Saturday ... The fishermen from the East Coast, who, in the mackerel season, now at its height, frequent the West Cornish ports, have never fallen in with this practice ...

**The Times**, 19 May 1896

**429** His [Dr Edward White Benson's] devotional, if somewhat archaic, type of mind impressed itself upon the eager, sensitive, Celtic Cornish character.

'Death of the Archbishop of Canterbury', in **The Times**, 12 October 1896

# 1897

**430** I might pause here to say much of the intense feeling which the Cornish cherish for their homes and for their own wild and beautiful country, a feeling which neither years nor exile can do aught but strengthen, and which, as far as I know, has been little recognised in literature. Perhaps the reason may be that which makes me stay my pen, and refrain from writing down for other men to wonder at what is too strongly felt to be easily expressed.

**Arthur H. Norway**, *Highways and Byways of Devon and Cornwall*, 1897

**431** ... I would with all my heart that I could see the whole number [of tall chimneys] belch forth smoke again as they did not many years ago, when the miners were prosperous at home, and the population had not been drained off from Camborne or Redruth to toil for foreign taskmasters at Johannesburg or Kimberley, while their wives, left behind to keep up the cottage whither the breadwinners hope always to return, look weekly for the remittance which never fails to come over the sea. For the men's hearts are in the valley underneath Carn Brea, though their bodies are sweating in the heart of an African mine.

**Arthur H. Norway**, *Highways and Byways of Devon and Cornwall*, 1897

## 1898

**432** The Cornishmen in London, who were the first to set on foot an annual county dinner in the metropolis, have now formed an association, with the object of carrying on the dinner, promoting social gatherings, and establishing a benevolent fund.

'London Cornish Association', in **The Times**, 30 March 1898

**433** Our aim is to produce a Magazine which will cost sixpence, and be worth more than sixpence to anybody, and considerably more than sixpence to any Cornishman; to fill it with sound and readable information, honest fiction, good illustrations; to satisfy the judges at home and carry to our kinsmen abroad a word of home and an assurance that their home remembers them, finally to do some good for Cornwall, or at least to earn the respect due to a brave attempt.

**Arthur Quiller-Couch**, *Cornish Magazine*, vol. 1, no. 1, July 1898

**434** I see her [Cornwall's] population diminishing and her able-bodied sons forced to emigrate by the thousand, the ruined engine-house, the roofless cottage, the cold hearthstone are not cheerful sights to one who would fain see a race so passionately attached to home as ours is still drawing vigour from its soil.

**Arthur Quiller-Couch**, *Cornish Magazine*, vol. 1, no. 1, July 1898

**435** There edn' no smell on earth like the smell of Cornish ground. An' there edn' no kingdom on earth to come up to Cornwall; nor no nation fit to stand up in the sight o' the Cornish nation.

Charles Lee, *Paul Carah, Cornishman*, 1898

**436** The Cornish descendants are scattering, and have almost lost their identity as a race. They do not hesitate to marry with other nationalities...

**L. A. Copeland**, 'The Cornish in Southwest Wisconsin', *Wisconsin Historical Collection*, 1898 [Bernard Deacon, *The Cornish Family*, 2004]

**437** Depreciation and defamation can only be the poisoned arrows of those who know *not* Cornish men and women. To understand the Cornish character is to admire and love it.

**'Open Eyes' [Mrs. C. Penberthy]**, *The Warp and Woof of Cornish Life and Character*, 1898

**438** There are thatched cabins here and there [in Cornwall] that might have been transplanted from Galway; hedges of stone, bogs and peat-stacks, pigs galore and a general aspect of dirt and happy laziness truly Irish. Also the people are very excitable ... and in their dress often remind one of the Irish peasantry.

**Herbert S. Vaughan,** *The British Road Book*, 1898 [Philip Payton, ... a vision of Cornwall, 2002]

**439** You can scarcely enter a farmhouse or labourer's cottage amongst the hills of Zennor or the moors of Wendron, or an engine-house amongst the mines of Camborne, without finding amongst the few books displayed a copy of Wesley's hymns.

**H. Arthur Smith**, 'Footprints of the Wesleys in Cornwall', in *Cornish Magazine* vol. I, no. 4, October 1898

# 1899

**440** In my view, it should be considered a duty by patriotic Cornishmen, each in the measure of his ability, to purchase and hold a few shares in Cornish mines.

**J. H. Collins**, in *Cornish Magazine*, vol. II, no. 1, January 1899

**441** I found the Cornishman everywhere the same sturdy, good-hearted, friendly fellow, able to hold his own with the best, and turning his opportunities to good account.

**Rev. Mark Guy Pearse**, in Arthur Lawrence, 'The Rev. Mark Guy Pearse, in *Cornish Magazine*, vol. II, no. 4, April 1899

**442** It may seem paradoxical, but I contend that for intellectual culture it is a great loss to the Cornish to have abandoned their native tongue. To be bilingual is educative to the intellect in a very marked degree.

**Sabine Baring-Gould**, A Book of Cornwall, 1899

**443** About the cliffs may still be seen the Cornish chough, with its scarlet legs, but the bird is becoming scarce. The south coast of Cornwall is now entirely deserted by the chough.

> **Sabine Baring-Gould**, *A Book of the West*, 1899

**444** The clannishness which is so marked a characteristic of Cornish people has for some time brought Cornubians resident in London, and in several of the great provincial cities, to meet together in a social fashion.

> **H. C. Shuttleworth**, 'The London Cornish Association', in *Cornish Magazine*, vol. II, no. 5, May 1899

**445** It is a well-established fact that there is a greater kinship between the inhabitants of Cornwall and Brittany than between any other pair of Celtic peoples ...

> **R. A. H. Bickford-Smith**, 'The Celtic Drama Revived', in *Cornish Magazine*, vol. II, no. 5, May 1899

**446** This Cornubia is a land of wonderment – historical, physical, spiritual. I'm not sure that it is part of the created universe.

> **Bishop Edward Benson**, in A. C. Benson, *The Life of Edward White Benson*, 1899

**447** ... a Cousin Jack sheds a lot of his clothes and perhaps more of his accent, in the land where his wages multiply by ten [the Transvaal].

> **F. J. Tiddy**, *The Cornishman*, 9 June 1899

## 1900

**448** ... there is really a greater Cornwall outside than inside.

> **Leonard Courtney**, in speech to the Midland Cornish Association, reported in *West Briton*, 20 February 1900

**449** ... the Cornish outside become more Cornish than the Cornish themselves.

> **West Briton**, 20 February 1900

**450** At last Cornwall have won a [rugby] match. It is so long that the county have won a game that one has almost despaired of their ability to win another. Since defeating Devon on the Redruth ground many years ago [1884], they have had nothing but a series of disasters. This year, however, there are signs of improvement, and by this win they have broken the spell of ill-luck that has been theirs.

> **West Briton**, November 1900

# 1902

**451** We are living off South Africa.
*Cornubian*, 31 January 1902

**452** All my blood is Celtic: the serum mainly Cornish, but the dancing red and white corpuscles derived from a maternal Welsh tributary, from a slender Highland torrent, and, far away back, from a rumoured Breton well-spring.
**L. C. Duncombe Jewell**, in *The Candid Friend*, 5 July 1902 [*Celtia*, vol. 2, no. 8, August 1902]

# 1904

**453** Between the ages of twenty-five and forty-five the death-rate from lung diseases among miners living in Cornwall has recently been from eight to ten times the corresponding death-rate among coal miners and ironstone-miners.
**Parliamentary Report on the Health of Cornish Miners**, 1904

**454** Why should Cornishmen learn Cornish? .... The question is a fair one, the answer is simple. Because they are Cornishmen.
**Henry Jenner**, A *Handbook of the Cornish Language*, 1904

**455** ... every Cornishman knows well enough, proud as he may be of belonging to the British Empire, that he is no more an Englishman than a Caithness man is, that he has as much right to a separate local patriotism to his little Motherland ... as has a Scotsman, an Irishman, a Welshman, or even a Colonial; and that he is as much a Celt and as little of an 'Anglo-Saxon' as any Gael, Cymro, Manxman or Breton.
**Henry Jenner**, A *Handbook of the Cornish Language*, 1904

**456** Cornish is a disappointing language in respect of swearwords, for it is by no means rich in these ornaments to conversation.
**Henry Jenner**, A *Handbook of the Cornish Language*, 1904

**457** The wildest of British wild sports is the pursuit of the seal in the almost inaccessible cliff caves to which it at times resorts. Of its haunts along the north coast of Cornwall ... from the Land's End to Tintagel, the caverns of Hell's Bay are perhaps those which it most frequents.
**J. C. Tregarthen**, *Wild Life at the Land's End*, 1904

**458** Yes, a magpie on a wind-clipt thorn bush, a yellow-hammer on a furze spray, gulls behind a ploughshare, a cormorant on a rock in the green water, and jack-daws about a broken mine-stack, are pictures downright Cornish; and they are always with us.

**J. C. Tregarthen**, *Wild Life at the Land's End*, 1904

# 1905

**459** 'As for Home Rule, I want local self-government not only for Ireland, but for Scotland, Wales.' At this point the interviewer interjected interrogatively 'Cornwall?' To Mr. Lloyd George's objection that Cornwall was small, the interviewer rejoined that it was 'inhabited by a separate race'.

Interview with **David Lloyd George** in *Pall Mall Gazette*, June 1905 [reported in a letter to *The Times* 28 October 1912]

**460** The gale of August 3 and 4, the most serious summer gale in the memory of Cornish fishermen, has worked sad havoc on the crab-pots and fishing gear of the little village of Cadgwith.

'Appeal for Cornish Fishermen'. Letter from **Henry Vyvyan**, in *The Times*, 15 August 1905

# 1906

**461**   Oh! Cornwall, barren, wretched spot of ground
Where nought but rocks and stones are to be found;
Thy barren hills won't find thy sons with bread,
Or wood to make 'em coffins when they're dead!
**Anonymous**, in *Cornish Notes and Queries*, 1906

**462** The Cornishmen whose deeds have been thought worthy of embalming in the great national record [*Dictionary of National Biography*] amounts to 303 persons ... The average of men of genius per county is ... 177

**J. Hambley Rowe**, in *Cornish Notes and Queries*, 1906

**463** The name 'Gwas Myhal' is my 'Bardic name' in the Gorsedd of the Bards of Brittany. It signifies the 'servant (or client) of St. Michael', and was conferred as appropriate to a native of the country of which St. Michael of the mount is Patron.

**H[enry] J[enner]**, in *Cornish Notes and Queries*, 1906

**464** My own belief is that Arthur was a Cornu-British chieftain, who fought the pagan Saxons successfully and was betrayed by one of his own relations.

**W. S. Lach-Szyrma**, in *Cornish Notes and Queries*, 1906

**465** I saw three Cornish Choughs wild at Gwithian sands about 1885.

**W. S. Lach-Szyrma**, in *Cornish Notes and Queries*, 1906

**466** As for Cornwall, whose dialect [language] is now extinct, she never produced much of a Celtic literature. What there is still extant is preserved in mss. of the fifteenth century, representing possibly all the ancient literature she ever had … With the exception of these [pieces] and another drama of the seventeenth century (1611), and the Lord's Prayer translated, the obsolete and defunct Cornish dialect has no literature to show …

> **Magnus Maclean**, *The Literature of the Celts*, 1906

**467** If the study of the language can be revived so as to enable us more fully to appreciate the few remains of its literature it will be very desirable, but we have no desire to see Cornwall aping the larger countries of Ireland, Wales and Brittany in their efforts after what they mistakenly suppose will lead to home rule.

> **Thurstan Peter**, *A Compendium of the History and Geography of Cornwall* … , 1906

**468** Nothing is more likely to attract the attention of a stranger who may happen to be in the mining district than the common use of the term 'Captain' (pronounced 'Cap'n)

> **Thurstan Peter**, *A Compendium of the History and Geography of Cornwall* … , 1906

**469** Cornish tin is the one famous product of ancient Britain.

> **William Page** (ed), *Victoria History of the County of Cornwall*, 1906

**470** When the button is pressed in Africa, the bell rings in Cornwall … a change in thought and action in South Africa affects the little western county which has contributed so much of the labour and enterprise to … the land of gold and diamonds.

> **Cornish Post**, 20 December 1906

**471** A Cornish Sunday to a man of cities is a weariness to the flesh, and a temptation to pray for Monday to come quickly …

> **J. Henry Harris**, *Cornish Saints and Sinners*, 1906

**472** … like a Cornishman's gift, what he does not want for himself.

> **J. Henry Harris**, *Cornish Saints and Sinners*, 1906

**473** As the pasty goes to the oven, so it comes out, puffed up a little with self-conscious pride at having gone through the fiery trial and come out a generous brown, with every cable-twist intact, and every curve swelling with inward importance … A pasty fresh from the oven sends up an incense which makes

a hungry man thankful to be alive.
**J. Henry Harris**, *Cornish Saints and Sinners*, 1906

**474** The Cornish genius has no great turn for architecture – its municipal buildings are plain and thrifty, like the dwelling-houses. To be 'wind and water tight' is the native idea of comfort; and then plenty of whitewash and a little paint.
**J. Henry Harris**, *Cornish Saints and Sinners*, 1906

## 1907

**475** A strange race these Cornish Celts, in whom the spirit of Wesley still moves freshly and newly, as when one hundred and fifty years ago, after much tribulation, he finally conquered the emotional Duchy and, so it is said, frightened the fairies away.
**C. Lewis Hind**, *Days in Cornwall*, 1907

**476** Time has not quite broken the ancient chain that links the Breton Celt to the Cornish Celt. Each year fantastic figures land on the coast of Western Cornwall, bearing yokes around their necks from which strings of onions dangle. They come from Brittany to sell their onions to Cornish fishwives; they talk in their native Breton and they are understood. Breton sailors and onion pedlars are treated like colonial cousins in Cornwall.
**C. Lewis Hind**, *Days in Cornwall*, 1907

**477** Cornwall has awakened, bridged the Tamar, admitted the railway, become civilised, accepted motor-omnibuses and the appellation of 'Riviera of England' to her shores; but Brittany lingers in Celtic twilight.
**C. Lewis Hind**, *Days in Cornwall*, 1907

**478** The extinction of Welsh by English is a chapter of history still incomplete, while the kindred tongue of Cornwall has long been driven from the field.
**Thurstan C. Peter**, *History of Cornwall for Schools*, 1907

## 1908

**479** Cornwall, peopled mainly by Celts, but with an infusion of English blood, stands and always has stood apart from the rest of England, much, but in a less degree, as has Wales.
**S. Baring-Gould**, *Cornish Characters and Strange Events*, 1908

**480** The isolation in which Cornwall has stood has tended to develop in it much originality of character ... and the underground life of the mines has a peculiar effect on mind and character: it is cramping in many ways, but it tends to develop a good deal of religious enthusiasm, that occasionally breaks forth in wild forms of fanaticism.

**S. Baring-Gould**, *Cornish Characters and Strange Events*, 1908

481 It was a famous victory, proclaim it all around,
How Cornwall beat Durham at the Recreation Ground:
That Durham tried their very best to everyone was plain,
But the Pasties were too hard for them, their efforts were in vain.
**Verse on a card celebrating Cornwall's victory over Durham** in the county championship, 28 March 1908 [Tom Salmon, *The First Hundred Years*, 1983]

482 From every town in England, crowds both great and small,
Came to witness Cornwall show Durham men football,
When the match was started the eyes of *One and All*
Keenly watched the movements of that bouncing Rugby Ball.
Determined on their victory, well bent for Ribbon Blue,
Durham had to lose the match, what other could they do?
Remember, only Miners far down in country West
Who've proved themselves at Football to be England's very best.
They twisted poor old Glo'ster, any shape they thought would do,
And Devon, they for mercy cried until the whistle blew;
Middlesex next on the scene, though plucky they may be,
Felt themselves quite honoured beaten 19 points to 3.
**Verse on another celebratory postcard** [*Tom Salmon, The First Hundred Years*, 1983]

483 The Cornish people, I take it, are Celts with less alien blood in their veins than any other branch of their race in the British Isles.
**W. H. Hudson**, *The Land's End*, 1908

484 The Cornish, like the Spanish, are passionate, and when anything goes wrong they are apt to wreak their fury on the poor unresisting beast – cow, calf, horse, donkey or sheep.
**W. H. Hudson**, *The Land's End*, 1908

485 ... in the chapels in West Cornwall ... the principle of any-house-good-enough has been carried to an extreme ... [the] square naked granite boxes set up in every hamlet and at roadsides, hideous to look at and a blot and

disfigurement to the village and to God's earth, are assuredly an insult to every person endowed with a sense of beauty and fitness.

**W. H. Hudson**, *The Land's End*, 1908

**486** The Cornish chough has not been seen for a score of years or more in many of its old haunts on the southern cliffs, though it is still a little less rare on the vaster precipices of the northern coast.

'The Cornish cliffs in Spring', in *The Times*, 2 May 1908

## 1909

**487** Cornwall's contribution to the Foreign Mission field is difficult if not impossible to gauge.

*Cornwall beyond the Seas*, 1909

**488** The Cornish miner is generally a man who can do his share of grumbling, and frequently reckons he knows how to run a mine better than the manager, so when Unionism caught on they realised that many injustices might have been remedied years ago had they been organised and pulled together, instead of merely growling as individuals.

**W. G. Spence**, *Australia's Awakening: Thirty Years in the Life of an Australian Agitator*, 1909

**489** With so many alien influences still alive around him to remind him of his ancient and diverse ancestry, it is not to be wondered at that the Cornishman's racial feeling is still very strong.

'The Prince in Cornwall', in *The Times*, 8 June 1909

## 1910

**490** The spoken language may be dead, but its ghost still haunts its old dwelling ...

**Henry Jenner**, 'Cornish Place Names', in *JRIC*, vol. 18, pt. 1, 1910

**491** The United Kingdom of Great Britain and Ireland comprises England, Scotland, Ireland, and Wales, to which a patriotic Cornishman might feel inclined to add Cornwall. And, if he did so, he would be in large measure justified, for Cornwall is not merely a county, although generally placed in that middle position between a mere shire and a distinct national identity. It is a Duchy, and, more than that, has something approaching a distinct nationality. Still the Cornishman may be heard talking of 'going into England', when he intends crossing the Tamar and entering Devon; and to this day all who would come westward across that stream are 'foreigners'. It is from no fantastic notion that he holds these views, but merely as a curious survival of ancient conditions, when Cornwall was still an independent country, the land of the Cornu-Welsh; the ultimate west, where the Saxon had not yet prevailed.

**Charles G. Harper,** *The Cornish Coast (North)*, 1910

492 The Cornish love their wild country as passionately as any other branch of the Celtic family their home, as the Scottish highlanders their lochs and glens, the Irish their bogs and mountains, or the Welsh their own beautiful land. But, unlike those nations, their love is dumb, and has never found expression in song and story. A Cornishman is never eloquent about Cornwall, but he always returns, if it be possible …

**Charles G. Harper,** *The Cornish Coast (North)*, 1910

493 With the object of attracting attention to the mildness of the climate of Cornwall during the winter months, the Great Western Railway are exhibiting in the windows of their principal receiving offices bunches of fresh-cut flowers sent direct from Cornwall.

'Flowers from the "Cornish Riviera" ', in **The Times,** 16 December 1910

## 1910–11

494 The [Cornish] natives have many traits in common with the Welsh, such as their love of oratory and their strong tribal attachment to the county.

*Encyclopedia Britannica*, 1910/1911

## 1911

495 The Cornish Riviera is England's Winter Resort. Cornwall offers winter warmth and sunshine, and a climate far more equable than that of foreign resorts. The Cornish coast scenery is the loveliest in England, and the climate is phenomenally mild.

**GWR** advert, in *The Times*, 5 January 1911

496     Not a soul in sight, poor Satan cried,
        It's giving me the pip, They're all gone
        In where I can't abide, Inside the
        Little Ship [Helston Free Methodist Chapel]
        **Anonymous,** c. 1911 [Thomas Shaw, *A History of Cornish Methodism*, 1967]

## 1912

497 … the Duchy has ever been celebrated, far above all other English counties, not only for its sturdy independence of character, but also, in its

intense local patriotism, for a somewhat contemptuous estimate as to the worth of mere intruders from the shires.

**J. Charles Cox**, *[County Churches]: Cornwall*, 1912

**498** Cornwall has suffered pre-eminently in the matter of the restoration of its church fabrics …

**J. Charles Cox**, *[County Churches]: Cornwall*, 1912

**499** Crass prejudice and vulgar lack of taste of the first half of the 19th century did more to bereave Cornwall of her once beautiful chancel screens than Reformation vehemence or Puritan malevolence.

**J. Charles Cox**, *[County Churches]: Cornwall*, 1912

**500** When gazing at the consummate skill, backed by clever steam or water-worked appliances, necessary for the hewing, polishing, and shaping of the granite, it is wonderful to think of the ability and pains that the Cornish workmen of the 15th century put forth in the cutting and shaping of the great monolith piers that support the arcades of so large a number of their churches.

**J. Charles Cox**, *[County Churches]: Cornwall*, 1912

**501** Sir, Please let me correct a mis-statement in the paragraph in today's 'West of England Views' on Dr. Bice's lecture on the Cornish language at St. Columb. I did not say a single word in any way referring to the revival of Cornish as a spoken language. I cannot imagine what I can have said to lead your reporter to think that I was referring to anything so fantastic and impossible.

**Henry Jenner**, in letter to *Western Morning News*, 8 January 1912

**502** At one moment the mass or school of pilchards … may be a quarter of a mile in length, and even as you look it elongates and shoots out into half a mile, only to thicken up a few minutes later into a regular ball, more or less spherical. Immediately the fish are sighted the huer's trumpet blares forth, and the cry of 'hevva! hevva!' goes up …

**John Harris Stone**, *England's Riviera*, 1912

## 1913

**503** The ancient Cornish game of hurling with a silver ball was played on Newquay Town beach on Saturday afternoon.

'An ancient Cornish game', in **The Times**, 25 August 1913

**504** At the meeting of the Royal Institution of Cornwall, at Truro, yesterday, it was announced that preparations were being made for a representation of the ancient Cornish miracle-play *The Life of St. Meriasek* ... It was not proposed to do the play in the Cornish language, but they might have a scene in Cornish.

'The Prince of Wales and a Cornish play', in **The Times**, 17 December 1913

**505** Novelists in large numbers have attempted Cornwall for their scenery and Cornish folk for their characters; and that I find the results almost uniformly distressing you may set down to jealousy if you will; but it must be the jealousy of a native, for as an artist I never had any.

**Arthur Quiller-Couch**, in preface to J. H. Harris, *Phyllis in Piskie-Land*, 1913

## 1914

**506** Considerable progress has now been made with the scheme to preserve a public path round the coastline of Cornwall ...

'The Cornish cliffs: proposed 300 miles coast-line path', in **The Times**, 18 April 1914

## 1916

**507** There has been much doubt concerning the identity of St. Piran.

**Thomas Taylor**, *The Celtic Christianity of Cornwall*, 1916

**508** Methodism on the old lines is moribund in Cornwall ... Revivals have almost become things of the past. Conversion, theoretically the starting point of Methodist religion, is no longer required to be sudden. The class meeting has lost much of its attractiveness ... Many of the old doctrines are being recast. Methodism is in a state of transition.

**Thomas Taylor**, *The Celtic Christianity of Cornwall*, 1916

**509** I like Cornwall very much. It is not England. It is bare and dark and elemental, Tristan's land.

**D. H. Lawrence**, 1916 in *Collected Letters* vol. 1, ed. Harry T. Moore, 1962

**510** They [the Cornish] are, of course, strictly *anti-social* and un-Christian ... each of them is like an insect isolated within its own scaly, glassy envelope, and running seeking its own small end. And how foul that is! How they stink in their repulsiveness ... they are entirely mindless ... They ought to be living in the darkness and warmth and passionateness of the blood, sudden, incalculable. Whereas thay are like insects gone cold, living only for money, for *dirt*.

**D. H. Lawrence**, 1916 in *Collected Letters* vol. 1, ed. Harry T. Moore, 1962

**511** All this week there has been running in the heads of the people of the Lizard peninsula, and in the memory of many a Cornish lad in the trenches of Flanders, a simple strain of ... music. It is as monotonous as the song of the cuckoo; and it means very much the same thing. For when spring has scattered abroad his first bounty of green and gold and flowers; when the downs are one cloth of gold and the hedgerows an embroidery of gorse and thorn, hyacinth and primrose, violet and daisy, then the inhabitants of the Lizard lay down their tools and make a day of festival which they call Flora Day ...

'Flora in Helston', in *The Times*, 12 May 1916

## 1917

**512** I am sure that if it [a proposed 'Celtic Union'] keeps clear of all traits of politics, and I am sure it will, Cornwall will be happy to join in.

**Henry Jenner**, in *The Celtic Conference, 1917*, ed. D. Rhys Phillips

## 1918

**513** Several persons were summoned yesterday with reference to a recent demonstration at Newquay against naturalised Germans being allowed to live directly facing the sea.

'Germans on Cornish coast', in *The Times*, 25 September 1918

**514** It is very tantalising ... to realise ... how narrowly we have missed several chances of adding to our Cornish vocabulary, or even possibly of keeping the language alive ... It maddens one to think of these learned laborious Cornishmen [William Borlase and William Pryce], misprinting earlier collections, misreading ancient manuscripts, fumbling their few Celtic or West Country English words with an indiscriminate hurling together of Cornish, Welsh, Breton and Irish from Lhuyd'd *Archaeologia Britannica*, compiling dictionaries and making cryptograms for Cornish students that take ten times as long to unravel as they did to write, while all the time the language itself was being spoken by the poor old 'backjowster' bringing fish round to the back door, or even by the bent old gardener mowing the grass from whom – alas! – it would have been infra dig to learn.

**R. Morton Nance**, 'Celtic words in Cornish dialect', in *RCPS* Report vol. 4, 1918–22

**515**     "Trelawny" was at Waterloo,
        At Alma, Marne, the North Sea, too,
        And at Gallipoli;
        With right and left he did his work,
        Smiting at Bulgar, Hun and Turk,

In air, on land, and sea.
**"Oneuno"**, 'Lest We Forget Trelawny', in *The People's Weekly*, c. 1918

## 1919

516 The Bishop of Truro yesterday gave judgment in the case against the Rev. L. S. Wason, vicar of Cury with Gunwalloe, who was charged with unlawfully performing the service of benediction in his parish church.
'Cornish Vicar Deprived', in **The Times**, 28 May 1919

517 Everybody is coming to Cornwall, but nobody seems ever to go away.
Correspondent from St. Ives, in **The Times**, 8 August 1919

## 1920

518 Cornwall ... differs from other counties in race and tradition. It is still partly Ivernian, partly Celtic, very little Teutonic. It was never Romanised and never Saxonised. Till comparatively modern times it had its own language.
**Arthur L. Salmon**, *Cornwall*, 4th edition, 1920

519 The Duchy is by no means in a stagnant or decadent condition; it is thoroughly alive and alert. It is no longer cut off from "the shires", but is being actively exploited by railway companies, financiers, artists and holiday-keepers from Britain and overseas.
**Arthur L. Salmon**, *Cornwall*, 4th edition, 1920

520 It has been stated by Devonians, in the ironical manner of near neighbours, that Cornwall does not grow wood enough to make a coffin.
**Arthur L. Salmon**, *Cornwall*, 4th edition, 1920

521 Gather ye the fragments that are left, that nothing be lost. *
**Motto adopted by St. Ives Old Cornwall Society**, c. 1920

## 1921

522 Cornishmen in the past have rarely known village life. Parish life there has always been, but in a very different sense from parish life beyond the Tamar.
**Charles Henderson**, 1921, *Essays in Cornish History* [1935]

523 Here we are on the verge of going to Cornwall. This time tomorrow ... we shall be stepping onto the platform at Penzance, sniffing the air, looking for our trap, and then ... driving off across the moors to Zennor – Why am I so incredibly and incurably romantic about Cornwall? One's past, I suppose.

**Virginia Woolf**, 22 March 1921, in *The Diary of Virginia Woolf 1920–1924* [1978]

**524** Cornish miners in want. Family of eleven on 15/- a week. Relief funds nearly exhausted.
Headline, in **The Times**, 8 October 1921

**525** Of all my books this is the most precious to me. There can be no doubt that it is the very one that "Q" used when a boy at Clifton. And now it is mine!
**A. L. Rowse**, 1921, in essay on rear end paper of Aristophanes' *The Clouds* [Sydney Cauveren, 'A Treasure from the library of A. L. Rowse' in *An Baner Kernewek* 103 February, 2001]

## 1922

**526** Mr. F. J. Symons, secretary of the London Cornish Association, informs us that he has received a letter from the secretary of the Cornish Association of the Transvaal stating that the latter had been discussing "the position of our folks in the Old Country and the gross injustice being done to the mining industry in Cornwall".
**The Times**, 2 February 1922

**527** The scenes on Saturday afternoon at the declaration of the poll beggared description … the enthusiasm of Nonconformist farmers, of earnest young preachers, of dark-eyed women and fiery Celtic youth had something religious about it. No such fervour could be seen elsewhere outside Wales.
**Cornish Guardian**, 3 March 1922

**528** No doubt if this were Italy, Greece, or even the shores of Spain, sadness would be routed by strangeness and excitement and the nudge of a classical education. But the Cornish hills have stark chimneys standing on them; and, somehow or other, loveliness is infernally sad.
**Virginia Woolf**, *Jacob's Room*, 1922

## 1923

**529** Had not the whole history of the language prepared us for such neglect, it would seem far less credible that as recently as 1891, the year of his death, John Davey's Cornish, like that of Dolly Pentreath or William Bodener a century earlier, was allowed to perish unrecorded; that at so late a date a man still lived who could recite some traditional Cornish, less astonishing, but even more sad, is it that not one word of all his store is known to his descendants today, although it is well remembered that he possessed it.

**R. Morton Nance**, 'John Davey of Boswednack and his Cornish rhyme', in *JRIC*, vol. 21, pt. 2, 1923

530 There are to-day ... other old people who are the sole possessors of certain words of Cornish that have not yet been written down, and that will as certainly be lost as Dolly's [Pentreath] unless they find some patriotic Cornish note-book ready for them within the next few years, months, or weeks.

**R. Morton Nance**, *A Glossary of Celtic Words in Cornish Dialect*, 1923

# 1924

531 The name 'South Africa' is cut deep in the heart of mining Cornwall, not so much engraved with an instrument of steel as jagged and ghastly with the malignant quartz that hid the gold and filled the lungs of the Cornish pioneers.

**Harry Pascoe**, in *The Cornishman*, 9 January 1924

532 On either side of Cornwall, across the Bristol or British Channel, we find with a British language a considerable body of British history and myth surviving: in Cornwall, the language gone, we have but a faint echo or two of our own Arthur, and something here and there that can only be explained by reference to the folk-lore of Wales and Brittany.

**R. Morton Nance**, *Folk-Lore Recorded in the Cornish Language*, 1924

533 The people of Cornwall, that strike one at once as being stranger and more foreign than Frenchmen, Danes, Dutch or Germans, are a people foreign to us but more native to our land than we are. As such they are marvellously at one with the changeless, bony, uncivilised land where they live.

**H. W. Massingham**, *In Praise of England*, 1924 [W. Arthur Pascoe, 'Some References to Cornwall and the Cornish', *Old Cornwall* vol 5, no. 6 (1955)]

534 It was the business of the E[nglish] C[hurch] U[nion] to re-Catholicise Cornwall – to bring Cornish people to the fold of the holy Catholic apostolic Church. Cornishmen are naturally Catholic.

As reported by **Rev. G. Doble**, *Royal Cornwall Gazette*, 13 August 1924

535 Complaints of the deprivation of public access to and along the Cornish cliffs and headlands are of frequent occurrence.

**L. C. Chubb**, Secretary of the Commons and Footpaths Society, reported in *The Times*, 16 September 1924

**536** Cornwall has always been a Liberal stronghold, and in 1923 the five devisions of the county returned five Liberal members. This year Liberal supremacy is being challenged by Labour in the two divisions of Camborne and Penryn and Falmouth.

> 'Cornish Seats', in *The Times*, 21 October 1924

**537** When the mightiest nations die out, language and all, the lesser Celtic ones cannot expect to live for ever, but the example of each of the others teaches us in Cornwall at least to die only when we must; and not, beacause we have ceased to take an interest in our own existance, to perish of inanition.

> **R. Morton Nance**, 'The Celtic Congress, Quimper, 1924'. Paper read at the Autumn Meeting of the Royal Institution of Cornwall, 21 October 1924

## 1925

**538** The Cornish peasant has a bluntness and a restful depth of ignorance ... a Mid African simplicity. His presence helps you to realise that you have travelled into a far and unfamiliar land.

> **C. E. Vulliamy**, *Unknown Cornwall*, 1925

**539** ... an Old Cornwall Society is not an Antiquarian Association, not a Celtic Society nor even a Cornish Social Club. It may seem all these by turns, but it is always something more. It gathers up these things of the past not as dead stuff to be learnedly discussed nor as merely amusing trifles, but as the Living Tradition of the Cornish People; the material in which the Sprit of Cornwall is to be handed on to future generations, keeping them Cornish still. Ours is thus the beginning at least of a National movement ...

> **R. Morton Nance**, in *Old Cornwall 2*, 1925

**540** The people of the Duchy of Cornwall have always resented any interference with their right to have unrestricted "free trade" with the sister Duchy of Brittany which was bound to them by ties of blood and long association, consequently they refused for many centuries to submit to the exactions of the English Customs duties.

> **A. A. Clinnick**, 'Cornwall and the Smuggling Trade', in *Old Cornwall 2*, 1925

## 1926

**541** The vicar of Zennor, Cornwall, announces that in future marble tombstones will not be allowed to be erected in the churchyard, for the reason that marble (the bulk of which comes from foreign countries) is unsuitable to the district. All memorials must be of granite or slate.

**542** It is wonderful that there should be any knowledge of Cornish today, seeing that Cornwall has been for a thousand years politically a part of England; but however near the process of making us "English" is to completion, it is far from complete yet, and our cousins in Wales, in Brittany and in Ireland, with a keener eye for what is Celtic, have recognized this even more than we have done.

> **W. D. Watson**, 'Nebes Geriow Moy Adro Dho Gernuak – A Few Words More about Cornish', in *Old Cornwall* 3, April 1926

**543** ... the growth of our movement [is] tending steadily towards the ideal that we have set before us, that of establishing something that shall be a national Cornish Festival, somewhat on the lines of the Welsh National Eisteddfod, or at least serving the same purpose in fostering Cornish National Sentiment.

> **[R. Morton Nance]**, 'Federation Report', in *Old Cornwall* 3, April 1926

**544** At Old Cornwall meetings and entertainments, especially those of the Federation, it is customary to sing "God Save the King" and a Cornish version of the Welsh Hen Wlad fy Nhadau in the Cornish Language.

> **[R. Morton Nance]**, 'Old Cornwall Publications', *Old Cornwall* 4, October 1926

**545** Those who seek display of Celtic fire in all the little ways of daily life will seek and ever seek again; but always just behind the old grey rocks, beyond the mist of the moorland, beneath the silence of the Cornishman, there lurks a sense of deep things seen and felt and well remembered, of beauty burning like a flame, of mystery that colours all the land.

> **C. C. Rogers**, *Echoes in Cornwall*, 1926

## 1927

**546** The Welsh Gorsedd members have in view the holding of a Gorsedd ceremony in Cornwall in September 1928 or 1929, for the purpose of bringing the ancient Land of Cornwall into more immediate association with Wales.

> **D. Rhys Phillips**, in letter in *Consortium Breton*, [*Old Cornwall*, October 1927]

**547** Cornish wrestling is *sui generis*

> **J. E. Morris**, *Black's Guide to Cornwall*, 25th edition, 1927

**548** Both feasts [St. Piran and Chewidden] ... were throughout their hey-day

regarded as commemorations of the first smelting of tin in Cornwall …
**A. K. Hamilton Jenkin**, *The Cornish Miner*, 1927

**549** Foremost of all … among the reasons for the peaceableness of the Cornish miner was the peculiar system of wages under which he habitually worked … For the month, or often longer period, during which he contracted to work a pitch, the Cornish miner was his own capitalist, and practically his own master.
**A. K. Hamilton Jenkin**, *The Cornish Miner*, 1927

**550** The idea that mining has been carried on in Cornwall "from the coming of the Phoenicians" to the present day is, of course, a complete fallacy, although a very common one.
**A. K. Hamilton Jenkin**, *The Cornish Miner*, 1927

**551** The shafts of Cornwall, could they be all numbered, would prove as the sands of the sea …
**A. K. Hamilton Jenkin**, *The Cornish Miner*, 1927

**552** 'Hes Cornwall a nashion, hes a a Hiland, or hes a ferren country?' an old school-dame, Peggy Combellack, would ask.

'He hedn't no nashon, he hedn't no highlan, nor he hedn't no ferren country,' the brightest of the scholars on one occasion answered.

'What hes a then?' asked Peggy.

'Why he's kidged to a furren country from the top hand,' was the reply which was heard by the whole school with much approval, including old Peggy herself.
**Anonymous** [Hamilton Jenkin, 1927]

**553** I am glad to be standing before you on this great day to speak to you a few words in Cornish … The Cornish are but a small people. It is a very good thing that there are other Celtic people ready to give us the hand of comradeship and kindness. It is often said that Cornish is dead. We are here to-day to show to you that there are Cornishmen in these days … who love their language; who are cultivating the knowledge of Cornish in all places. The Cornish Language is not dead while those faithful ones are living, though they are but few. *
**W. D. Watson**, in speech to Inter-Celtic Festival at Riec, Brittany, *Old Cornwall*, October 1927

**554** Round about that time [1824] … a custom, or unwritten law, prevailed in these parts, to the effect that if you could build a house in one night you might forever claim the freehold of it.

**J. C. Hoare**, 'Quaint Houses in Cornwall', in *Old Cornwall* 6, October 1927

# 1928

555 King Arthur is not dead; he will come again. *
**From the Cornish Gorsedd ceremony**, 1928

556 Brunel's Royal Albert Bridge at Saltash … is the means, and an almost magic means, of transporting travellers from a county, which, if richer than others, is yet unmistakably an English county, to a Duchy which is in every respect un-English.
**S. P. B. Mais**, *The Cornish Riviera*, 1928

557 Everybody has dreamt of a land where the sun always shines but never proves harmful, where it is always warm but never enervating, where we may bathe in the winter and take active exercise in the summer. We had to have a name for this Elysium, so we called it the Cornish Riviera.
**S. P. B. Mais**, *The Cornish Riviera*, 1928

558 The impression I want to leave … is that our object is to restore in Cornwall the idea that it is a Celtic country. The Gorsedd is not political or anti-English, but we want to foster the self-respect of Cornish people by making them regard themselves as one of the Celtic nations.
**R. Morton Nance**, *Western Morning News*, 21 September 1928

559 If Celtic nationality is denied to English-speaking Cornishmen, it must equally be denied to those many members of the other Celtic nations who speak no Celtic language – which is absurd.
**Henry Jenner**, *Who are the Celts and what has Cornwall to do with them?*, 1928

560 "Anglia et Cornubia" was as common an expression as "England and Wales" is now. There is not much mediaeval evidence of what the Cornish thought of themselves as regards nationality, but a good deal to show that the English looked upon them as a separate nation.
**Henry Jenner**, *Who are the Celts and what has Cornwall to do with them?*, 1928

# 1929

561 … the uplands of Cornwall, could they but speak, would tell of generations of song.
**J. C. Tregarthen**, in foreword to Ralph Dunstan's *Cornish Song Book*, 1929

**562** There is nothing "Cornish" whatsoever in this shield [the fifteen bezants] – not one iota that relates to Cornwall's sea or soil, its mankind or its History!
**Arthur L. Mata**, *On The Shield of Arms for the Duchy of Cornwall*, 1929

**563** … the arms of Cornwall are based upon a misconception, and are, in fact, not of native but of foreign origin, and many ancient Cornish families are today quartering the Poitevin peas. They have, of course, by usage become the authentic arms of the Duchy.
**C. W. Scott-Giles**, *The Romance of Heraldry*, 1929

**564** So successful is the Cornish pichard season this year that the fishermen of Newlyn, Mousehole, Porthleven, and other parts are enjoying a period of unparalleled prosperity.
'Cornish Pilchard Season', in **The Times**, 23 August 1929

**565** The wrestling contest between Cornwall and Brittany was held at Pool, Camborne, on Saturday … Last year, when the Cornishmen paid a visit to Brittany, it was found that the wrestlers in both countries used almost the same style, which is the ancient British, the only difference being the type of jacket worn.
**The Times**, 2 September 1929

**566** Sun-bathing in trains. Special glass in Cornish Riviera Expresses.
Headline in **The Times**, 2 November 1929

## 1930

**567** Cornwall is *not* an improvised playground; it is *not* a "Riviera", and the use of that word, whoever first applied it to Cornwall, was and has been a commercial "inexactitude". To any right Cornishman, Cornwall is a mother with a character, a most egregious one, definite and clear. Having that character, she has a character to lose.
**Arthur Quiller-Couch**, in *Cornwall, A Survey*, ed. W. H. Thompson, 1930

**568** Prior to 1750 roads were so bad that county families kept Christmas in their own spacious homes after the old English fashion.
**Charles Henderson**, in *Western Morning News*, 2 April 1930

**569** Happily [the] loss to British life [of the chough or "Cornish daw"] is much less imminent to-day, whilst in other respects the chough has been reinstated to something of its former prominence through being adopted by the Old Cornwall Societies as their emblem …
**A. K. Hamilton Jenkin**, in letter to *The Times*, 10 July 1930

**570** Cornwall has an inexhaustible supply of granite of the finest quality, and a wealth of orders would pour into the country if firms could quote competitive prices …

> **Alfred Soyes**, Secretary of the Cornish Granite Merchants and Quarry Masters' Association, reported in *The Times*, 25 November 1930

**571** The likenesses between Cornwall, the next smallest Celtic nation, and the smallest, the Isle of Man, are in some respects closer than those that we see in comparing our own with any other Celtic country.

> 'An Idea from the smallest Celtic nation', in **Old Cornwall** 12, Winter 1930

## 1931

**572** We have more information as to the cult paid to S. Perran at Perranzabulo before the Reformation than about the cult of any other Cornish saint, and, standing at the lonely oratory amid the sand hills, or the great stone cross close by, we feel, more than anywhere else in the country, that we are treading in the footsteps of one of those makers of Christian Cornwall whose names remind us of the strange and picturesque Celtic Church which flourished here long before English Christianity existed.

> **Gilbert H. Doble**, *Saint Perran, Saint Keverne and Saint Kerrian*, 1931

**573** … in the British Isles… the Chough only nests in Cornwall, Wales, the Isle of Man, Ireland, South-west Scotland and the Hebredes [sic] – the haunts of the remains of the great Celtic people.

> **F. C. H.**, 'The Chough', in *Old Cornwall*, vol. 2, no. 1, Summer 1931

**574** Dialect is … a gateway to our National Language, and since our older dialect-speakers are our nearest to the "native-speakers", who are the accepted guides to other Celtic languages, learners of our Brythonic tongue must forget academic English, and as a first step acquire dialect …

> **E. G. Retallack Hooper**, 'Dialect as a gateway to Cornish', in *Old Cornwall* vol. 2, no. 2, Winter 1931

**575** The Cornish Language is more and more taking its place as the chief token of Celtic nationality in Cornwall.

> 'Cornish Books', in **Old Cornwall**, vol. 2, no. 2, Winter 1931

**576** Cornish did not appear a century ago, as is usually supposed; it lingered on in remote districts even into the twentieth century, and I know personally two scholars who speak it, but its days are probably numbered, and it is destined to fade away forever.

> **Rev. G. Hartwell Jones**, 'Celtic Renaissance and how to forward it', Y Cymmrodor, vol. 42, 1931

**577** When I come home to die I shall not feel that I have lived in vain. I have seen the earth turn red at evening, the dew sparkling in the morning, and the snow shining under a frosty sun; I have smelt the rain after drought, and have heard the stormy Atlantic beat upon the granite shores of Cornwall.

> **Bertrand Russell**, *The Scientific Outlook*, 1931 [Hawkey, A Cornish Chorus, 1948]

## 1932

**578** A performance of *The Little Ass*, a Cornish comedy by Mr. Bernard Walke, will be relayed to-night at 8 o'clock from St. Hilary, Cornwall, to the National programme.

> 'Broadcasting: A Cornish Comedy', in **The Times**, 21 April 1932

**579** Remain forever Cornish.

> **Henry Jenner**, in *Western Morning News*, 31 December 1932

**580** Conditions are so closely similar in Cornwall and Man that everything that has been done in the island can equally well be done in the peninsula.

> **R. Morton Nance**, 'Old Cornwall and the Celtic Congress', in *Old Cornwall*, vol. 2, no. 4, Winter 1932

**581** Wrecking ... was by no means confined to the lower orders of Cornish society, its greatest and most successful practitioners being those to whom rank and privilege had granted the power to pillage and plunder on a scale undreamt of by the poor.

> **A. K. Hamilton Jenkin**, *Cornish Seafarers*, 1932

**582** ... smuggling and Methodism long went hand in hand, and impossible as the association may seem today it is none the less true, that in the past some of the most notorious of Cornish smugglers were also staunch supporters of the dissenting cause.

> **A. K. Hamilton Jenkin**, *Cornish Seafarers*, 1932

**583** By the forties of the last century, the palmiest days of Cornish smuggling were over.

> **A. K. Hamilton Jenkin**, *Cornish Seafarers*, 1932

**584** In the year 1847, the exports of pilchards from Cornwall amounted to

40,883 hogsheads or 122,000,000 fish, whilst the greatest recorded number ever taken in one seine was that of 5,600 hogsheads or 16,500,000 fish, at St. Ives in 1868.

**A. K. Hamilton Jenkin**, *Cornish Seafarers*, 1932

# 1933

585 Combined with it [the 1870 Education Act], a depression in the mining industry began to cause that outward flow of emigration which has since exerted a far-reaching influence upon the character of the Cornish people.

**A. K. Hamilton Jenkin**, *Cornwall and the Cornish*, 1933

586 'Who's that fella you was spakin' to just now?' a miner was once overheard inquiring of a friend.

'Why, Cap'en Trevanion!'

'What, the new cap'en from ovver to Wheal Rose?'

'No, that's another chap.'

'Aw, so he's a say cap'en, I s'pose?'

'No, 'e edn'; nor yet a Salvation Army cap'en neither. He's a horse-sojer.'

'There, now, I thoft he was only a army cap'en. He didn't look like nothin' more 'n that.'

**A. K. Hamilton Jenkin**, *Cornwall and the Cornish*, 1933

587 The history of Cornwall is that of a county with a strong personality, priding itself on its peculiarities and alive with a local patriotism rooted in racial differences and fed by geographical isolation.

**Mary Coate**, *Cornwall in the Great Civil War*, 1933

588 The period of the Civil War and Interregnum is the most important in the history of Cornwall, for never before or since had she contributed so largely to the general course of events.

**Mary Coate**, *Cornwall in the Great Civil War*, 1933

589 Throughout their history the Cornish have been a religious people responsive to the emotional rather than to the intellectual element in religion.

**Mary Coate**, *Cornwall in the Great Civil War*, 1933

590 The formation, by the younger generation, of 'Tyr ha Tavas' ... must give pleasure to the pioneers of the Cornish Celtic movement, as it affords evidence that their work will be carried on and developed when they lay aside their armour.

**B. Y. Couch**, 'The Cornish Youth Movement', in *Old Cornwall*, vol. 2, no. 5, Summer 1933

**591** Under the influence and inspiration of scholars it [the Cornish language] has arisen from the dust and (happy omen for its future!) a band of young Cornishmen have thrown themselves with ardour into the scientific study of the language and the remnants of its literature.

> **Rev. G. Hartwell Jones**, 'Brittany and Wales', speech delivered at the Celtic Congress [*Y Cymmrodor*, vol. 44, 1935]

**592** Food, Cornish food, was the lecturer's topic, and even in that homely subject Cornwall keeps herself to herself, fastidiously eluding the ordinary.

> **The Times**, 26 October 1933

**593** The [Cornish] pasty is extraordinary in being entirely commonplace yet uniquely good to eat.

> 'Four Good Things', editorial in **The Times**, 26 October 1933

# 1934

**594** The system of leasing property on 'lives' formerly proved of immense advantage to Cornish landowners, as by this means thousands of acres of utterly waste land were brought under cultivation which might otherwise have remained unused and unusable to this day.

> **A. K. Hamilton Jenkin**, *Cornish Homes and Customs*, 1934

**595** ... until almost the end of the last [19th] century many Cornish houses knew no other fuel than that which came to them from within a short distance of their doors [turf].

> **A. K. Hamilton Jenkin**, *Cornish Homes and Customs*, 1934

**596** When a pig was killed the Cornish people had a use for everything 'except the squeal'.

> **A. K. Hamilton Jenkin**, *Cornish Homes and Customs*, 1934

**597** It is said that in the early days of the Cornish emigration to the Rand the curiosity of the postal authorities at Johannesburg was aroused by the number of strange-smelling packets passing through their hands ... [O]n inspection its contents [saffron] were adjudged to be a rank poison, and the package was accordingly returned to the sender, accompanied by a stern warning pointing out the nature of the offence.

> **A. K. Hamilton Jenkin**, *Cornish Homes and Customs*, 1934

**598** The Cornish language should be revived – nay, is being revived, for am I not myself reviving it? What more effective protest against imperialism (in art as in other matters) could you or I make than by adopting, as a pure ritual, a speech, a nationality, that no longer exist – for you to make your dwelling [Bosigran] the centre of a Celtic rebirth – the rebirth of a something that never was born ...?

**Peter Warlock** [Philip Heseltine], in Cecil Gray, *Peter Warlock*, 1934

**599** From that time on [1920] Mr. Jenner took his rightful place as the central figure in our effort to rouse Cornish people from the indifference to their own past.

**R. E. Morton Nance**, "Gwas Myghal' and the Cornish Revival', in *Old Cornwall*, vol. 2, no. 8, Winter 1934

**600** The last conscious words uttered by him [Henry Jenner] regarding the movement which was so close to his heart, although spoken to one, may be taken as intended for a farewell message of good cheer to all his fellow Bards and Old Cornwall Workers. They were, 'You will go on,' and were answered, for us all, 'We will'.

**[R. Morton Nance]**, 'Federation of Old Cornwall Societies', in *Old Cornwall*, vol. 2, no. 7, Summer 1934

**601** It is to the enterprise and enthusiasm of Mr. A. S. D. Smith that we owe the appearance of *Kernow*, a paper almost entirely in Cornish, that is to be issued monthly ... It has been adopted as the official organ of 'Tyr ha Tavas' ...

**[R. Morton Nance]**, 'Cornish Books', in *Old Cornwall*, vol. 2, no. 7, Summer 1934

**602** "The Cornish nation" – the enigma of the West. Of the hundreds of thousands who come here for holidays only one in a thousand can hope to see below the surface. The other nine hundred and ninety-nine ... merely turn Cornwall temporarily into London ...

**Stanley R. Baron**, *Westward Ho! From Cambria to Cornwall*, 1934

**603** In the subconscious mind of Cornwall, England is but a land to which the Cornish nation has allied itself.

**Stanley R. Baron**, *Westward Ho! From Cambria to Cornwall*, 1934

**604** ... the discovery of [The Life of St. Meriasek] in 1869 by Mr. Wynne of Peniarth among the Hengwrt manuscripts in Wales, and its subsequent publication by Whitley Stokes... in 1872, proved an epoch-making event in the history of the revival of the study of the ancient Cornish language ...

**Gilbert H. Doble**, 1934 in *The Saints of Cornwall* Pt. 1, 1960

**605** So much of my effort nowadays, working hard to make money and saving, is directed towards someday going there [to Trenarren House] to live.

    **A. L. Rowse**, 1934 in *The Diaries of A. L. Rowse*, 2003

**606** It is hardly likely that there will be a clamour for compulsory Cornish in the schools, but that a voluntary pride should be taken in the language is all to the good. It fosters patriotism, brings out the meaning of hundreds of mysterious place names, and reminds the Saxon that the Duchy has, when it likes to wear it, a culture which is beyond that of the more standardized counties to the east.

    'A Revival of Cornish', in **The Times**, 25 August 1934

## 1935

**607** A passionate loss to his friends – and they were many, for all serious students of Cornwall and Cornish history the untimely death of Charles Henderson cropped the most confident hope of a generation.

    **Arthur Quiller-Couch**, in preface to Charles Henderson, *Essays in Cornish History*, 1935

**608** Many older hearts were heavy as we filed out from the memorial service in Truro Cathedral. Two or three of us walked away to the building where his legacy is to be stored, the artillery he was ever collecting for his great Parochial History.

    **Arthur Quiller-Couch**, in preface to Charles Henderson, *Essays in Cornish History*, 1935

**609** One of the most serious charges brought against Cornishmen of old days was their propensity for 'wrecking'. By this is usually meant the luring of unhappy vessels on to the rocks in order to provide pillage for the natives of the district. I have never seen any documentary evidence of such an inhuman practice, though there is only too much evidence to show how the Cornish people of some districts pillaged and plundered ships and seamen who were cast ashore.

    **Charles Henderson**, *Essays in Cornish History*, 1935

**610** The fact that Count Robert [of Mortain] had St. Michael for his patron was probably the reason why Cornwall and so many Cornish churches were also under his invocation.

    **Charles Henderson**, *Essays in Cornish History*, 1935

**611** They are a *mean* people, the Cornish, because organised Nonconformity is organised meanness.

**A. L. Rowse**, EUL ms. 113/2 Journals and notebooks/5/4, 20 June 1935
[Payton 2005]

**612** The Cornishman excels in handling stone and dealing with water. He understands their nature and how best they may serve his purpose. He has worked with water during centuries of tin-washing, and leads it where it can be of service as a mother takes a child by the hand. He treats stone with the same quiet understanding of its nature.

**Bernard Walke**, *Twenty Years at St. Hilary*, 1935

**613** Although I have lived among them [the Cornish] for over twenty years I am still a stranger at St. Hilary, so much is there in their lives that remains as secret as the land they serve.

**Bernard Walke**, *Twenty Years at St. Hilary*, 1935

**614** His [Bernard Walke's] interesting chapters on Cornish life and Cornish character show that he appreciates none the less the difficulty, for a person of his views, in overcoming the reserve of a peasantry with such strong traditions of its own.

Review of *Twenty Years at St. Hilary*, in **The Times**, 28 June 1935

**615** The champion was a young man with a pale, serious face, who might have been a Greek athlete but for his Cornish profile. The game was in his blood, for his father had been a wrestler before him.

'At a Harvest Fair', in **The Times**, 23 September 1935

**616** The scheme for a Cornish gathering similar to the 'Manx Homecoming', which has been unknowingly revived by Sir Arthur Quiller Couch ... has been simmering for almost a year, but a meeting to decide its possibility is to be held almost immediately.

'The Cornish Fortnight', in **Old Cornwall** vol. 2, no. 10, Winter 1935

**617** A schoolboy will say that the chief event of 1815 was Waterloo; the old Bible Christians will say that it was the birth of their society; but the old Wesleyans of West Cornwall will say that it was the erection of the pretty little church at Gwithian.

**Laurence Maker**, *Cob and Moorstone*, 1935

**618** Think of such names as Rehoboth, Zion, Bethel, Ebenezer, Salem,

Providence, Bethesda, Siloam – Cornwall has them all …
**Laurence Maker,** *Cob and Moorstone,* 1935

619 In Cornwall the older and middle-aged men who pass one in the lanes with a 'Good day to you' almost always raise their hands to one in this way [with the hand raised about in a line with the face and with the palm outwards]. But the young men too often touch their foreheads with a finger, or a nod: which are merely English fashions, and not Cornish at all.
**'Gwas Gerrans',** 'The Cornish Salute', in *Old Cornwall* vol. 2, no. 10, Winter 1935

## 1936

620 The Cornish language was used for a service in a Cornish cathedral for the first time at Truro this afternoon. No word of English was spoken or sung throughout the service of evensong …
'Cornish Service in Cathedral', in **The Times,** 17 August 1936

621 If we took to this reputed cross-banner of Cornwall … we should probably have Cornwall more in evidence on occasions when the flags of all nations decorate Cornish streets.
'The Banner of Cornwall', in **Old Cornwall** vol. 2, no. 11, Summer 1936

622 The earliest record of ONE AND ALL in Cornwall seems to go back to more than 300 years ago, but then it was not Cornish at all … but … a phrase then common to all English-speaking sailors in revolt.
'One and All', in **Old Cornwall** vol. 2, no. 11, Summer 1936

623 Yesterday afternoon a prophet was honoured in his own country, a Cornishman in his own county, Sir Arthur Quiller-Couch in his native city, Bodmin.
**The Times,** 25 September 1936

624 To raise laughs, at least one of the characters [in dialect sketches] is a simpleton, and it is he or she who usually talks the broadest Cornish. Surely this is not the way to gain respect for our dialect.
**W. M. Symons,** 'Dialect', in *Old Cornwall* vol. 2, no. 12, Winter 1936

## 1937

625 If we are quite truthful we have to admit that the revival of the Gorsedd

has scarcely touched the lives of the common people of Cornwall.
**'Cornishman'**, 1937 [Den Toll, *Gorseth Kernow: the first 50 years*, 1978

626 ... all I want to be is a spokesman for the Cornish people.
**A.L. Rowse**, *Cornish Labour News*, May 1937

627 It is noteworthy indeed that for the first time this year Cornish phonology is included among the compulsory courses for graduation in the school of Celtic Studies [at Liverpool University].
**L. C. J. Orchard**, 'A Liverpool Venture', in *Old Cornwall* vol. 3, no. 2, Winter 1937

628 Dorothy Pentreath, who lived in Mousehole, and died here in 1777 ... is often said to be the last to speak Cornish. That is not exactly true, for there are some in Cornwall who have some fragments of Cornish still when they speak among themselves.
**Arthur Mee**, *Cornwall*, 1937

629 Some places ask us to come to them, but Cornwall has never offered allurements to others to share its life; yet it is this tinge of aloofness in race and history and atmosphere that makes it so enchanting to the stranger.
**Arthur Mee**, *Cornwall*, 1937

630 There is nothing in this country to beat our wild Atlantic coast, and there is nothing else like Cornwall. It is unique. Its coast and its moors are like something apart, and the traveller may feel that its people are a little less English than any other English people in the land.
**Arthur Mee**, *Cornwall*, 1937

# 1938

631     From the fisher's little cottage in the sandy cove below,
          To the farmstead, in the churchtown upalong,
          We are "One and All" united, we all know that we are right,
          Did you ever find a Cornishman far wrong?
**Vyvyan Pellow**, in *Western Whispers*, 1938

632 Newquay and other Cornish coast resorts are keenly interested in the movement to encourage a wider spread-over of the summer holiday period in this country.
'Spread-over holidays', in **The Times**, 5 April 1938

**633** Two very different points of view may be taken in the attitude of people, and especially those who are not Cornish, towards mining and mining matters. The most general one is that the mining industry is an utterly sordid and soulless occupation, or at its best but a gambling venture, that those engaged in it are people to be looked upon with suspicion and distrust, and that the miners themselves are people of the lowest possible description, brutal and corrupt. Hence the great abandoned dumps or "burrows", as the Cornishmen call them, with the remains of massive engine-houses cropping up in all sorts of unexpected places, are by such people looked upon as excrescences, eyesores and blots on the countryside, memorials of little else than bygone follies, and the fleecing in the past of some unfortunate individuals of their own class.

On the other hand there are the few who, given broader vision, can see what real triumphs of skill and energy, of brain and invention, such silent witnesses really stand for. To these they are records not merely of a sordid money-getting industry of long ago, but of the bold attempts of long-passed-away generations to wring from the depths the secrets and wealth of mineral deposits, in which often they were defeated, but sometimes surprisingly successful.

F. J. Stephens, 'The Romance of Mining', in Old Cornwall, vol. 3, no.3, Summer 1938

**634** The closest link of all [between Brittany and Cornwall] ... has been formed by our common adoption of the Gorsedd as a focus of patriotic feeling in each country ...

'Cornish Delegations', in **Old Cornwall**, vol. 3, no. 4, Winter 1938

**635** For years I have made a note of every little incident or word or phrase which I think may be different in spirit and show in any way a Cornish trend of thought. Never was it more urgent than now to put them down in writing before they escape from memory ...

**James H. Hodge**, 'Records', in Old Cornwall, vol. 3, no. 4, Winter 1938

**636** During the Reformation and the succeeding centuries of indifference, all the written lives of the patron saints of Cornish parishes were deliberately or negligently destroyed.

**Gilbert H. Doble**, Saint Petroc, 1938

**637** On looking through the numbers of 'Old Cornwall' ... a lover of Cornwall finds in the scope of 'Old Cornwall work' a veritable university – one whose studies are more closely related to daily life than the separate subjects of the schools, yet which may lead the way to higher branches of knowledge by showing him where these begin at home.

E. G. Retallack Hooper, 'Our Own University', in *Old Cornwall*, vol. 3, no. 4, Winter 1938

638 ... it must be above all in the Cornish Language that the Cornishman of this university will find himself, for this it is which proves to him his own nationality and his own place among mankind.
E. G. Retallack Hooper, 'Our Own University', in *Old Cornwall*, vol. 3, no. 4, Winter 1938

# 1939

639 The tribute system, that is, one of no fixed wage, but a certain proportion of the ores won by the miners, has always been more attractive to the real Cornishman, than the securer weekly or monthly wage system, and it bred a miner who now is nearly, if not quite, extinct, a type of man who learned to use his acumen and brain as well as his muscles.
F. J. Stephens, 'The Romance of Cornish Mining', in *Old Cornwall*, vol. 3, no. 5, Summer 1939

640 Old Cornwall members who find more relief from gloomy conditions in some absorbing occupation than in any mere distraction may well consider the value to themselves of Cornish as against the short-lived fascination of crossword-puzzles, etc.
R[obert] M[orton] N[ance], 'Cornish Simplified', in *Old Cornwall*, vol. 3, no. 6, Winter 1939

641 As long as the place-names last, Cornwall will continue to speak to its inhabitants in the old language, and if we are not there told the whole tale it is possible at least to listen to this talk more intelligently by using the Cornish Dictionary to explain it.
R[obert] M[orton] N[ance], 'Hints for Place-Name Study', in *Old Cornwall*, vol. 3, no. 6, Winter 1939

642 The Cornish live, like their fellow-Celts, on the W. fringe of Europe, driven there by pressure from the E. There, in a climate both wet and warm, they are fighting all the time, mainly against the elements. Therefore they are in no way soft; yet they often display a remarkable indolence, and again a startling capacity for intense effort. This contradiction is carried right through their character; harshness and gentleness, cruelty and tenderness, gaiety and melancholy, you will find inextricably mixed up – if you get to know them well enough. But they are not an easy people to know well ...
J. W. Lambert, *[Penguin Guide] Cornwall*, 1939

**643** For some obscure reason attempts are being made to revive the use of this language [Cornish] which is quite adequate for announcing that the pig is in the river, but useless for buying a packet of cigarettes. A Gorsedd is held annually when a number of self-styled bards dress up like Druids, stand on an exposed piece of moor and chant it at each other.

**J. W. Lambert**, *[Penguin Guide] Cornwall*, 1939


## 1940s

**644** A better knowledge of the Cornish past should give us the understanding and the grit whereby we become better Cornishmen, more useful-to-Cornwall Cornishmen today.

**John Legonna**, in a letter to A. L. Rowse, n.d. [Payton, 2005]


## 1940

**645** The business of the Vice-Warden of the Stannaries was, owing to the decline in the Cornish tin trade, so much less exacting than it had once been that the main part of it could [in the mid 1880s] be dispatched in four sessions of a fortnight each at Truro.

**H. A. L. Fisher**, *Unfinished Autobiography*, 1940


**646**    A flame of rushlight in the cell
On holy walls and holy well
And to the west the thundering bay
With soaking seaweed, sand and spray,
Oh good St. Cadoc pray for me
Here in your cell beside the sea.

**John Betjeman**, *Saint Cadoc*, 1940


## 1941

**647** No peoples are so haunted by memory as the Celts: therein lies their distinctiveness in Europe. Moreover so much of the folk-memory of the Celtic peoples ... seems to have attached itself to the Cornish scene.

**A. L. Rowse**, *Tudor Cornwall*, 1941


**648** Tin-mining was the industry in which Cornwall was pre-eminent; it marked the county off from all other counties, except Devon, which shared in it to a decreasing extent; it gave Cornwall its distinctive place in the economy of Europe.

**A. L. Rowse**, *Tudor Cornwall*, 1941

**649** Altogether Cornwall, through the dubious distinction of its liaison with the Duchy, was a fine milch-cow for the Crown and remained so for centuries: a long-continuing mark through the pages of history of its original condition as a conquered country. No wonder Cornishmen as late as the sixteenth century remembered that they were a conquered people, and resented it. They had cause to.

**A. L. Rowse**, *Tudor Cornwall*, 1941

**650** … the Rebellions of 1497 and 1549 were to Cornwall what the '15 and '45 were to the Highlands.

**A. L. Rowse**, *Tudor Cornwall*, 1941

**651** Up to the 16th century, Cornwall was the last outpost of the known world.

**A. L. Rowse**, *Tudor Cornwall*, 1941

**652** One has always to remember in dealing with a Cornish name that the present spelling is likely to be misleading.

**R. Morton Nance**, 'Hints for Place-name Study', in *Old Cornwall*, vol. 3, no. 9, Summer 1941

**653** The Cornish personality has been strong enough to withstand the influence of the summer visitor …[and] the mass disseminated culture of the B.B.C. It does not need, therefore, to be bolstered up by a resurrected language, of which even the pronunciation lies in doubt, to foster its patriotism and remind it of Cornwall's long and honourable history.

**[Claude Berry]**, Editorial in *West Briton*, 11 August 1941 [Payton, 2005]

## c. 1942

**654** As a rule Cornishmen know nothing of compromise or half-measures. Whatever they like they are enthusiastic about, and whatever they dislike they detest very thoroughly and either ignore it or attack it …

**Edwin Chirgwin**, 'A Critical Essay on the Work of A. L. Rowse', unpublished ms., Institute of Cornish Studies [Payton, 2005]

**655** Being individuals par excellence they [the Cornish] have a marked tendency to intolerance and bigotry, and down to the outbreak of the war of 1914 this intolerance pervaded the whole religious and political life of the county.

**Edwin Chirgwin**, 'A Critical Essay on the Work of A. L. Rowse', unpublished ms., Institute of Cornish Studies [Payton, 2005]

# 1942

**656** I was so delighted with Scott for this last reference to our National Emblem [the Cornish Chough in *Redgauntlet*], the very essence of all that Arthur and his legends stand for, written more than a hundred years before the revival of a Cornish Gorsedd, that I felt I would like to see the name of Walter Scott emblazoned on a "Roll of Honour" along with those of other strangers, such as Lhuyd, Daines Barrington, Norris and Stokes, who have like our own Cornish writers done something to keep our Celtic Spirit and language going and make a Cornish Gorsedd possible in the 20th century ...

> **C. S. Murrish**, 'Scott and "Celtic Spirit"', in *Old Cornwall*, vol. 3, no. 11, Summer 1942

**657** Almost every Cornishman is superstitious, and even to-day the numerous once-religious rites of "breaking the charm", often perhaps reluctantly or shyly performed in public, are so instinctive in us, that they have fully as much force as the commands of Church or Law.

> **C. C. James**, 'Cornish Parish Feasts', in *Old Cornwall*, vol. 3, no. 11, Summer 1942

**658** ... the legend that Cornwall has always been sparsely wooded cannot be upheld. Woodland can be said to be really absent only on the exposed plateau surfaces of the Land's End district, the North Coast, and the Lizard peninsula.

> **N. J. G. Pounds**, 'The Ancient Woodlands of Cornwall', in *Old Cornwall*, vol. 3, no. 12, Winter 1942

**659** There never was a greater joke than 'One and All' as the Cornish motto, for Cornish people, like all Celts, are notoriously individualistic and incapable of co-operating.

> **A. L. Rowse**, *A Cornish Childhood*, 1942

**660** Mother talked the Cornish dialect her mother had talked before her, minus the 'h's' which even granny was not entirely without; nor was my father, though he used them sparingly, as they might be aspirins rather than aspirates.

> **A. L. Rowse**, *A Cornish Childhood*, 1942

**661** What Thomas Hardy is to Wessex, 'Q' is to Cornwall.

> **A. L. Rowse**, *A Cornish Childhood*, 1942

**662** To be Cornish is to be Celtic, and all Celts seem to exhibit a sort of aristocratic intransigence. They have natures that quickly and thunderously cloud over, and they are touchy in a way that the Anglo-Saxon finds incalculable.

**Elizabeth Bowen**, Review of *A Cornish Childhood*, in *Tatler*, 15 July 1942 [Payton, 2005]

# 1943

663 It must be true that Cousin Jacky *enjoys* bad health, for he will very seldom own that he is really well.

**M. W. Rogers**, 'Enjoying Bad Health', in *Old Cornwall*, vol. 4, no. 1, Summer 1943

664 The Annual Meeting of the Cornish Gorsedd recognises the close kinship of Cornwall and Brittany and approves the formation of a group to be called "Friends of Brittany" which … shall do all that is possible to help Brittany in the future …

**Annual Meeting of the Cornish Gorsedd**, 4 September 1943

665    Cornwall, that little world apart, whose essence,
    – Not whose existence – is to establish men
    As different from those of any other land
    As Chinaman from Dutchman!

**Hugh MacDiarmid** [Christopher Murray Grieve], 'Cornish Heroic song for Valda Trevlyn', 1943

666 Some of those who bear Saxon names may … be now more Celtic than many who carry a fine old Cornish *Tre*-name, for it must be allowed that the most aristocratic of Cornish surnames may record only the loot, by a Norman, of the estate of a Saxon, who dispossessed the heir of a Cornishman, who founded it and gave it to his own name with *Tre*- before it; while the Cornish founder's heirs may still walk among us bearing perhaps, like so many Celts in Wales, some name such as Williams, Thomas, or Richards that tells nothing of their long Celtic pedigree.

**R. Morton Nance**, 'Celtic Personal Names of Cornwall', in *Old Cornwall*, vol. 4, no. 2, Winter 1943

667 … the Cornish are an emotional, literal people with no art of their own through which to free themselves; these compensations [religion and drink] have therefore become necessary to balance the psychological conflict set up by the severity, insecurity and peninsula nature of their lives …

**Sven Berlin**, *Horizons*, 1943

# 1944

**668** A Cornishman, who is sufficiently of them [the English] to appreciate them and yet is different enough to see them with a certain objectivity, may say that [the English are amongst the most brilliant of modern nations].

**A. L. Rowse**, *The English Spirit*, 1944

**669** All Cornishmen love their country. It is in their blood. They cannot help it – But this love fails to extend to their brethren Cornishmen when they return home …

**W. H. Rowe**, in *Western Morning News*, 12 February 1944 [Payton, 2005]

**670** The Cornish Tin Mining Advisory Committee, in a memorandum dealing with the future of metalliferous mining in Cornwall, states that unless the Government intervene immediately the war ends, British non-ferrous mining in this county will become extinct.

***The Times***, 1 April 1944

# 1945

**671** With the outbreak of Civil War the Duchy [of Cornwall] reached, perhaps, the apex of its importance …

**A. L. Rowse**, *West-Country Stories*, 1945

**672** It is first necessary to clear out of the way the popular confusion between the Duchy and the county of Cornwall. They are, of course, two entirely separate entities, utterly differing in character.

**A. L. Rowse**, *West-Country Stories*, 1945

**673** Though in latter years becoming known as 'England's Riviera', the essential attributes of Cornwall are in truth the reverse of tropical luxuriance.

**A. K. Hamilton Jenkin**, *Cornwall and its People*, 1945

**674** It is not without reason that the Cornish people have always been regarded as a race apart. Even to-day, despite the loss of their native language, they retain, to a surprising degree, the characteristics which mark them still as Celts.

**A. K. Hamilton Jenkin**, *Cornwall and its People*, 1945

**675** … no other Cornishman has ever known Brittany as familiarly or made so many personal friends there as he [Canon G. H. Doble] did in following up the footprints of the Saints.

'A Loss to Cornwall', in **Old Cornwall**, vol. 4, no. 4, Summer 1945

**676** I found [on the Cornish coast] long stretches of 'coastguards' path still plain on the ground ... and I could see no reason why all should not readily be linked up again with continuous public rights of way.

**John Dower**, *National Parks of England and Wales*, 1945

## 1946

**677** There are few parts of the earth's surface that have been more dug, excavated, disgorged, sifted, and puddled, in the elusive search for mineral riches, than that known as the Mining District of Cornwall.

**F. J. B. MacDowell**, 'The Field-Names of Redruth Parish', in *Old Cornwall*, vol. 4, no. 5, Summer 1946

**678** I am haunted by Cornwall, the obsession that awaits me around the corner when I am away from my friends, nearly all of them English ...

**A. L. Rowse**, *Notebook*, 1946 [Richard Ollard, *A Man of Contradictions*, 1999]

## 1947

**679** It [Cornwall] has all the possibilities of an earthly Paradise, but not in terms of rose wreathed hovels, picturesque slums and mummified beauty preserves. Not in terms of patronising visitors and parasitic natives, but as a regenerated Nation, proud of its own industries, able to contribute to Britain things that England cannot contribute; standing finally on its own feet ...

**Peggy Pollard**, *Cornwall*, 1947

**680** There are those who pretend to take a poor view of the Cornish Gorseth because it was inaugurated in 1928 A.D. instead of B.C. In a thousand years' time they will be sorry they spoke. All things must have a beginning.

**Peggy Pollard**, *Cornwall*, 1947

**681** "Bedheugh bynytha Kernewek." "Be forever Cornish." That is the best we can wish Cornwall.

**Peggy Pollard**, *Cornwall*, 1947

**682** All things considered, the wonder is not that Cornish ceased to be spoken about 1800 A.D., but that it managed to survive so long.

**A. S. D. Smith**, *The Story of the Cornish Language*, 1947

**683** ... membership of the Celtic Congress did much to awaken in Cornish people a consciousness of their affinity with the other Celtic nations.

**A. S. D. Smith**, *The Story of the Cornish Language*, 1947

**684** It [the revival of the Cornish language] has enabled many Cornishmen to find an outlet for the Celtic spirit within them, which otherwise would have but little scope and no apparent objective. In other words, it provides the incentive and the means to become Cornish in speech as well as in name. For without her language, Cornwall in the eyes of the world is just another English county. The Revival is beginning to put Cornwall on the map.

**A. S. D. Smith**, *The Story of the Cornish Language*, 1947

**685** The "foreigner" from a northern city who comes in summer to taste, perhaps superficially, of the pleasant, unhurried life of Devon and Cornwall, may condemn its people for being stupid and backward, even while secretly he considers the peaceful, picturesque, isolated village as an ideal spot in which to end his days. But let him retire into that village permanently; let him live there for years, winter or summer, with little means of leaving it, and with no contact with urban life – and in time he will begin to understand from within himself that strange mentality of people in remote rural parts.

**Survey Committee, University College of the South West**, *Devon and Cornwall: A Preliminary Survey*, 1947

**686** … the persistence of high unemployment in Cornwall suggests a post-world war depression problem more chronic than in either England or Devon.

**Survey Committee, University College of the South West**, *Devon and Cornwall: A Preliminary Survey*, 1947

## 1948

**687** The best-informed authorities are emphatic that there is as much mineral left in Cornwall as has been produced here through the ages. Mining is now practically extinct in the county, but tin is worth £540 a ton.

**W. Tregonning Hooper**, reported in *The Times*, 26 January 1948

**688** The Chough's existing stronghold to-day lies within a coastline stretch of about thirty miles on our Northern sea-board. Outside this, the birds are to be found nowhere in Cornwall unless very occasionally as casual wanderers.

**B. H. Ryves**, *Bird Life in Cornwall*, 1948

**689** The Duchy of Cornwall may be regarded as the home of the giants par excellence, indeed no other part of Britain can present such an array of titanic love as does this storied peninsula. The group of the Cornish giants is well-nigh unique in British tradition.

**Lewis Spence**, *The Minor Traditions of British Mythology*, 1948

**690** Expressed in this book ... is the Cornwall we know: the Cornwall of the sea-holly and the samphire, the vernal squill and the mesembryanthemum: the banners of weed, the salt in the air, the primrose, thrift, and campion, wings flashing in the sun, seals asleep, the fuchsias' dazzling arras, gulls behind the share, grey stone, glittering mica, a fisherman's trawl, mine-fingers against the blue, the deep, tangled valleys, the sand burrows, hilly fields and stunted elms, the eager present and the overwhelming sense of the past. Cornwall, proud and independent still, is not to be patronised loftily or carelessly exploited: it remains a land apart.

**J. C. Trewin**, in preface to *A Cornish Chorus*, ed. Muriel Hawkey, 1948

**691** In the heart of Cornwall, there are so many quiet roads and bylanes which seem to begin in no particular place, and end without having served any particular purpose – unless it be to delight the heart of the solitary traveller.

**W. P. Hodgkinson**, 'The Under-Road', in *A Cornish Chorus*, 1948

## 1949

**692** The Cornishman who has stayed at home is not really aware that he is in any way different from other Englishmen. Least of all is he concious of being Cornish. A Camborne man, a St. Ives man, yes, but not *especially* a Cornishman.

**Ivor Thomas**, 'County or Country', *Cornish Review 2*, Summer 1949

**693** ... when a Cornishman talks about cream he *means* cream, and not the 'milky trade' which up-country people pour from little jugs over their fruit, puddings, and jellies.

**Claude Berry**, *Cornwall*, 1949

**694** ... some "foreigners", egregiously obtuse and impulsive, provoke hostility in a Cornish community here and there by trying, in the name of progress, or some such thing, to turn the place upside down "in forty minutes". Not so is the way of life to be drastically changed in Cornwall ...

**Claude Berry**, *Cornwall*, 1949

**695** No People cling more tenaciously than the Cornish to the things that custom has ordained 'do belong to be' ...

**Claude Berry**, *Cornwall*, 1949

**696** Mr. Claude Berry's 'Cornwall' ... to many of us will seem the Cornishman's own book about Cornwall.

**Old Cornwall**, vol. 4, no. 10, Winter 1949

**697** ... in 1935 ... I denounced the Cornish "national" movement as a misguided, futile and wasteful effort – a view which I still hold.

　　Jack Clemo, *Confession of a Rebel*, 1949

**698** ... I am one of those writers whose creative work cannot be fully understood without reference to certain broken boundaries in their private lives.

　　Jack Clemo, *Confession of a Rebel*, 1949

**699** Local gentry who knew my plight well enough, and cast sometimes a pitying glance at me when they passed me in their cars as I slouched about the Goonamarris lanes, at once sent along fat cheques to the Scholarship Fund to enable poor Cornish boys to get a University education. Neither Q nor any other educationalist thought of launching a fund for Cornish misfits whose 'schooling' is a raw, elemental grapple with life itself...

　　Jack Clemo, *Confession of a Rebel*, 1949

**700** A forgotten larger part of the population of Cornwall is overseas ... They come home when they can (and always send back gifts generously), and to die when they can, but it is a small proportion over which to erect perpetual angels of nostalgia. The granite in those that go away is more typical of the backbone of the country than the lichen that remains.

　　R. Glynn Grylls, 'Reflections on the Cornish', in *Cornish Review* 1, 1949

**701** It was Cornwall that helped to release and develop this thing [stone carving] which, I began to see, was an extension of my painting and drawing...

　　Sven Berlin, 'My World as a Sculptor', in *Cornish Review* 1, 1949

## 1950

**702** The Cornish acre was a hopelessly indefinable area, varying according to the fertility of the ground, and perhaps from other factors, from place to place. In the eighteenth century Tonkin wrote that it could vary in size from 40 to 200 common acres.

　　Rev. W. M. M. Picken, 'Landiok', in *Old Cornwall* vol. 4, no. 11, Summer 1950

**703** Cornwall, Cornubia, is named scores of times [in Geoffrey of Monmouth's *Historia Regum Britanniae*], several times as often as Cambria, Demetia or Venedotia, and far oftener than any smaller region of Britain...

　　J. S. P. Tatlock, *The Legendary History of Britain*, 1950

**704** The Cornishman is not double-faced but multiple-faced, facets of character which add up to a sort of innocence. He is never still himself except in death, but all the conflicts which lead to a game of hide and seek between native and the so-called 'foreigner' are part of a process which constantly surfaces the most diverse and conflicting factors.

**Peter Lanyon**, 'The Face of Penwith', in *Cornish Review* 4, 1950

**705** Sooner or later every stranger – "foreigner" to the local people – who goes to Cornwall falls under her spell and before long is convinced that she has revealed to him the secret of her magic. Once let him voice this conviction, however, and proceed to analyse, interpret, or explain the magic, and he is lost. And so is the magic. It has a way of vanishing inexorably in a cloud.

**Claude Berry**, in *Devon and Cornwall in Pictures*, 1950

**706** The measuring-rod that we use in our backyard and parlour is ill adapted for surveying national, international or cosmic boundaries, and we Cornishmen who are now setting out to cry up our own goods must beware of falling into the snare that entraps certain minor European nations and a few addicts of regional literature … What should they know of Cornwall who only Cornwall know? Bearing these things in mind, we shall be wise enough to refrain from making extravagant claims for Cornish celebrities.

**C. C. Vyvyan**, 'J. C. Tregarthen', in *Cornish Review* 4, 1950

# 1951

**707**   Romantic Cornwall's dead and gone,
　　　With Stephen Hawker in his tomb;
　　　The Western Ocean breaks upon
　　　The Land's End Point in a froth of foam…
**John Heath-Stubbs**, 'Last Will and Testament of the Cornish Chough', in *Cornish Review* 8, Summer 1951

**708** It is odd to remember that when Father Wason said Mass in the Latin tongue in Cury Church, he came up against the same stubborn Cornish resistance to innovation which, in Queen Elizabeth's reign, had refused to accept the Service of Holy Communion in the English language, then, of course, a foreign tongue to the Cornish.

**Frank Baker**, 'The Perpetuate curate of Cury-with-Gunwalloe', in *Cornish Review* 8, Summer 1951

**709** Cornwall possesses little of the highest aesthetic quality though much that is lovable and much that is moving. Nearly always, however, in analysing one's emotions one will find that what is remembered is more the setting of architecture than architecture itself.

**Nikolaus Pevsner**, *Cornwall*, 1951

710 The view from the churchyard [of St. Euny, Redruth] is towards Norman keeps and obelisks all in ruin. They are in fact the remains of Cornish tin-mining in a more prosperous era, every one now appearing a folly of follies.

**Nikolaus Pevsner**, *Cornwall*, 1951

711 With the approval of the Transport and General Workers Union, 100 Italian miners are to be brought to Cornwall to help to improve tin production.

*The Times*, 30 August 1951

# 1952

712 ... the Cornish are a strange and unquenchable race – to-day they are capable of a loyal friendliness and often of gracious actions, but we must not forget that we are meeting the descendants of folk who still have a leaven of paganism in their blood.

**R. Thurstan Hopkins**, *Cornwall*, 1952

713 Port Isaac is Polperro without the self-consciousness, St. Ives without the artists.

**John Betjeman**, *First and Last Loves*, 1952

714 Some think of the farthest away places as Spitzbergen or Honolulu. But give me Padstow, though I can reach it any day from Waterloo without crossing the sea. For Padstow is in Cornwall and Cornwall is another country.

**John Betjeman**, *First and Last Loves*, 1952

715 A working-class child who admired the aristocracy, a one-time Labour candidate who has recently out-Toried the Tories in some of his views, an emotional Celt who set out to suppress his emotions in favour of intellectual rationalism – Rowse is made up of many paradoxes. But then so are the Cornish people, and there is no doubt that he understands them well, too well for their liking.

**Denys Val Baker**, 'Cornish Literature', in *Cornish Review* 10, Summer 1952

716 This is the tenth and final issue of the *Cornish Review*. Born Spring, 1949; died Summer, 1952. Cause of death, lack of local support ... Financially, the whole venture has been a disaster ...

**Denys Val Baker**, in *Cornish Review* 10, Summer 1952

**717** For two years a growing group of Cornish people have been concerned with the problem of how to preserve the Cornishness of Cornwall, in other words, to prevent the disappearance of the Cornish by emigration and by assimilation into other peoples.

> **Mebyon Kernow Press Statement**, c. 1952 [Charles Thomas, 'An Dasserghyans Kernewek', *Old Cornwall*, vol. 6, no. 5, Autumn 1963]

**718** Let it not be thought that there is anything rebellious in this Cornish Nationalism. The more loyal we are to our own little nation, the more loyal shall we be to the wider community of nations. The man who does not care is the great menace, in local and world affairs.

> **Richard Gendall**, 'Cornish Nationalism', in *Cornish Review* 10, Summer 1952

**719** Threat to Cornish Fishing Industry. Effect of Tourist Trade.

> Headline in **The Times**, 4 September 1952

## 1953

**720** It might be rightly said that the sea has played a greater part in the life of the Cornish people than the land whereon they dwelt.

> **John Rowe**, *Cornwall in the Age of the Industrial Revolution*, 1953

**721** Farming, till recent times, was the Cinderella of the Cornish economic order.

> **John Rowe**, *Cornwall in the Age of the Industrial Revolution*, 1953

**722** The custom of periodical meetings of the tinners of both counties [Cornwall and Devon] in the so-called *stannary parliaments*, to renew and, if necessary change and add to the body of stannary law, conferred what might almost be termed territorial semi-independence …

> **John Rowe**, *Cornwall in the Age of the Industrial Revolution*, 1953

**723** When I first went away from Gorran to live, I felt like an old Cornish lady who went to visit her daughter in Birmingham. She said, ' 'Tes wonderful, my dear, wonderful. 'Tes like some great day up there all the time with all the people. Only I can't breathy.' I felt like that. I couldn't 'breathy'. I was always coming back for a whiff of Gorran air.

> **Anne Treneer**, in 'Coast and Country' [Radio Broadcast], May 1953

**724** We cannot claim that the inventor of the steam railway, Richard

Trevethick [sic], was a Welshman, though he was the next best thing, Cornish, and probably understood a language very like Welsh ...

*The Welsh Republican – Y Gweriniaethwr*, October-November 1953

# 1954

**725** This [the 18th Century] was the last century in which the majority of Cornish regarded themselves as Cornish first and English merely as an afterthought, before the failure of the mines spread Cornishmen throughout the globe, before the railway brought the visitors who have done so much to destroy that which they profess to come to see.

**P. A. S. Pool**, 'William Borlase', in *Old Cornwall*, vol. 5, no. 5, 1954

**726** One of the first impressions that comes inevitably to the sensitive traveller in Cornwall is the awareness of a landscape that has a unity and a quality of its own. Although of England it is quite un-English.

**W. G. V. Balchin**, *Cornwall: an illustrated essay on the history of the landscape*, 1954

**727** The Cornish never took kindly to town-life.

**W. G. V. Balchin**, *Cornwall: an illustrated essay on the history of the landscape*, 1954

**728** Cornwall is very largely a product of its own environment.

**W. G. V. Balchin**, *Cornwall: an illustrated essay on the history of the landscape*, 1954

**729** Although the wind is so great an element in the Cornish weather, the windmill has never been a conspicuous feature of the scene.

**W. G. V. Balchin**, *Cornwall: an illustrated essay on the history of the landscape*, 1954

**730** I am sure that all Cornishmen will be grateful if they could depend on *The Times* to keep alive the ancient and only correct name for the Helston festival of May 8 – the Furry Dance, derived from the Cornish fer (festival).

**Sydney E. Allsop**, letter in *The Times*, 13 May 1954

**731** The parish of which Mr. Grigson writes is in south-east Cornwall, a few miles inland from Polperro, and he has the freedom of it by the best of all titles: that of a native.

Review of *Freedom of the Parish*, in **The Times**, 22 May 1954

# 1955

**732** In the war with Spain Cornwall was in the front line ... and in the 1590s the conflict was on her doorstep ...

A. L. **Rowse**, *The Expansion of Elizabethan England*, 1955

**733** One very important characteristic distinguished the Celts from some other Western peoples, and above all from the English; they are ever haunted by memories, and brood over the past, especially over harsh treatment which they may have experienced, feeding their hearts on 'laments and myths' ... The Cornish people never forget that they were a conquered race, compelled to live under an alien rule.

L. **Elliott-Binns**, *Medieval Cornwall*, 1955

**734** The Cornishman abroad shows amazing powers of adaptability and displays little of the insularity that marks the Englishman.

W. **Arthur Pascoe**, 'Some References to Cornwall and the Cornish', in *Old Cornwall*, vol. 5, no. 6, 1955

**735** It is surprising that, in the one part of Cornwall (Camborne and Redruth) which has been industrial for over a century, so many old dialect terms, many quite rare, can still be heard.

**Charles Thomas**, 'Camborne Words and more Camborne Sayings', in *Old Cornwall*, vol. 5, no. 6, 1955

# 1956

**736** 'Inland Cornwall has no interest.' Nonsense.

A. L. **Rowse**, 1956, in *The Diaries ...*, ed. Richard Ollard, 2003

# 1957

**737** The Cornish are reticent about their secret heritage, partly from a half-conscious desire to hide it from the ravages of modernity; partly perhaps from a folk-memory of the epochs of persecution.

**Ithell Colquhoun**, *The Living Stones: Cornwall*, 1957

**738** Cornwall is the only county with a patron saint of its own, because it is in fact a country with its St. Michael as a peer to St. David of Wales ... yet some still prefer the claim of St. Petroc, patron of Bodmin, as Cornwall's patron too.

**Ithell Colquhoun**, *The Living Stones: Cornwall*, 1957

**739** It is refreshing to hear a Celtic language spoken effortlessly and with gusto, for the Cornish tend to speak in flat Anglicised tones with little *blás*. The contrast with the intonation of native speakers is instructive, showing how difficult it is to resuscitate a language that has been moribund for almost two centuries.

> **Ithell Colquhoun**, *The Living Stones: Cornwall*, 1957

**740** As if, when the old language was exchanged for the new, no English had seemed ready to replace them, many words of Cornish lived on in local speech.

> **R. Morton Nance**, 'Cornish for cul-de-sac', in *Old Cornwall*, vol. 5, no. 8, 1957

**741** Hockings, Dunstans and Bolithos were in my Cornish maternal ancestry, so that now to think that there was a language peculiar to Cornwall, that all around me were place-names not English at all, but Cornish names – this made me feel like the man of whom John Keats tells us, who stood 'Upon a peak in Darien' and viewed the broad Pacific Ocean.

> **Wm. Daniel Watson**, 'How Cornish came to me', in *Old Cornwall*, vol. 5, no. 8, 1957

**742** In Cornwall guide books greet the English tourist by telling him, gently and humorously, but still telling him that, as long as he is on Cornish ground, he must consider himself a foreigner.

> **Leopold Kohr**, *The Breakdown of Nations*, 1957

## 1958

**743** Cornwall may be a small county, but you will find its sons and daughters all over the world... And when the world comes to Britain for its mining knowledge, it is to Cornwall it comes.

> **Holman Bros.** Advert, in *Cornish Magazine*, vol. 1, no. 2, June 1958

**744** The River Fal has been named as the most radioactive river in the country, and we are told ... that the search for uranium is to continue in Cornwall.

> *Cornish Magazine*, vol. 1, no. 5, September 1958

**745** Yes, there is something about Redruth that stirs Cornish hearts and when, for instance, there is a vital Rugby County Championship Match it seems only natural that we all congregate on that lovely Redruth ground. Everyone feels 'at home' there and win or lose, rain or fine, it's here that Cornwall give of their very best – why?

'Focus on Redruth', in *Cornish Magazine*, vol. 1, no. 6, October 1958

**746** Our symbolic use of Arthur and his sword is based on the cry, "Arthur is not dead!" which is traditionally said to have been raised at bardic gatherings in the Middle Ages. It may well have been taken literally a thousand years ago and less, but as meaning that there is still a hope of reviving the Celtic spirit of Cornwall it seems apt enough today.

**R. Morton Nance**, in letter to the *Cornish Magazine*, vol. 1, no. 7, November 1958

**747** [T]he most recent Cornish dictionary, that of Mr. Morton Nance ... displays that scarecly scientific revivalist local paatriotism which is still so commonly associated with Cornish studies.

**C. L. Wrenn**, 'Saxons and Celts in South-West Britain' (O'Donnell Lecture), *Transactions of the Honourable Society of Cymmmmrodorion*, 1959

**748** Home for Paul Feast ... no liquorice and broad figs from the Isle of Man, brought by the returning fishermen to their families, but my supper of marinated pilchards and saffron cakes compensated for the memories of when the Newlyn pilchard fleet followed the herring northwards to the Manx ports of Peel, Douglas, Derbyhaven and Castletown and even beyond. Like the nomadic shoals of pilchards I had come west for Harvest and the Feast Day.

**John Harvey**, 'The Expatriate's Dream', in *Cornish Magazine*, vol. 1, no. 7, November 1958

**749** The Cornish were afraid of the Mysterious People, as was obvious from the way their houses huddled down into hollows, like frightened sheep, always shrouded with elms or evergreens. None of these houses ever had a view, except in situations where it was impossible to avoid. And all the little farms and cottages I knew looked out on to a tiny square of garden, enclosed in high banks, and then a shroud of rhododendrons, aescalonias, fuchsias or any other rare shrub filched from the manorial gardens, backed with stunted pines or elms leaning away from the west, whose tops were clipped into dwarf forms by the fierce wind.

**Frank Baines**, *Look Towards the Sea*, 1958

# 1959

**750** ... in spite of foreign invasion that culture has not been altogether lost in the Celtic kingdom of lost causes and lost industries – for although their numbers continue to shrink there are still thirty times ten thousand

Cornishmen, independent, clannish, parochial even, proud of their separate history symbolized by quoit, saint, huer's hut and sky fingering mine-chimney.

**F. E. Halliday**, *A History of Cornwall*, 1959

**751** The independent political history of Cornwall may be said to have ended at the Restoration.

**F. E. Halliday**, *A History of Cornwall*, 1959

**752**    The four wheels of Charles's Wain,
        Grenville, Godolphin, Trevanion, Slanning, slain.

ANONYMOUS, in **F. E. Halliday**, *A History of Cornwall*, 1959

**753** The Cornish people themselves are like their land, an old and knowing race, withdrawn to strangers, living as much in the past as the present; without, as has been said, much creative inspiration.

**Denys Val Baker**, *Britain's Art Colony By the Sea*, 1959

**754** ... one generation has set Cornish on its feet. It is for another to make it walk.

**R. Morton Nance**, c. 1959

**755** The mantle of Gwas Myghal [Henry Jenner] fell on to the shoulder of Mordon [Robert Morton Nance], and Mordon wore it with the natural air of a sage.

**J. H. Martin**, in *West Briton*, 28 May 1959

**756** While thousands in Cornwall had never heard of his [Robert Morton Nance's] work as a ship modeller, thousands beyond the Tamar knew of him as a modeller of antique ships who also happened to be "a druid or something down in the West Country".

**J. H. Martin**, in *West Briton*, 28 May 1959

**757** Cornwall will not soon forget the white-haired scholar... who worked to give us a new vision of our past and deeper feeling for the enduring spirit of our homeland.

**J. H. Martin**, in *West Briton*, 28 May 1959

**758** Camborne's street names are linked very closely with those great families which once controlled its destiny – the Vyvyans of Trelowarren, the Bassets of Tehidy, Pendarves, and, of course, John Wesley.

'Focus on Camborne', in **Cornish Magazine**, vol. 2, no. 5, September 1959

**759** ... the very life of modern Camborne is so closely associated with Holman Bros., Ltd., that it is quite the usual thing for a son to follow his father and grandfather as a skilled tradesman in one of the Holman factories.

'Focus on Camborne', in *Cornish Magazine*, vol. 2, no. 5, September 1959

**760** A Cornishman is not an Englishman. Cornwall is half-way between England and America.

**A. L. Rowse**, 1959, in *The Diaries* ... , ed. Richard Ollard, 2003

# 1960s

**761** Cornwall's Right: Internal Self Government. Assemblies for Scotland and Wales: Why Not Cornwall?

**Mebyon Kernow poster**, 1960s

# 1960

**762** Although addicted to the vices of the age, the average Cornishman was no whit the worse than his English contemporary and the change effected in him by the evangelical revival was a re-awakening of his spiritual faculties which had lain dormant since the Reformation when there was imposed on him a mode of worship foreign to his sympathies and for which he could raise no enthusiasm.

**T. R. Harris**, *Methodism and the Cornish Miner*, 1960

**763** In Cornwall it has been popular to perpetuate family surnames as Christian names, and this might be an idea if grandparents or parents have names suitable ... Most holders of Cornish names that I know are proud of it, and with a number of names to choose from I do not think parents who are, as they say, Cornish patriots, will go far wrong.

**Cecil H. Beer**, in letter to the *Cornish Magazine*, vol. 2, no. 12, April 1960

**764** ... there are three things which go to make Cornwall what she is; first, the land itself, with its strong individuality and its man-supplied additions, such as grey granite hedges and fishing craft; second, the Cornish people, with their particular characteristics and long ancestry of some four thousand years' occupancy of that land; third, the Cornish language, embracing those same people with their hedges and fishing boats in a trinity which is Cornish in the most particular and absolute sense.

**Richard Gendall**, 'Cornish Language Lesson I', in *Cornish Magazine*, vol. 3, no. 1, May 1960

**765** There can hardly be a region in the world more influenced by water than

Cornwall, penetrated and almost surrounded as it is by the sea, rained upon, and criss-crossed with streams, so it is hardly surprising to meet POL frequently.

**Richard Gendall**, 'Cornish Language Lesson II', in *Cornish Magazine*, vol. 3, no. 2, June 1960

**766** An Englishman's home is his castle, but a Cornishman's home is his life.

**D. M. Taylor**, in *Cornish Magazine*, vol. 3, no. 6, October 1960

# 1961

**767** Today, 102 years after the completion of the Brunel masterpiece, the principal topic of conversation in Saltash is still "the bridge". "The bridge", however, has come to mean not the "old faithful", but a modern masterpiece – the new Tamar road bridge, scheduled to be completed this year.

*Cornish Magazine*, vol. 4, no. 2, June 1961

**768** It is rather shocking to see how little the average Cornish man and woman cares for the relics of their more recent past. So much of the work of preservation, from houses to kitchen utensils of past generations, and the support for Old Cornwall Societies, seems to be done by outsiders with a love for the county's history. Perhaps this is a symptom of Celtic arrogance – we are, and not by gee-games shall we be remembered.

**Valerie Bussey**, 'Cornwall for the Cornish', in *Cornish Magazine*, vol. 4, no. 3, July 1961

**769** *New Cornwall* ... now reports that an enterprising firm in Truro is ready to take orders for the Cornish kilt. It is proposed that the kilt should be plain black, as the Duke of Cornwall's arms are gold on black, and St. Piran's flag is white on black ...

*Cornish Magazine*, vol. 4, no. 3, July 1961

**770** The Cornish Gorsedd was held at Bude at the beginning of September, with all its impressive and traditional ceremonial. The beginnings of a new tradition – or the revival of an old one – were to be seen in the Grand Bard's wearing of the Cornish kilt.

*Cornish Magazine*, vol. 4, no. 6, October 1961

**771** Sensible people here do not wish the outer world to imagine they are producers only of broccoli and Cornish cream; they want their sons and daughters to take part also in enlightened movements of the ever-changing times.

**G. E. O. Knight**, in letter to *Western Morning News*, 1961, re. A Cornish University

# 1962

772 Cornish children have the right to learn their own language.

**Retallack Hooper**, reported in *The Times*, 29 March 1962

773 Cornish Methodism has been marked by an emotional approach to, and expression of, religion, an independent and conservative spirit, and an intense and ascetic spirituality, all of which are characteristic of a Celtic people.

**Thomas Shaw**, *Saint Petroc and John Wesley*, 1962

774 The parochial organisation in Cornwall has always been something of a Saxon imposition laid rather uneasily upon an older pattern of community, and it was to this original pattern that the new Methodism unconsciously related itself.

**Thomas Shaw**, *Saint Petroc and John Wesley*, 1962

775 This was Cornwall, and out of this grew the Cornish people: the puckish, friendly, devil-ridden, treacherous, destructive, much loved and much hated Celtic clan who had changed little since they had slept in their stone beds set in these hills only two thousand five hundred years before.

**Sven Berlin**, *The Dark Monarch*, 1962

776 So there was the façade, the drop-cloth to Cuckoo Town [St. Ives], created by the visitors, the foreigners who had invaded the peninsular fort of Cornwall; and this had now become its industry, behind which the sullen, astute Cornishmen hid their pride and took their revenge.

**Sven Berlin**, *The Dark Monarch*, 1962

# 1963

777 His life's works are his true memorial. *

**Part of the inscription on the grave of Robert Morton Nance** in Zennor churchyard, 1963

778 His [Robert Morton Nance's] love of Cornwall was so intense that, in his later years, when on the other side of the Tamar, he felt insecure and restless, and longed for the day when it would lie again to the eastward of him.

**A. K. Hamilton Jenkin**, in R. Morton Nance, *A Glossary of Cornish Sea-Words*, 1963

779 Nobody but a plastic rhinoceros could fail to be conscious of the past in Cornwall. This very dark brooding spirit of the past. Here you learn to live with ghosts.

**Charles Causley**, in *Cornish Magazine*, vol. 6, no. 1, May 1963

**780** Three hundred years ago a beautiful language was lost to the Cornish people because they were taught to be ashamed of it. Let us make sure that what remains of the Cornish voice is not allowed to slip away for very similar reasons.

'Around and About', in **Old Cornwall**, vol. 6, no. 4, Spring 1963

**781** If Glasney College had not been destroyed at the Reformation Penryn might now have a University for the south-west.

**M. Geach**, 'Glasney College', in *Old Cornwall*, vol. 6, no. 5, Autumn 1963

**782** The uninformed regard the entire Old Cornwall and Gorsedd movement as a waste of time, bogus to the core and simply an excuse for an annual escapist junket of picturesque appearance. All that one can say is that it is the business of the movement to see that the uninformed become the informed, and I think that slowly this is being accomplished.

**Charles Thomas**, 'An Dasserghyans Kernewek', address to Celtic Congress, 16 – 20 April, 1963 [*Old Cornwall*, vol. 6, no. 5]

**783** There is, in my opinion, only one living writer of dialect who is really outstanding, and that is Herbert Lean of Camborne: there are any number of others, but to me their work lacks authenticity.

**Charles Thomas**, 'An Dasserghyans Kernewek', address to Celtic Congress, 16 – 20 April, 1963 [*Old Cornwall*, vol. 6, no. 5]

**784** I believe much of the romantic glamour attributed to Cornwall is bogus and sentimental, and I have never subscribed to the extreme nationalist ideals in the county, though I would preserve what is picturesque and of historical interest.

**Jack Clemo**, in Michael Williams, 'The World of Jack Clemo', *Cornish Magazine*, vol. 6, no. 4, August 1963

**785** A great deal that was Cornwall has already gone, and in this age of mass entertainment, mass planning, mass everything, with its ruthless extermination of the individual, it is vital that a minority, with such worthwhile aims and objects as the Gorsedd, should live.

**Frank Ruhrmund**, 'Gorsedd of Cornwall', in *Cornish Magazine*, vol. 6, no. 6, October 1963

**786** Being Cornish, for me, is terribly important. Cornwall's part of you; you have to go away to realise this … you're Cornish … 'No, I'm not English, I'm Cornish!' Everybody laughs when you say it, but it's true.

**Margo Maeckelberghe**, in Michael Williams, 'Margo Maeckelberghe', *Cornish Magazine*, vol. 6, no. 7, November 1963

# 1964

**787** When Cornwall gets its new University, I hope it will shame some of the established institutions in the larger countries of our bloc by instituting a Chair of Inter-Celtic Relationships, in which the efflorescence of industrial Wales and Cornwall in their heroic ages will be studied not only for its own sake but in relation to the Celtic Presence, that great tapestry, frayed and faded and tattered though it be which has still to be fully woven on the loom of time.

    **Harri Webb**, 'From Across the Severn Sea', in *New Cornwall*, vol. 12, no. 2, March 1964

**788** We are 'home-along' when we cross the Tamar from Devon and we like things as 'they do belong to be'!

    'Whither Cornwall?', in **New Cornwall**, vol. 12, no. 2, March 1964

**789** Cornish Heath [is] the only true Cornish bloom among those under consideration [for the National Flower of Cornwall], and has already been used in past years in wreaths etc. on public occasions, representative of Cornwall.

    **Richard Gendall**, in 'A National Flower for Cornwall', *New Cornwall*, vol. 12, no. 3, May-June 1964

**790** The Cornish themselves are not dreamy and unpractical as the "foreigners" sometimes suppose. Like most Celts, they combine a deep sense of religion with a shrewd gift for business.

    **John Betjeman**, *Cornwall: a Shell Guide*, 1964

**791** Visitors to Cornwall, "foreigners" as they are rightly called by the Cornish...

    **John Betjeman**, *Cornwall: a Shell Guide*, 1964

**792** ... Bodmin is not much more than a moorland village, Truro is a dozy little cathedral town, while the hybrid Redruth-Camborne is nobody's idea of a pulsating heart.

    **Geoffrey Moorhouse**, *Britain in the Sixties: The Other England*, 1964

**793** Though the activities of Mebyon Kernow may be inflated out of all proportion, and though they take themselves a sight too seriously, it would be a very stupid Englishman who didn't recognise that this extravaganza expresses a fundamental resentment shared by many Cornishmen outside the movement.

    **Geoffrey Moorhouse**, *Britain in the Sixties: The Other England*, 1964

**794** To me it is not any international recognition that matters in my Art, because such a thing is transitory, but the force of old events in the soil of Cornwall.

> **Peter Lanyon**, 'Peter Lanyon – Marghak an Gwyns', in *New Cornwall*, vol. 12, no. 5, October – November 1964

**795** Cornwall has shared many experiences with England, some pleasant, others unpleasant, but Cornwall originated in a different tradition from that of England and after a thousand years the Cornish community is still determined to remain Cornish.

> 'Regionalism and Cornwall', in **New Cornwall**, vol. 12, no. 5, October–November 1964

**796** The subject of wind power has been surprisingly ignored by Cornish historians. The musical sound of falling water and the hiss of steam have deafened Cornish ears to the one sound of which they should need no reminding, the soughing of the wind.

> **H. L. Douch**, *Cornish Windmills*, 1964

**797** The opening of the Wesleys' work in Cornwall was quite unconsciously ill-timed. The native caution of the Cornish in dealing with strangers and the prevailing political conditions rendered it considerable disservice.

> **H. Miles Brown**, *The Church in Cornwall*, 1964

**798** The Wesleys and their itinerants restored *heart religion* to Cornwall.

> **John Pearce**, *The Wesleys in Cornwall*, 1964

**799** If it be concluded that the Great Emigration is the crown of the Cornish accomplishment, then John Wesley is seen to be its brightest jewel.

> **John Pearce**, *The Wesleys in Cornwall*, 1964

**800** Whatever may be said of the Reformation in England, in Cornwall, as in Wales, it snuffed out many candles which have never been relit.

> **John Pearce**, *The Wesleys in Cornwall*, 1964

**801** I have not lived in Cornwall for twenty-five years... I have few relatives left there and the houses where we once lived are in other hands. I had been back only once in ten years, for a fortnight of missionary meetings. Yet, despite all that, I share the eternal home-sickness of the Cornishman. This is something that goes deeper than mere loyalty to a county. It is found in the Welsh and the Scot and the Breton who cares more for Brittany than he does for France. There is nationalism in it of course, and all the deep-running

emotion of the Celt. It is often inexplicable to the Englishman, with his mixed racial inheritance, who regards Cornwall as 'just another English county'...
   **Cyril Davey**, *Cornish Holiday*, 1964

# 1965

802 The emergence over the last fifteen years of a thoughtful, vocal and consciously Cornish group [Mebyon Kernow] is one of the most promising signs that Cornwall will continue to exist as a Celtic country and not decline into merely an administrative division of England.
   **Richard and Ann Jenkin**, *Cornwall: the hidden land*, 1965

803 The continuing family links with America, Australia and South Africa give the Cornish a different outlook on the world from that of the English ...
   **Richard and Ann Jenkin**, *Cornwall: the hidden land*, 1965

804 To the Cornishman these ruined relics of past industry [engine-houses] have a significance greater than that of any Norman castle.
   **Richard and Ann Jenkin**, *Cornwall: the hidden land*, 1965

805 ... it is impossible to visit Cornwall, and especially western Cornwall, without feeling that there is a difference between its people and the people of the rest of England. They seem to be as different at least as the Welsh are, and the impression of a foreign country is heightened by distinct differences of language evident in place-names.
   **Sean Jennett** (ed), *Cornwall and the Isles of Scilly*, 1965

806 Cornwall is something more than a place of refuge for people in war and for Prime Ministers in peace. Our crime is that we live on the periphery.
   **A Davey**, in *West Briton*, 30 September 1965

807 Wesley's Cornish societies had been planted in a Celtic soil in which the emotional elements in Methodism had full and free play.
   **Thomas Shaw**, *The Bible Christians 1815–1907*, 1965

808 Like a kiss of rebirth Caradar [A. S. D. Smith] came, urged his Cornish classes across Cornwall, translated St. Mark and was gone.
   **John Legonna**, in *New Cornwall*, vol. 13, no. 6, December 1965

# 1966

809 They shall have a name perpetual and a flame permanent and immortal.
   **Plaque to Michael Joseph and Thomas Flamank** at St Keverne, 1966

810 All good Cornishmen must sympathize with the Smith's revolt against taxes imposed by the English ... If only the Tamar boundary were a real frontier!

**A. L. Rowse**, in letter to the Secretary of Mebyon Kernow, 1966 [*New Cornwall*, vol. 14, nos. 4 and 5, Winter 1966]

811 Miners' wives abroad, in the early days, craved for the flavouring [saffron] and it was customary for their Cornish relations to send a weekly package, enclosed with the West Briton, to their friends. Life, to the exiles on the Rand and elsewhere, would have lost its savour without either of them.

**Old Cornwall**, vol. 6, no. 10, Spring 1966

812 I would not like it to be thought that the Old Cornwall movement is opposed to mining in principle or the winning of tin by methods other than open-cast. Personally, I think we are taking a very grave risk in Cornwall today by putting too many restrictions on people who are genuinely trying to develop mines for the winning of tin.

**A. K. Hamilton Jenkin**, at spring meeting of the Federation of Old Cornwall Societies, 1966

813 ... it is necessary that Cornish boys and girls see what is Cornish tradition and what is English influence. Otherwise an English education is being applied to Cornish children making them less Cornish. Some do this innocently, some ought to know better.

**Mebyon Kernow**, *The Education of Cornish Children*, 1966

814 The ogre of eighteenth century Cornwall was the tinner, the hard-drinking and lawless patron of many an ale-house and grog-shop.

**H. L. Douch**, *Old Cornish Inns*, 1966

815 Cornwall and its people, in the forty and more years that I have known them, have always seemed to me to be closer to those values that are important in human life than in many other places. Perhaps this is because they belong to the 'Celtic fringe'.

**Dora Russell**, 'Whither Cornwall?', in *Cornish Review* 3, 1966

# 1967

816 The opening of the Saltash [Railway] Bridge produced what might be called 'the second English Invasion' of Cornwall.

**W. G. V. Balchin**, *Cornwall*, 1967

817 Religion, to the Cornish, is bred in the bone …
**Daphne du Maurier**, *Vanishing Cornwall*, 1967

818 There is in the Cornish character, smouldering beneath the surface, ever ready to ignite, a fiery independence, a stubborn pride.
**Daphne du Maurier**, *Vanishing Cornwall*, 1967

819 I have no sentimental feelings about giving up England. After all, I am a Cornishman …
**A. L. Rowse**, 1967, in *Diaries* …, ed. Richard Ollard, 2003

820 The popular image of a Methodist as a non-drinker and non-gambler is of comparatively recent origin.
**Thomas Shaw**, *History of Cornish Methodism*, 1967

821 Lake's *Parochial History of Cornwall*… was the gate through which I first entered the field of Cornish history…
**Thomas Shaw**, *History of Cornish Methodism*, 1967

822 Politically, Cornish Methodists have tended to be Liberals despite the Toryism of their founder, but they feared radicalism and rejected Chartism…
**Thomas Shaw**, *History of Cornish Methodism*, 1967

823 Launceston was of course one of the most important places on the North Cornwall line, the frontier town between England and Cornwall, with a sense of division about it – here the Celtic land really began, here lush Devon was left behind and austere Cornwall lay ahead. The fact that the GWR had a terminus here accentuated this – it had reached the foreign land but could go no further.
**T. W. E. Roche**, *The Withered Arm: Reminiscences of the Southern lines West of Exeter*, 1967

824 The harsh truth of the Cornish miner's working life is … [that] it was a miserable, dangerous, and even squalid, existence … he was more frequently the rent-owing occupier of a damp cottage, gaunt on a diet of potatoes and pilchards, and addicted to the local beer-shop.
**D. B. Barton**, *A History of Tin Mining and Smelting in Cornwall*, 1967

825 … one academic critic irately described him [Robert Morton Nance] as 'a scarcely scientific revivalist local patriot', but there are perhaps many worse things to be.
**P. A. S. Pool**, 'The Cornish Language', in *Cornish Review* II, 4, New Year 1967

**826** The only good thing that ever came out of Devon was the road to Cornwall.

**Robert Dunstone**, reported in *The Times*, 18 March 1967

**827** We have had similar enquiries for such a stamp previously but we felt that regional stamps were intended to recognise both the ancient status and current constitutional position of the regions concerned. Each one had in some degree a measure of local autonomy and special representation... Cornwall, on the other hand, although a Royal Duchy with distinctive Celtic history, was on a par with other English counties; and if we had issued a Cornish regional stamp we would, in fairness, have had to allow them similar recognition. That would have been quite impracticable.

**Postmaster General**'s reply to the request of the Celtic Congress for a regional stamp for Cornwall, reported in *New Cornwall*, vol. 15, no. 3, Oct-Dec, 1967

**828** I want to see devolution of power away from Whitehall and London to the people in the regions and nations of the United Kingdom. I look forward to a Parliament for Wales, Scotland, Cornwall and Brittany, and hope that eventually all regions of England will have greatly increased powers.

**John Pardoe, MP**, reported in *New Cornwall*, vol. 15, no. 3, Oct-Dec 1967

**829** It is our contention that the Cornish people have the same right to control their country, its economy and its political future as the other Celtic peoples of Scotland and Wales.

**Peter Bessell, MP and John Pardoe, MP**, in letter to *The Times*, 1 December 1967

**830** I feel sorry for the Cornish – they cannot help being an inferior race.

**Lord Arran**, in *The Independent*, [*New Cornwall*, vol. 15, no. 3, Oct–Dec 1967]

**831** I have been made a Member of the Nationalist Party of Cornwall, called Mebyon Kernow (Sons of Cornwall) and given a badge to wear, and a thing to stick on my car, and I can hardly wait to go and blow up a bridge, like your Welsh Nationalists!

**Daphne du Maurier**, 10 November 1967, in *Letters from Menabilly*, ed. Oriel Malet, 1993

**832** I'm not an extremist nationalist who wants to blow up the Tamar bridge or anything. But by standing as a Tory I believe I can do more for Cornwall than as a nationalist.

**David Mudd**, reported in *The Times*, 16 December 1967

**833** ... the differences between social groups [in 19th century West Cornwall] were never as clearly marked as elsewhere. There were no great families in the English sense.

**A. C. Todd**, *Beyond the Blaze: a biography of Davies Gilbert*, 1967

**834** It seems reasonable to suppose that Cornwall lost at least one third of its population [during the nineteenth century]...

**A. C. Todd**, *The Cornish Miner in America*, 1967

**835** The Tamar is our last frontier and we may have to make it the issue of our time.

**Royston Green**, c1967, [*New Cornwall*, vol. 15, no. 3, Oct–Dec 1967

## 1967–8

**836** Many beautiful flowers grow in Cornwall, but the Cornish national emblem is not one of these. That honour is reserved for the bramble, because the bramble is a Cornishman, and every true Cornishman is a bramble.

Wherever there are the most stones and least earth, the bramble flourishes and grows to a huge size. Poverty is a stimulus and not a handicap, to brambles and Cornishmen. Indeed, wherever in the world there are deserts and rocks, there you will find brambles and Cornishmen flourishing. The brambles are most obviously brambles; you cannot mistake them for any other plant. The Cornishman is always and unmistakeably Cornish, because God put Cornwall into his soul, and no man can take it away.

Many people regard the bramble as an ugly and savage weed, and the Cornishman as a wild and savage barbarian. Actually, the bramble bears a rather beautiful flower, but very few ever notice it. The Cornishman has his virtues also, but he must not expect any great praise or reward for them.

But at least everybody agrees its fruit is delicious; the bramble may be a weed, but it is a useful weed. And when we think of those men who have been most useful in the world, it is surprising what a large proportion of them turn out to be Cornishmen.

At blackberry time, little children can, and do, handle this vicious and spiky plant without harm. So can anyone who takes the trouble to understand it. And indeed, some people regard us, not as savages, but as quaint and amiable comedians who need not be taken too seriously. But you try to push rudely through a bramble bush, and see what happens!

It is true that you can, with some difficulty, chop a bramble to pieces, burn it, and clear the ground of all the roots you can find. But next year, what comes up? Brambles!

It's no good, they're immortal; they have it in them to conquer the world. And we must always remember; God did not put us into the world to be nice respectable copies of a well-educated Englishman. He put us here to be tough and thorny fanatics, content to have little in our minds but righteousness, little in our souls but the love of God and our barren native rock, and if need be, little or nothing in our pockets.

If we can remember this, and live like this, we also can conquer the world.

**William Blewett**, 'The Bramble', in *Cornish Nation* 3, 1967/1968, reprinted in *New Cornwall*, vol. 16, no. 3, May 1969

# 1968

**837** English influence has put an Englishman inside every Cornishman. Without destroying the Cornish character – so far – the English influence has made it difficult to be a Cornishman without inhibition.

**Robert Dunstone**, in *Cornish Magazine*, vol. 11, no. 1, March 1968

**838** Nothing could do more to foster the growth of Cornish economy and the whole spirit of this area than to say – 'You are on your own. Get on with it. No welfare payments from the English.' This is the pattern of the future, Party politics will matter less. The essential thing is to bring power back to the people. This is not nationalism; it is simply the natural progression of democracy.

**John Pardoe, MP**, reported in *New Cornwall*, vol. 15, no. 4, March 1968

**839** ... I am convinced that over the past few generations the Cornish have been steadily losing their self-respect in the same measure as they have been losing their traditions ... Too remote from the South East to ever be truly in the 'national' swim ... Cornwall must, I am convinced, be Cornwall, take a pride in herself, recognise herself for the entity she is.

**R. R. M. Gendall**, 'Cornish as an optional subject in schools', in *New Cornwall*, vol. 16, no. 1, June 1968

**840** To claim that *Kernow* is *Bys Vyken* is a discrepancy and a fallacy when so much Kernewek in manuscript is left on book-shelves unnoticed, unwanted, forgotten.

**D. H. Watkins**, 'Kernewek – some fallacies and discrepancies', in *Old Cornwall*, vol. 7, no. 3, autumn 1968

**841** To a Cornishman who knows the history and the problems of his own nation, Brittany is almost a second home.

**Richard G. Jenkin**, 'The Celtic Congress', in *New Cornwall*, vol. 16, no. 2, Oct–Nov, 1968

**842** Piers Dixon, prospective Conservative candidate for Truro, said that Cornwall and England were united to each other like man and wife, and one could not be half married. Perhaps we should sue for divorce on the grounds of England's illicit unions with Scotland and Wales!

**'P[asco] T[revyhan]'**, in *New Cornwall*, vol.16, no. 2, Oct-Nov, 1968

**843** The sea brought the world to the Cornishman's doorstep and kept him in touch with the centres of trade and government in his own nation, and any estimate of Cornish culture and economic life in former times must keep that in mind.

**V. M. and F. J. Chesher**, *The Cornishman's House*, 1968

**844** The observant reader will notice we use the terms "region" and "regional" a good deal in referring to the county. We consider that, in the context with which we are concerned, Cornwall was geographically and culturally a region in its own right, and that this is reflected in its buildings.

**V. M. and F. J. Chesher**, *The Cornishman's House*, 1968

**845** ... Cornish men and women should have preference in appointments to Cornish jobs, other factors being equal.

**Mebyon Kernow**, *What Cornishmen Can Do*, 1968

# 1969

**846** All Cornish people experience that wonderful healing feeling they receive returning to Cornwall from some distant shore.

**Robert Dunstone**, in William Greenberg, *The Flags of the Forgotten*, 1969

**847** It is a fact that the growth of nationalist movements on the Celtic fringe in Scotland, Wales, the Isle of Man and Cornwall has been in direct proportion to the growth of bureaucracy at the centre in London ...

**William Greenberg**, *The Flags of the Forgotten*, 1969

**848** Only a Cornishman can feel, and takes for granted, that surge of loyalty and affection for this curiously shaped, sea-girt tongue of land thrusting out into the Atlantic. Land's End is England's end, and the other side of the Tamar is, to a Cornishman, where England begins.

**Malcolm Saville**, *Come to Cornwall*, 1969

**849** Side by side the two great bridges span the boundary between Cornwall and the rest of England and the last geographical barrier is down – but that does not make Cornishmen into Englishmen. Bridges may come and bridges may go, but those born and bred to the west of the Tamar know that this peninsula, with its rocky coasts and historic interior, is still their 'own dear land'.

> **Malcolm Saville**, *Come to Cornwall*, 1969

**850** Nowhere better than in Cornwall can one feel the mysterious link between man and the whole of his planet, down to the very substance of its rocky foundations.

> **Dora Russell**, 'Thinking about time', in *Cornish Review* 12, 1969

**851** The Cornish are warm-hearted, friendly, kind, a strong and courageous race. But even as, charmingly, they take your cash, they will leave you in no doubts as to whose land you are visiting – you, the eternal 'foreigner'.

> **Henry Trevor [Denys Val Baker]**, 'Why Cornwall?', in *Cornish Review* 12, 1969

**852** An unexpected result of teaching Cornish to Cornish children has been improvement in their English writing – they understand that their 'Cornicism' is a trace of their own language with its own dignity of expression, neither a quaint relic nor merely a 'west country' dialect of the imaginary district of the British Broadcasting Corporation.

> **E. G. Retallack Hooper**, *The Story of the Cornish Language*, 1969

**853** Historical evidence of nationality is good and exists, if one looks for it, in Cornish history, but the plain, forthright demonstrable proof is possession of a distinct language …

> **E. G. Retallack Hooper**, *The Story of the Cornish Language*, 1969

**854** Down in Hellfire Corner many visiting hopes have perished. Teams – and players – of great reputation have met their Passchendaele there.

> **Michael Tresillian**, in *Cornish Magazine*, vol. 12, no. 1, March 1969

**855** In Cornwall, the majority knows nothing at all about Cornwall's Celtic history – so well have the people been severed from their roots.

> **Peter Berresford Ellis**, *The Creed of the Celtic Revolution*, 1969

**856** The ideal of Celtic unity was stated by the Welsh author of 'Armes Prydain Fawr' (ironically translated as 'The Prophecy of Great Britain') but the Great Britain of the Celtic vision was the unity of the Welsh, Irish, Scots, Cornish, and Bretons who would drive the English from their countries ... and 'Armes Prydain Fawr' was written in the 10th Century!

**Peter Berresford Ellis**, *The Creed of the Celtic Revolution*, 1969

**857** The only way forward is by co-operation between the [Cornish] National Party and Mebyon Kernow.

**Colin Murley**, in *Cornish Magazine*, vol. 12, no. 3, September 1969

**858** In the Civil War the sympathies of the democratic Cornish – monarchy and aristocracy meant little to them, unlike the more conservative English – were naturally with the North against slavery.

**A. L. Rowse**, *The Cornish in America*, 1969

**859** There is plenty of evidence that Cornwall has a quite exceptional capacity to draw and retain the hearts of its children, wherever they may be.

**A. L. Rowse**, *The Cornish in America*, 1969

**860** Dr. Johnson said that the finest road a Scot ever sees is the high road that leads from Edinburgh into England; much the same could be said of the Cornish and the high road that leads across the Tamar into England.

**A. L. Rowse**, *The Cornish in America*, 1969

**861** What is the most neglected minority group in America? Why, the Cornish, of course.

**New York Times Book Review**, 23 March 1969 [Payton, 2005]

**862** It's a hard struggle convincing people that the Cornish are quite exceptional in the way they have got round the world.

**A. C. Todd**, in letter to A. L. Rowse, 27 September 1969 [Payton, 2005]

**863** I have heard black men at Speakers' Corner refer to Welshmen and Cornishmen as facing the same troubles as themselves.

**Peter Evans**, 'Tribal custom in the human jungle', in *The Times*, 4 October 1969

## Late 1960s

**864** The Only Region For Cornwall is Cornwall.

**Mebyon Kernow** slogan, late 1960s [Bernard Deacon, Dick Cole and Garry Tregidga, *Mebyon Kernow and Cornish Nationalism*, 2003]

# 1970

**865** The fact is that of all the Celtic nations, despite the loss of the language, Cornwall is the most homogeneous. Partly, this is due to its easily comprehended geographical unity, partly to its small size and partly to the tenacity of its inhabitants. Cornwall has all the attributes of a nation; the only next thing is whether the Cornish people think they are.

   **James Whetter**, 'Cornwall into the 21st Century', in *Cornish Review* 14, Spring 1970

**866** ... the language is the summation of the Cornish identity, the facet of Kernow and its people which will always distinguish them from the rest of the world ...

   **James Whetter**, 'Reasons for learning the Cornish language', in *Cornish Nation*, vol. 2, no. 2, December 1970

# 1971

**867** [In St. Ives] I noticed, on coming out of the café, that 'Pirates' and 'Mermaids' are written over the doors of the places nearby. There is a strange mixture of the ancient and tasteful atmosphere of Cornwall and the atmosphere of Blackpool or Butlins. *

   **Harri Williams**, *Crwydro Cernyw*, 1971

**868** As we see the simple and stark black and white banner [of St. Piran] fluttering in the wind, a tremble of pride goes through our hearts. We are in contact, in unison with our Celtic ancestors. We are emboldened to do great things.

   **James Whetter**, *The Celtic Background of Kernow*, 1971

**869** They [Cornish revivals] have surely been glamourised, for if one speaks of the great revivals of Cornish Methodism one must in all honesty speak also of the great slumps of Cornish Methodism.

   **John C. C. Probert**, *The Sociology of Cornish Methodism*, 1971

**870** Much of it [Cornish Methodism] sad to say, was built on intensive denominational competition bearing strong resemblance to the competition of various grocery chains today. It has left a vicious heritage.

   **John C. C. Probert**, *The Sociology of Cornish Methodism*, 1971

**871** We know of no Cornish Methodists in the county family class... Doctors, solicitors, auctioneers rarely appear in the Methodist trust deeds, and teachers and bankers appear only occasionally.

   **John C. C. Probert**, *The Sociology of Cornish Methodism*, 1971

**872** It would be unfair to charge all Cornwall's Members [of Parliament] of the past with [the] general indictment of financial motive and a lack of integrity and responsibility towards their constituents, although Cornish nationalists would no doubt cynically observe that Cornwall got no more nor less than it deserved for irresponsibly supporting English candidates to represent Cornish interests!

**David Mudd**, *Cornishmen and True*, 1971

**873** ... though her [Cornwall's] cliffs are certainly the most spectacular in England, and worthily comparable with the finest in Scotland or on the Atlantic coastline of Ireland, and though she possesses 'a little Dartmoor' in the shape of the stern granite uplands of Bodmin Moor, one yet instinctively thinks of her as a sun-bathed and generally soporific westwards extension of the land, walled by granite to resist the onslaught of the Atlantic Ocean, offering seclusion, warmth and comfort, beauty for the taking, and a strangely persuasive peace which baffles understanding to the extent that one comes to accept it readily and without conscious question.

**Garry Hogg and John Tomes**, *The Shell Book of Exploring Britain*

**874** It is still meaningful to speak of Methodism as being the established religion of Cornwall...

**John D. Gay**, *The Geography of Religion in England*, 1971

**875** The fact that we are a nation should be written into the constitution and the Tamar border guaranteed by statute.

***Cornish Nation***, vol. 2, no. 5, September 1971

**876** As things are, the economic disparity of the "Two Nations", Kernow and Pow Saws (England) is likely to continue to grow in the future. Wage levels are unlikely to catch up with those in England, more and more young Cornish will have to leave the land to find employment, the coastal areas will increasingly be bought up by the English, Cornish farms will be taken over by newcomers and the land exploited for short-term profits while the heavy work, the economic drudgery will continue to done by Cornish people living in the poorer housing districts.

**James Whetter**, 'The Two Nations', in *Cornish Nation*, vol. 2, no. 6, December 1971

# 1972

**877** The Irish problem is part of the Celtic problem... But the Irish is only one of the Celtic problems. There are also the Cornish, the Breton, the Welsh, the Manx,

the Scottish problem. Why should not all these Celtic peoples have their freedoms?
**Cornish Nation**, March 1972

878 Inside each one of us, no matter how Anglicised we may be, is the Celt screaming to be let out. We must aid his re-emergence.
**P. J. Payton**, 'Language Revival', in *New Cornwall*, vol. 17, no. 3, Summer 1972

879 The thing about the Cornish is that they are not nice: exciting and attractive, but not nice. They have colour enough to turn the spectacles of most onlookers pink, but it is not fast to light. The impulsiveness that goes as far as magnanimity does not sustain generosity; the devotion, loyal to fanaticism, has no fidelity; the forthcomingness keeps much more back than reticence – like an iceberg the two-thirds under the water, if there were not anything less like an iceberg than the Celt.
**R. Glynn Grylls**, 'Who are the Cornish?', in *Cornish Review* 21, Summer 1972

880 ... Cornwall was the Eden of her [Virginia Woolf's] youth, an unforgettable paradise ... She was to love other places, but for Cornish people and Cornish things she had a kind of patriotic emotion; they seemed to be made of some particularly fine matter which made them more romantic and more distinguished than the products of any other soil.
**Quentin Bell**, *Virginia Woolf: a Biography*, 1972

881 Cornwall today is a mecca for tourists, a canvas for painters, and a dream-world for industrial workers on the edge of retirement.
**A. C. Todd and Peter Laws**, *The Industrial Archaeology of Cornwall*, 1972

882 ... throughout the length and breadth of the county ... it has been suggested there may have been as many as three thousand mills operating at one time or another during the last few centuries.
**D. E. Benney**, *Cornish Watermills*, 1972

883 Steeped in curious ancient practices and traditions, and offering to the beholder such varied spectacles as the high drama and excitement of a "Hevva!", the poetry of a tuck, and the animated bustle of a curing cellar when bulking fish, seining must be classified as one of the most romantic of all Cornish industries.
**Cyril Noall**, *Cornish Seines and Seiners*, 1972

**884** Few other fish can have had such honours heaped upon them; yet the pilchard abdicated his Cornish realm, deserting the seas which he had once dyed with his royal purple, and leaving his palaces ashore empty and untenanted.

**Cyril Noall**, *Cornish Seines and Seiners*, 1972

**885** ... the Tamar has come to acquire a symbolic, almost mystical significance for Cornishman... for countless thousands of them it has stood – and stands – as the place of parting or return, the end or the beginning of home ...

**John Fleet**, 'The Cornish Border', in *The Celtic Experience: Past and Present*, ed. F. G. Thompson, 1972

# 1973

**886** The early inhabitants of Cornwall were of Celtic origin. The Anglo-Saxon settlement of England did not extend to their territory and the people of Cornwall continued to be Celtic.

**The [Crowther-Kilbrandon] Report on the Royal Commission on the Constitution,** 1973

**887** The creation of the Duchy of Cornwal l... established a special and enduring relationship between Cornwall and the Crown. Use of the designation on all appropriate occasions would serve to recognise both this special relationship and the territorial integrity of Cornwall.

**The [Crowther-Kilbrandon] Report on the Royal Commission on the Constitution,** 1973

**888** What they [the Cornish] do want is recognition of the fact that Cornwall has a separate identity and that its traditional boundaries shall be respected.

**The [Crowther-Kilbrandon] Report on the Royal Commission on the Constitution,** 1973

**889** With the possible exception of geology, Cornish studies all, ultimately, reflect the activities of Man – Cornishmen and Cornishwomen – in Cornwall, past, present, and future.

**Charles Thomas**, *The Importance of Being Cornish in Cornwall*, 1973

**890** I think ... that Cornwall is approaching some sort of internal social crisis. It is increasingly difficult to *be* Cornish. It is correspondingly important ... for those who *are* Cornish, and who presumably value their identity, to stand up and to be counted.

**Charles Thomas**, *The Importance of Being Cornish in Cornwall*, 1973

**891** ... Revived Cornish, as to its spelling, an increasing part of its vocabulary, and most of its pronunciation, cannot be regarded as genuine and this is why it is viewed with such suspicion and reserve by almost all Celticists... This does not amount to failure... the major achievement of Henry Jenner, Robert Morton Nance, and their contemporaries was the establishment of a sense of Cornishness, of national consciousness ... An obliquity of direction in the matter of Revived Cornish is unfortunate, perhaps rectifiable; it hardly detracts from the plain fact that, had this overall Cornish Revival not been attempted, and accomplished, it would by now be quite impossible to construct the particular platform on which the linguistic, cultural, nationalistic and environmental movements in Cornwall all perform.

**Charles Thomas**, *The Importance of Being Cornish in Cornwall*, 1973

**892** Between the ages of 18 and 65, the population of Cornwall is annually creamed off ... This missing middle-generation ... deprives Cornwall, permanently, of a great chunk of its native population at the height of their operational efficiency, whether truly indigenous or not.

**Charles Thomas**, *The Importance of Being Cornish in Cornwall*, 1973

**893** If we define 'Cornish' as meaning no more than 'having been born in Cornwall', the 1951 Census, which for once gave birthplace by counties, showed this figure as 69% ... I emphasize that this has nothing to do with parentage, and would cover a Congo pygmy or a Chinaman who happened to be born here; if a cat has kittens in the oven this doesn't make them into pasties.

**Charles Thomas**, *The Importance of Being Cornish in Cornwall*, 1973

**894** It would be difficult to drum up much romantic excitement about 'going to Essex' or 'going to Bucks' or 'going to Leicestershire' – yet even to this day there remains an intangible yet very real romanticism about 'going to Cornwall'. It is going west, towards the sun, into the mysterious land of Lyonesse, into another world.

**Denys Val Baker**, *The Timeless Land*, 1973

**895** It is not they [the Cornish people] who have created the timeless land that has exerted such a strange and strong influence on so many artists. It is, in fact, the timeless land that has created the Cornish people ...

**Denys Val Baker**, *The Timeless Land*, 1973

**896** Cornwall does not need to create differences to emphasize its apartness from the rest of England. It *is* apart, solidly and unmistakably, and in the fullest

geographical sense.
**Denys Val Baker**, *The Timeless Land*, 1973

**897** Identity is ... difficult, for Cornwall is a kingdom, not a county. Mosaic might be a better word. With a language and a heritage of her own, Cornwall defies neat easy classification. No true Cornishman would call her English. Study our south and north coasts, one soft, the other harsh. Who would connect the two? Who would give them a common adjective other than Cornish?
**Michael Williams** (ed), *My Cornwall*, 1973

**898** We see a filching of our resources, our amenities, our environment and our identity all in the service of this great influx dictated by statistics, statisticians and planners. All this is decided without reference to the people who live in Cornwall.
**Mebyon Kernow**, *Strategy or speculation*, 1973

**899** ... the unusual and sometimes inconvenient placing of our churches is due in many cases to the Celtic origin of the Christian community in Cornwall, on which foundation later ages built.
**H. Miles Brown**, *What to look for in Cornish churches*, 1973

**900** When the spinners of tales for the visitors and the romantics have come and gone, there still remain the ancient stone circles, the menhirs, the wayside granite crosses, the traces of the 'old men', the strange Cornish place names, the Cornish character itself to testify to the length of history in these regions and its difference from the English story.
**H. Miles Brown**, *What to look for in Cornish churches*, 1973

## c. 1974

**901** Trebetherick ... may have been a suburb by the sea and for all our crabbing, fishing and bathing, nothing to do with the real Cornish who regarded us as the foreigners we still are. But for me it was home for the eyes, the nose and the ears.
**John Betjeman**, c1974, in Michael Williams, *People and Places in Cornwall*, 1985

## 1974

**902** What I hope to see is the Cornish language used again by ordinary people, not just an esoteric minority. A first step must be the introduction of the language as an optional subject in schools. There was great enthusiasm among schoolchildren when I conducted an experimental session and we played games in Cornish.

**Mary Truran**, in *Sunday Times* 7 April 1974

**903** ... this powerfully built articulate young man could charm the pastry off a Cornish Pasty ...

**Daily Telegraph**, Summer (?), 1974 [Annette Penhaligon, *Penhaligon*, 1989]

**904** If a Cornishman begins to think, he's a rebel!

**Stannator Alsop**, reported in '24 Cornishmen are nailing their colours to the Magna Carta', *The Times*, 26 October 1974

**905** However much money tourism brings into Cornwall, you must remember that it comes in on one train and goes out on the next ...

**Stannator Brian Hambley**, reported in '24 Cornishmen ...'

**906** The Kilbrandon Report controversy provides us with a heaven-sent opportunity to press the claim of Cornwall... Cornwall should demand her own devolutionary Cornish Parliament with administrative, legislative and executive powers at least equal to those already proposed for Scotland.

**Cowethas Flamank**, *Towards Self-Government*, 1974

**907**    Here in the late October light
See Cornwall, a pathetic sight,
Raddled and put upon and tired
And looking somewhat over-hired;
Remembering in the autumn air
The years when she was young and fair –
Those golden and unpeopled bays,
The shadowy cliffs and sheep-worn ways,
The white unpopulated surf,
The thyme- and mushroom- scented turf,
The slate-hung farms, the oil-lit chapels,
Thin elms and lemon-coloured apples –
Going and gone beyond recall
Now she is free for "One and All".

**John Betjeman**, from 'Delectable Duchy', in *A Nip in the Air*, 1974

**908** The growth of the Cornish political national movement is inseparable from that of the language revival; you cannot revive a language without reviving the idea of nationhood and the aspiration of nationhood is independent statehood.

**P. Berresford Ellis**, *The Cornish Language and its Literature*, 1974

**909** One recognizes the Celtic temperament in the Cornish: warm and generous, if not hurt or offended, touchy and quick, easily resentful and apt to nurse ill-feelings a long while. Anglo-Saxons be wary! for we are also secretive, reserved, mistrustful; not at all on the surface, or obvious, or so easily read as you think; very individualist and clannish, we hang together in an instinctive way, if not so good at cooperating; hospitable to foreigners – and all outsiders are 'furriners' in Cornwall – if they treat us well (you won't get much out of us if you don't); spirited and brave enough, with all the effort and struggle, the hard lot through the ages of wresting a living from a scanty soil, the perils of mining and the sea. In spite of everything, and above all, we are interesting and *different*, an individual people in our own Little Land.

**A. L. Rowse**, in John Betjeman and A. L. Rowse, *Victorian and Edwardian Cornwall from old photographs*, 1975

## 1975

**910** Lhuyd's visit was perhaps the most important event in the modern history of Cornish …

**P. A. S. Pool**, *The Death of Cornish*, 1975

**911** If ever a language was lost by apathy and indifference, then it was Cornish.

**P. A. S. Pool**, *The Death of Cornish*, 1975

**912** That a local pressure group [Mebyon Kernow] should have to campaign for signs in Cornish welcoming visitors to the county is a pathetic comment, not on those supporting the idea, but on the authorities.

**Tony Deane and Tony Shaw**, *The Folklore of Cornwall*, 1975

**913** The re-appearance of the Cornish Stannary Parliament is not a huge joke or something "dreamed up" by a group of cranks or hot heads. It is the Right of Cornwall and without it Cornwall is not legally governed.

**E. Trewin-Wolle,** in *Cornish Stannary Gazette*, No. 1, January 1975

**914** There can be no doubt that a great number of Cornish people are thinking in terms of self government for Cornwall. Unfortunately so many of our country men and women are so imbued with English orientated political thinking that they can see no other way of obtaining Cornish self-determination but through the Westminster polls.

**Anonymous**, 'The Polls to Perdition', in *Cornish Stannary Gazette*, No. 2, 1975

**915** Cornwall's Celtic fire died down long ago, but as they blow on the embers, there are many who believe that Cornishness can be kept alive.

**Trevor Fishlock**, 'Mixed feelings as Cornishmen consider two-sided coin of tourist traffic', *The Times*, 24 March 1975

**916** ... a large element of the story of Cornwall is of insiders fighting to get out and outsiders fighting to get in.

**Trevor Fishlock**, 'Mixed feelings as Cornishmen consider two-sided coin of tourist traffic', *The Times*, 24 March 1975

**917** ... I recognise the validity of much of the [Cowethas Flamank] Report's case and feel that, on balance, Crown Dependency status [for Cornwall] is the most realistic goal.

**David Mudd**, in letter to Cowethas Flamank, 13 May 1975, [Payton, 1993]

**918** On 28th May 1975 at Truro a number of former members of Mebyon Kernow met and decided to form a new party, the Cornish Nationalist Party. The basic aim of the new party is the achievement of self-government for Kernow by democratic and constitutional means.

**Dr. James Whetter and Grenville Smyth**, Press statement on behalf of the Cornish Nationalist Party, 1975

**919** Michael Joseph fought and died for Cornwall and he was proud to boast that his people would not forget him. He was sure the Cornish Nation would endure and remember. We must fight to ensure that our land remains Cornish and that as long as Cornwall remains it will be the homeland of the Cornish people. We shall not disappear and we shall not be dispossessed of our Cornish heritage.

**Richard Jenkin**, speaking at St. Keverne, June 1975

**920** The effect of the Cornish Revival upon Methodism, though limited, has been to reawaken a sense of the links with Celtic Christianity, with which early Methodism had so much in common ...

**G. Pawley White**, *A Half-Century of Cornish Methodism 1925–1975*, 1975

**921** Here [Camelford in 1930] there were three chapels, locally nicknamed "High and Mighty", "Spite and Envy" and "The Old Folks at Home"! Anyone previously unacquainted with the turbulent history of Methodism in this part of Cornwall would soon have become aware of it, because of the feeling of rivalry between Chapels of different Methodist origins.

**G. Pawley White**, *A Half-Century of Cornish Methodism 1925–1975*, 1975

**922** A long historic past, during which many myths and traditions had developed, delayed recognition of the fact that, early in the twentieth century, Cornish mining had so drastically declined that in realistic terms it was only of minor significance.

**John Rowe**, 'The Declining Years of Cornish Tin Mining' in *Education and Labour in the South West*, ed. Jeffrey Porter, 1975

**923** … the tradition of the Cornish people means that they are not, and never have been, a herd of people at the beck and call of some impersonal master.

**John and Elizabeth Saxton** (ed), *About Cornwall*, 1975

**924** In the circles in which I move these islands are considered to be occupied not by four nations… but by six, the Scottish, Irish, Manx, Welsh, Cornish and English.

**James Whetter**, in letter to *The Times*, 28 October 1975

## 1976

**925** Cornwall is a hard land. The mind of a man is incised by the power of sharp rocks and monstrous seas. Winter and night are the times when this power is most manifest.

**James Turner**, *The Stone Peninsula*, 1976

**926** At its [the A30's] far end, here at the Land's End, is the vision of Lyonesse where the road splitting Cornwall ends or begins. Here is the land of Arthur whose soul is gone into a bird, the chough. And the chough, too, has long since gone from Cornwall, except for the one old fellow who still haunts the cliffs above Newquay. I have seen him peering into Fox Cove and into Pepper Cove. But there is no Guinevere for him any longer.

**James Turner**, *The Stone Peninsula*, 1976

**927** From now until the end of September, Cornwall is an occupied country … [F]rom cove to cove there is the ringing of tills, the campanology of Cornwall.

**Trevor Fishlock**, 'Pressures that arouse a sense of Cornishness', *The Times*, 19 April 1976

**928** Cornwall's contribution to Rugby is much greater than the number of matches it has won. Cornwall, more than anyone else, has imbued the County championship with competitive enthusiasm and fired it with their own heat.

    **Alan Gibson**, *A Mingled Yarn*, 1976

**929** On every issue we are told that we are an English county, a part of an English Region, and the answer always means more English exploitation and even less Cornish well-being ... Cornwall was a Country, it is a Country and will be a Country as long as there are Cornish people who assert their historic nationhood.

    **Leonard Truran**, *For Cornwall – A Future!*, 1976

**930** The Cornish do not like the direct statement. Even the affirmative 'yes' does not fall naturally from them as a definite agreement. It is spoken with a slightly rising tilt, often followed by the word 'you'. "Iss, you." Or it may be heard as no more than a sibilant. "Ss." A kind of hiss, conveying a hint of doubt. He is not going to give too much away, this Cornishman.

    **Frank Baker**, *The Call of Cornwall*, 1976

**931** To this day I find the Cornishman hard to sum up. He is such a remarkable compound of many contradictory qualities. Essentially individualistic, of course; yet he is conservative too and jealously guards his native customs. He can appear to be cautious, then suddenly seems reckless. As opportunist he has travelled all over the world – mining wherever there is anything to be mined.

    **Frank Baker**, *The Call of Cornwall*, 1976

**932** It soon became customary for a Cornish evensong to be sung on the Sunday after the Cornish Gorsedd in the parish church of the parish where the Gorsedd was held.

    **H. Miles Brown**, *A Century for Cornwall – The Diocese of Truro 1877–1977*, 1976

**933** The Cornish people united in a wholesome nationalism are unbeatable.

    **James Whetter**, 'The Cornish People United', in *An Baner Kernewek*, vol. 1, no. 4, Merth 1976

# 1977

**934** What fools we Cornish are – kick us, humiliate us, usurp our power, steal our jobs and livelihoods, rape our countryside and buy up our homes – and what do we do? We turn out and vote for those centralist parties that have

never done us any good, are doing us no good and never will do us good.
**L. H. Truran**, 'The Only Answer', in *An Forth 2*, 1977

**935** Far from the possibilities of further expansion being exhausted, there are more than 20 areas in Cornwall where there appear to be good prospects of making additional discoveries of tin, tungsten, lead, zinc and, possibly, even of copper ...
**Cornish Chamber of Mines**, *Mining in Cornwall Today*, 1977

**936** ... Cornwall is a country as different from England as is Wales and Scotland. And certainly was in Medieval times and up to this century, when people like my own family have invaded it and thankfully have been accepted.
**Angela du Maurier**, 'What a diocese can mean' in *One hundred years a diocese*, ed. Roy Standing, 1977

**937** On the map the isolation may seem imaginary, yet Cornwall is quite distinct from the rest of England. Its people and customs are different, and for centuries it spoke a language all its own ...
**Reginald J. W. Hammond and Kenneth E. Lowther**, *Complete Cornwall*, 1977

**938** If the view of Cornwall, as seen from London, is that of a colony whose raw materials and labour are to be exploited for the relative well-being of a non-productive central bureaucracy, while at the same time maintaining the appearance of raising regional incomes, then the regional policies of successive governments begin to make some sense ...
**Cornwall Industrial Development Association**, *The Economy of Cornwall*, 1977

**939** No hundred years has been more crowded with daring deeds, acts of supreme courage and self-sacrifice than the century of lifeboat service which has elapsed since the founding of the first Cornish station at Padstow in 1827.
**Claude Berry**, *The Story of Padstow's Lifeboats*, 1977

## 1978

**940** Nowhere in history has been found mention of bards in Cornwall, but life here was so very similar to that in Wales that it is unthinkable that the Cornish kings and princes did not have their bards.
**Den Toll (Hugh Miners)**, *Gorseth Kernow: the first 50 years*, 1978

**941** At least one Celtic tribe appears to have derived its name from the god

Cernunnos and he may well be perpetuated in Cornwall, the Celtic name for which is Kernow.

**Ward Rutherford**, *The Druids and their Heritage*, 1978

942 For all their Celtic awareness and occasional separatist fervour, most Cornishmen could not deliver as much as the time of day in their ancient Brithonic language.

**Alan Hamilton**, 'Revival of interest in the Cornish language', *The Times*, 25 July 1978

943 When I refer to England, I am usually referring to the area outside Cornwall.

**David Penhaligon, MP**, in House of Commons Debate, 4 December 1978

944 It [the creation of a Cornwall and Plymouth European Parliamentary Constituency] is the first time in any election that the boundary of Cornwall, which is sacrosanct and important, has been ignored ... the Celts of Cornwall regard this as a sad day in their history, for it was the day when their boundary was ignored and denied.

**David Penhaligon, MP**, in House of Commons Debate, 4 December 1978

945 The history of Cornwall as one of England's peripheral areas is relatively little known, as is the fact that it is the only part of England to have given rise to and sustained a nationalist/autonomist movement that has been neither spurious nor ephemeral.

**Adrian Lee**, 'Cornwall: Aspects of Regionalism and Nationalism', unpublished paper, 1978 [Payton, 1993]

## 1979

946 The little chapels out in the china-clay district were virtually Liberal recruiting stations in my time.

**A. L. Rowse**, *A Man of the Thirties*, 1979

947     Lib · Lab · Tory have had their day
       Vote Mebyon Kernow the Cornish way.
**Mebyon Kernow** slogan for the Parliamentary election, 3 May 1979

948 A need that the Cornish still have ... is to be among their own people and to share the quite extravagant love they have of their homeland.

**Tom Salmon**, in *Sunday Independent* 11 November 1979

**949** The closest degree of lexical relationship is that between Breton and Cornish … The most distant relationship is that of Breton and Welsh … [T]he degree of lexical relationship between Cornish and Welsh is about halfway between the two extremes.

    **R. W. Elsie**, *The Position of Brittonic …*, D. Phil. Dissertation, University of Bonn, 1979

**950**    I never thought before how much my country belonged to me,
    Till I had gone many miles from my home by the sea…
    Cornwall the land I love –
    Kindred is strong, this is where I belong:
    In the land I love.
    **Richard Gendall**, from 'Cornwall the land I love', c. 1979

**951** When he [David Penhaligon] catches the train to Paddington, he is a Cornish rebel going to battle in an alien land, not a carpet-bagger going home.

    *Guardian*, c. 1979 [Penhaligon, 1989]

# 1980

**952** It [the Duchy of Cornwall] owns 160 miles of foreshore for which it makes charges. So there is no doubt that it is big business and that it is exploiting every acre, every river and every shore on which it can lay its hands.

    *The Financial Times*, 1980, [Royston Green, *What is the Duchy of Cornwall*, c1984]

**953** It has always mattered enormously to people whether they are from Cornwall or Devon. And people living on the banks of the Tamar will be all the more staunchly Devonian or Cornish than those living further into the counties, not wanting to lose their identity.

    **Sarah Foot**, *Following the Tamar*, 1980

**954** You're not really Cornish unless you're from west of Hayle River.

    **Anonymous** [Gerald and Sylvia Priestland, *West Of Hayle River*, 1980]

**955** … it is the capitalist system itself which still today menaces the national culture of the approximately quarter million people of Cornish origin in Cornwall, and correspondingly… the future of all people in Cornwall depends upon securing the reality of democratic control over economic, social and cultural life which socialism alone can bring.

    **Royston Green**, *The National Question in Cornwall*, c1980

**956** ... the awareness of a Cornish identity finds expression... in other than linguistic fields.

D. B. Gregor, *Celtic: A Comparative Study*, 1980

**957** In Cornwall we [tourists] are called Emmets, and if you are a true Corn you stick "Kernow" on the back window of your car and "Non-Emmet" on the front. Emmet is an old word for ant: that is how bad it is.

Michael Ratcliffe, 'Grockles, emmets and county guides', in *The Times*, 26 June 1980

**958** The mines of Cornwall were the wonder of the contemporary world.

T. A. Morrison, *Cornwall's Central Mines: the Northern District 1810–1895*, 1980

# 1981

**959** I claim exemption under Cornwall's stannary laws.

Census objector's statement, April 1981 [*West Briton* 3 December 1981]

**960** There [at Tehidy] dwelt generations of Bassets amidst unbelievable luxury derived from the mining industry in which innumerable violent deaths and crippling accidents were monotonously termed 'By misadventure'.

Michael Tangye, *Carn Brea*, 1981

**961** Henry VII will always be remembered for his heartless slaughter of the ill-armed Cornish at Blackheath in 1497. Was the tower [of St. Euny, Redruth] built shortly after that date whilst anger still burned in the minds of the Cornish speaking sculptors who depicted this distant English sovereign with hands pulling his mouth abroad in a grotesque grin to compete with the ugliness of the surrounding gargoyles?

Michael Tangye, *Carn Brea*, 1981

**962** A notable minor party vote [in the European parliamentary Election of 1979] was Mebyon Kernow's 5.9 per cent in Cornwall and Plymouth ...

David Butler and David Marquand, *European Elections and British Politics*, 1981

**963** The twentieth century offers either the prospect of [Cornwall's] total incorporation into England, or a cultural revival spearheaded by the several small, national and cultural organisations which now exist.

Rosalie Eastlake, 'Cornwall: The Development of a Celtic Periphery', 1981 [Payton, 1993]

**964** A Celtic nation and a county of England, Cornwall appears to be the centre of a struggle between the forces of territory and function.

>**Ian Wight**, 'Territory Versus Function in Regional Development: The Case of Cornwall', unpublished paper, 1981 [Payton, 1993]

**965** The [Royal Albert] bridge was supposed to let in the Devil. What in fact trickled in were all kinds of national unifying influences – to the true Cornishman, of course, these were the very Devil.

>**David St. John Thomas**, *A Regional History of the Railways of Great Britain, vol 1: The West Country*, 5th edition, 1981

**966** Some among the population of nineteenth-century Britain were obviously very parochial. Others, however, were equally remarkable for their readiness to uproot themselves and re-settle in distant places, or to move continually around the country and overseas in response to shifting economic opportunities... Cornish miners provide a[n] ... example – so many of them moved to the Scottish coalfields that public libraries there took the Cornish newspapers.

>**E. H. Hunt**, *British Labour History 1815–1914*, 1981

**967** The world would not echo with mourning if Cornish were fully lost, but we believe it is a cultural flower which should not be allowed to perish.

>**William Brown**, *The Times*, 26 August 1981

**968** It is MK's aim to concentrate on creating nationalists rather than on winning superficial support and it is logical that MK should declare itself to be republican.

>**Motion passed at Mebyon Kernow's annual conference**, November 1981 [*West Briton* 5 November 1981]

# 1982

**969** From now [962 AD] on, the Cornishman's genius for independence was maintained only by his ignoring, to the best of his ability, the land to the east.

>**Crysten Fudge**, *The Life of Cornish*, 1982

**970** [John] Cornwall and [Richard] Pencrych... were largely responsible for the replacement of French by English in schools, a major victory in the campaign to halt the decline of English. It must have seemed a hollow victory to the writers of Cornish at Glasney.

>**Crysten Fudge**, *The Life of Cornish*, 1982

**971** I must admit that, during the last one hundred years, the Cornish canvas has become somewhat frayed around the edges; in fact, as we stumble towards the end of the century, it is looking tattered; that it needs cleaning is obvious, but the remedy is less so. Do you use merely soap and water, or pass it over to a London expert who may restore it to the original colour and shape, but at what price?

> **John Mehennick**, 'A Cornish Canvas', in *An Baner Kernewek* 27, February 1982

**972** One of the first flags to be flown in East Falkland was Helston School Pasty Club's flag depicting the St. Piran black cross with a super-imposed pasty and a Union Jack in the corner ... The 15-inch by 18-inch flag represents a number of teachers at the school who ... are "pro-Cornish, and eat pasties in the staffroom" ... The words, "We done good" are embroidered in Cornish ("Ny a druk da") on the flag along with the Latin equivalent.

> **Western Morning News**, 1982 [*An Baner Kernewek* 29, August]

**973** Occasionally a letter appears in the *Cornishman* requesting information on why people go to Lamorna on Good Friday, but in the corner of Penwith where I grew up, it was the most natural thing in the world and the oft voiced phrase between friends and relatives would be 'Are you going to Lamorna?'

> **Sylvia Pender Johns**, 'Good Friday', in *Old Cornwall*, vol. 9, no. 7, autumn 1982

**974** A proposal to end the ancient Cornish custom of tin-bounding has been dropped. Parliament is to be asked to remove its abolition from a Bill before the Commons.

> **Craig Seton**, 'Reprieve for the bounders of Cornwall', in *The Times*, 10 November 1982

## 1983

**975** Integrating factors have been so powerful that, by rights, a separate Cornish identity should have been obliterated long ago.

> **Bernard Deacon**, 'Is Cornwall an Internal Colony?' in *For A Celtic Future*, ed. Cathal O'Luain, 1983

**976** When contesting Westminster elections Cornish nationalists suffer from the same factors as all minor parties in the UK. An electoral system that positively encourages tactical voting, lack of access to the media, in particular television, the adversarial structuring of General Election campaigns by the Press, lack of financial resources all make electioneering an uphill task for the nationalists.

**Bernard Deacon**, 'The Electoral Impact of Cornish Nationalism' in *For A Celtic Future*

**977** Rugby became, in some strange way throughout those years, a quite special inspiration – an inspiration almost religious in its intensity. It was as if it was not individuals who were finding themselves again (as people tend to do in religious revivals) but almost as if a land – or a very old nation – was rediscovering itself, and finding something at which it was especially good, during a time when so many other things had gone tragically sour.

**Tom Salmon**, *The First Hundred Years: The Story of Rugby Football in Cornwall*, 1983

**978** As all the Cornish know, the definition of 'foreigner' is: a person, or persons, essentially English-speaking and British-born, but with the misfortune of having first seen the light of day on the wrong side of the Tamar.

**Tom Salmon**, *The First Hundred Years: The Story of Rugby Football in Cornwall*, 1983

**979** In many respects the development of Rugby in Cornwall has been closer to its Welsh rather than its English counterpart. In both, it is primarily a working-class game, and this undoubtedly accounts, along with the common Celtic temperament, for the passion traditionally associated with both Cornish and Welsh Rugby. It was at once an assertion of manhood, and of national identity.

**C. D. Galbraith**, in *The First Hundred Years* …

**980** Cornish rugby occupies a place in the hearts of the game's followers – even those who have never seen them [Cornwall] play.

**David Hands**, 'Cornwall celebrate hundred years of rumbustious play', in *The Times*, 21 September 1983

**981** Rumbustious, forthright, practical are the adjectives likely to attach themselves to Cornish sides, who play a game stripped of frills and fripperies, whose virtues may so frequently seem overlooked because of their geographical distance from more recognized centres of rugby.

**David Hands**, 'Cornwall celebrate hundred years of rumbustious play', in *The Times*, 21 September 1983

**982** If any living creature is regarded in Cornwall as being one hundred per cent Cornish it is the pilchard.

**Richard Pearse**, *The Land Beside the Celtic Sea*, 1983

**983** Cornwall's virtual independence of the central government in the thirteenth and fourteenth centuries was not true self-government or real autonomy. It was a form of autonomy imposed from above as part of the king's design to strengthen the nation's war potential.

**Richard Pearse**, *The Land Beside the Celtic Sea*, 1983

**984** The Cornish never took kindly to town life.

**W. G. V. Balchin**, *The Cornish Landscape*, 1983

**985** Dolcoath was beyond doubt the greatest of all the Cornish mines. Its influence on Cornish mining history was profound. It supported hundreds of families for generations. Whatever other mine was a great one, Dolcoath was greater.

**T. A. Morrison**, *Cornwall's Central Mines: the Southern District 1810–1895*, 1983

## c. 1984

**986** Deep within the Duchy's greedy possession is the territorial patrimony of the Cornish kings.

**Royston Green**, *What is the Duchy of Cornwall?* c1984

**987** It [the Duchy of Cornwall] is a changeling, albeit not with full success, for the residual political memory that Cornwall, being not English, was once a separate state.

**Royston Green**, *What is the Duchy of Cornwall?* c1984

## 1984

**988** 'Unified' Cornish is unsatisfactory because it does not have a firm phonological base.

**Ken George**, *Phonological History of Cornish*, unpublished thesis, 1984

**989** The old Celtic speech of Cornwall died out two centuries ago. It is still dead, and will evermore remain so … In the past, the term 'Cornish' has been used with reference both to the traditional and authentic language of Cornwall and to modern pseudo-Cornish, but I shall reserve the term for genuine Cornish and shall refer to pseudo-Cornish as 'Cornic'.

**Glanville Price**, *The Languages of Britain*, 1984

**990**    Cornwall, near England.
Into Cornwall, out of England.

**Sayings** quoted by Philip Payton in *The Cornish Miner in Australia*, 1984

**991** The visitors have come to Cornwall. I'm a visitor. 'Visitors', 'foreigners' we're called by the Cornish. We litter the cliffs with our houses. We litter the cliffs with our shacks. When I was a boy, all this place was open fields.

    **John Betjeman**, in *Betjeman's Cornwall*, 1984

## 1985

**992** The rise of this political national consciousness had been a remarkable achievement, after it had long been considered that Cornwall had been totally assimilated into the English ethos.

    **Peter Berresford Ellis**, *The Celtic Revolution*, 1985

**993** In Cornwall, before the recent attempt to breathe life into the dry bones, the Cornish nation has been nothing but a spirit hovering above a cemetery, a smile on the face of a cat which is quickly disappearing. *

    **R. S. Thomas**, 'Unity', 1985, in *Selected Prose*, 1995

**994** [In the nineteenth century] Cornwall was probably an emigration region comparable to any in Europe.

    **Dudley Baines**, *Migration in a Mature Economy*, 1985

**995** To be a true Cornishman a man must have mastered the 'three Rs' of Rugby Football, Religion and Rhythm.

    **Kenneth Pelmear**, in Hubert Julian, 'A true Cornishman', *Cornish Scene*, vol .1 no. 2, Aug/Sept, 1985

**996** 'Up country' folk are still to some extent a strange and alien race and the Tamar is still a frontier when seen through Cornish eyes.

    **Richard Muir**, *Shell Guide to Reading the Celtic Landscapes*, 1985

**997** The Cornish Revivalists [of the early 20th century], more than their Celtic colleagues, positively wallowed in the un-reason of Romanticism.

    **Bernard Deacon**, 'The Cornish Revival: An Analysis', unpublished paper, 1985 [Payton, 1993]

## 1986

**998** ... Cornwall's present inhabitants, native-born and newcomers alike, might still manage a wry smile of satisfaction at the opinion of a Plymouth correspondent to the *Western Morning News* that 'we may have built the Tamar Bridge between us but there is still something pretty odd at the western end of it'!

    **Ian Soulsby**, *A History of Cornwall*, 1986

**999** A good Cornish [rugby] side takes a lot of beating because we are playing against the rest of the country every game.

**Brian 'Stack' Stevens**, in Michael George, *Sportsmen of Cornwall*, 1986

**1000** When travelling outside of his beloved homeland, every Cornishman takes with him a burning passion and fierce pride to sustain him through his exile, however short it may be.

**Michael George**, *Sportsmen of Cornwall*, 1986

**1001** Slump, a moderate and faltering revival, recession and depression again, these were the successive stages of Cornish tin mining in the 1920s, making a gloomy chapter in the county's economic history.

**John Rowe**, 'Cornish Mining Crisis in the 1920s', in *An Baner Kernewek* 45, August 1986

**1002** ... it may well be another century before most native Cornish cease to think, subconsciously and automatically, in terms of 'Cornwall' and 'England', an Us-and-Them syndrome sharpened by distance from central government and, recently, by post-war revivals of a Cornish national-consciousness movement.

**Charles Thomas**, *Celtic Britain*, 1986

**1003** The British may not be as *centraliste* as the French with their Buonapartist legacy, but the almost universal misuse of 'English' to convey the meaning 'British' overlooks from a southeast English standpoint the fact that majorities in Wales and Scotland would not dream of calling themselves anything other than Welsh or Scottish. There are also plenty of Cornish and Manx to support them in this practice.

**Charles Thomas**, *Celtic Britain*, 1986

**1004** The real Cornish are difficult to find: many have emigrated, and those who remain distrust the English, a people they hold in scarcely higher regard than they do Devonians.

**Gwyn Headley**, Follies: A National Trust Guide, 1986

**1005** The Tamar is... the traditional frontier of Cornwall... even today, as the CORNWALL-KERNOW signboards on the bridge announces, west of Tamar is another people, another little world.

**Donald R. Rawe**, A Prospect of Cornwall, 1986

**1006** A Harvard Cornishman told me that, of all the British stocks in the

United States, the Cornish were the most addicted to going back to their native heath, if only on visits.

**A. L. Rowse**, *The Little Land of Cornwall*, 1986

1007 Myself, a primitive inhabitant, indigenous and autochthonous, one of the natives …

**A. L. Rowse**, *The Little Land of Cornwall*, 1986

1008 I have enough atavistic sympathy with Cornish nationalism to wish that we could loosen our subjection to the mainland sufficiently to enjoy a reasonable system of taxation.

**A. L. Rowse**, *The Little Land of Cornwall*, 1986

1009 The founding of the diocese and the building of a cathedral… released an astonishing stream of Cornish patriotism …

**A. L. Rowse**, *The Little Land of Cornwall*, 1986

1010 The process of colonization was emphasised by Athelstan around 930 when he deported British speakers across the Tamar, which was fixed as the border of the Cornish. They were left under their own dynasty to regulate themselves with West Welsh [Cornish] tribal law and customs, rather like Indian princes under the Raj.

**Michael Wood**, *Domesday*, 1986

1011 The fate of Cornwall at the hands of the colonists may be taken as a metaphor for the general relationship between the Celts and the English.

**Philip Dodd**, in *Englishness: Politics and Culture 1880–1920*, ed. R. Colls and P. Dodd, 1986

## 1986–87

1012 If Cornwall was an independent state, he [David Penhaligon] should have been its President …

**SNP member**, in letter to Annette Penhaligon, 1986/1987 [*Annette Penhaligon*, 1989]

## 1987

1013 Don't get me wrong. I'm not against emmets. I like to see them come. And I like to see them go. But what I can't stand is seeing them queueing up to get into the estate agents.

**Radio Cornwall interviewee**, 14 June 1987 [Deacon, George and Perry, *Cornwall at the Crossroads?* 1988]

**1014** They [Mebyon Kernow and the Cornish Nationalist Party] played a part in making the Cornish think about who they were and made other parties do something and think about Cornwall.

> **Donald Rawe**, in Alan J. P. Dalton, *Turn Left at Land's End*, 1987

**1015** The [Fleet Street] sub-editors have a view of Cornwall based on the film "Straw Dogs", sodomy and yokel type stories are what they want.

> **Graham Smith**, in Alan J. P. Dalton, *Turn Left at Land's End*, 1987

**1016** ... the picture that emerges from our study is of a Cornwall swamped by a flood of middle-class, middle-aged, middle-browed city dwellers who effectively imposed their standards upon local society.

> **Ronald Perry**, *Counterurbanisation: International Case Studies of Socio-Economic Change in Rural Areas*, 1987 [Deacon, George and Perry, 1988]

**1017** ... 'Trelawny' ... *does* encapsulate the spirit of Cornish patriotism, and therein lies its popularity and its success as Cornwall's national song.

> **Car Dyvresow**, 'More Notes About Trelawny', in *Cornish Scene* vol. 2, no. 5, Mar/April 1987

**1018** For the price of a poky flat or a boring semi, you could move to Cornwall, buy one of these super properties AND have a fistful of change.

> ***Private Eye*** 21 August 1987

**1019** Cornwall is like a quiet little beach, which some 5,000 people propose to visit on the same day to savour its peace and quiet. Is there a solution? Does anyone care?

> **Letter to the *West Briton*** 1 October 1987

**1020** Cornish factories NOT Tesco's.

> **Part of An Gof press statement**, October 1987 [*Camborne Packet* 8 October 1987]

**1021** This book is dedicated to the likes of High George and Tommy Blue, Old Robbie and his maid, Sarah. To Silas Rouncefield, Martha Polglase, Mary Trenowden, Quizzy Maggie and Steve Trevorrow, all of whom are fictitious, though I have borrowed a nickname here and there. They represent the last of the Cornish, who are following their beautiful language into oblivion.

> **N. R. Phillips**, *The Saffron Eaters*, 1987

**1022** The greatest *deficiency* in Cornwall's mineral wealth was without doubt its lack of *coal*. This proved to be a near fatal flaw in terms of the county's general industrialisation and long-term economic welfare.

**Roger Burt** (ed), *Cornish Mines*, 1987

# 1988

**1023** ... Cornwall is almost an island with natural boundaries fixed by the coastline. It is largely isolated from the rest of the country. It has a strong separate identity with its own history, traditions, customs, language and (to some degree) laws and institutions. Many of these attributes are firmly rooted in its Celtic past. It seems anomalous that such a community should not have its own separate voice in the European Parliament.

**Cornwall County Council**, *European Parliamentary Elections Act 1978 (as amended): Representations to the Boundary Commission for England ...*, 1988

**1024** It remains obvious from much of the evidence given at the enquiry that the Cornish people, in spite of being joined with England, have remained separate and have pursued their own cohesion through language, culture and emblems.

**G. D. Flather Q.C.,** Boundary Commission Report, 1988

**1025** The Cornish have not been much of a literary folk – their genius has been all for mining, science and technology – and Cornwall has been mostly written about by others.

**A. L. Rowse**, *Quiller Couch: A Portrait of 'Q'*, 1988

**1026** One has the feeling that all West Penwith is distinctly numinous.

**A. L. Rowse**, *A. L. Rowse's Cornwall*, 1988

**1027** The Tamar is a decisive boundary such as no other county possesses – but, then, Cornwall is not an ordinary county, it is a "Little Land" of its own.

**A. L. Rowse**, *A. L. Rowse's Cornwall*, 1988

**1028** I am 100 per cent native, irremediably Cornish ...

**A. L. Rowse**, *A. L. Rowse's Cornwall*, 1988

**1029** The Cornish are a named group or community, with a self-awareness (albeit of differing degrees) of a separate identity, being long established in a well-defined territory, and according to this definition do qualify for the label 'ethnic group' or 'ethnic community'.

**Mary McArthur**, *The Cornish: a case study in ethnicity*, unpublished M.Sc. thesis, 1988

1030 ... unless the category of Cornish is submerged (which currently seems unlikely) it is possible that ... the incomers of today will become (or produce) the Cornish of tomorrow.

**Mary McArthur**, *The Cornish: a case study in ethnicity*, unpublished M.Sc thesis, 1988

1031 Cornwall has so much potential it is unbelievable. When you think how people are falling over themselves in the South East for a tiny parcel of development, Cornwall is a gold-mine.

**Peter de Savary**, in *Daily Telegraph* 23 August 1988

1032 If the Cornish people are not there underpinning it [the Cornish identity], then all the talk in the world about 'Cornish culture' or 'the Cornish heritage' will be just idle talk. We will have an empty culture with a disjointed identity. Cornwall will be populated only by ghosts of its past – it will no longer be Cornwall in any real sense of the word but merely another spot on the map.

**Deacon, George and Perry**, *Cornwall at the Crossroads*, 1988

1033 Cornwall is at the crossroads. Do we continue on a path of aimless population growth, one that doesn't even solve our economic problems and, indeed, creates new ones, at the same time as putting the distinctive quality of Cornwall under a growing threat? Or do we evolve a new strategy, one that does not see Cornwall as a 'remote periphery', that puts the needs of our own people at the forefront, that aims to build sustainable and dynamic communities rooted in our land and its traditions, and that respects our environment while avoiding the dead-end of preservationism for its own sake.

**Deacon, George and Perry**, *Cornwall at the Crossroads*, 1988

1034 On the one hand plenty, and on the other near poverty. This is Cornwall in the late '80s.

**Deacon, George and Perry**, *Cornwall at the Crossroads*, 1988

1035 The Cornish – shunted onto windswept council house reservations on the outskirts of our coastal villages – have seen their communities disintegrate in front of their own eyes within just one generation.

**Deacon, George and Perry**, *Cornwall at the Crossroads*, 1988

1036 ... Cornwall is administratively 'in' England, but is not 'of' England. Culturally the River Tamar is a national boundary ...

**Ivan Rabey** (ed), *Cornwall: An Official Guide* ... , c1988

1037 English Go Home. Celtic Cornwall.
**Graffiti on Carn Brea Monument,** September 1988 [*Camborne Packet* 22 September 1988]

1038 Cornwall is very beautiful and a great fund and fount of experience for me, but I don't see why one should be necessarily proud of an accident of birth … If I seem to write with a Cornish accent, fine, but I certainly don't want to go down the road of professional Cornishry …
**Charles Causley,** in Brian Merrick, 'With a Straight Eye: an Interview with Charles Causley', *Children's Literature in Education*, vol. 19, no. 3, Fall 1988

# 1989
1039 Last one out of Cornwall switch the lights out.
**Bill Bishop,** on the eve of Cornwall's County Championship final against Durham at Twickenham, 1 April 1989 [Colin Gregory, *Cornwall: Rugby Champions*, 1991]

1040 Like the Welsh, the Cornish take the view that rugby and community are the same thing.
**The Guardian** 2 April 1989

1041 Twenty thousand Cornishman used the great ground [Twickenham] for a statement, if not of Celtic nationhood, then at least of their distinct identity …
**The Independent** 3 April 1989

1042 I have heard some people saying indignantly, 'I don't speak Cornish, but I am Cornish!' Surely. But will their great-grandchildren be Cornish?
**Peter Berresford Ellis,** 'The Celtic People: the linguistic criterion', in *Kernow* 4, Aug-Sept, 1989

1043 During the late fifteenth-century, Scotland, Ireland and Wales were left largely to their own devices and even smaller communities such as the Isle of Man and Cornwall … enjoyed a good deal of independence.
**Hugh Kearney,** *The British Isles: A History of Four Nations*, 1989

1044 The paradox of Arthur as a figure in Cornish culture… becomes more intelligible if the Severn is thought of as a unifying factor, linking the Britons of the south-west with their countrymen ('Cymry') in what is now 'Wales'.
**Hugh Kearney,** *The British Isles: A History of Four Nations*, 1989

1045 In the colonial situation which existed in England after the Conquest, it was not surprising that royal lawyers should work hard to sharpen a distinction between the 'natives' and the newcomers ... There was, finally, Celtic-speaking Cornwall, which was incorporated into 'England', governmentally if not culturally.

**Hugh Kearney**, *The British Isles: A History of Four Nations*, 1989

1046 ... those Methodist chapels in Cornwall which contain monuments remember, through this means, not usually old landed families but "captains of industry", who often bore the title "Captain" before their name, or wealthy merchants and businessmen.

**C. J. Appleby**, 'Methodism and Industry in and around Hayle', in *Gain Save Give: some Methodist businessmen in West Cornwall*, 1989

1047 ... Cornwall to me is a country of the mind, a construct of the historical imagination in which I live.

**A. L. Rowse**, *Friends and Contemporaries*, 1989

1048 What all workers for Cornish must always remember is that, whatever their feelings or standard is, they are the trustees for all their fellow Cornishmen (past, present and future) of the language and, therefore, of the very Identity of Cornwall.

**Brian Coombes**, 'Unified Cornish, Common Cornish and other Cornishes: some thoughts', in *An Baner Kernewek* 55, February 1989

1049 Mordon [Robert Morton Nance] was not merely a great scholar, but also a patriot and a prophet, the greatest Cornishman of our time. What was good enough for him should be good enough for us all, and for Cornwall.

**P. A. S. Pool**, 'A Plea for Unified Cornish', in *Old Cornwall* vol. 10, no. 9, 1989

1050 Mutual comprehension is being replaced by a situation akin to a Celtic Babel. The revival of our language, one of the marvels of our time, is grinding to a halt, and may even go into reverse.

**P. A. S. Pool**, 'A Plea for Unified Cornish', in *Old Cornwall* vol. 10, no. 9, 1989

1051 Never was the nationalist influence more transparent than at the Truro by-election [in 1987] when each main candidate strained to prove his Cornish credentials, even though it was quite clear none had a complete set.

**Andy Smith**, in *Western Morning News*, 8 March 1989

**1052** The concept of the Duchy rests on the existence of a separate and ancient territory of Cornwall. That separate territory has never been assimilated formally into England.

    **Paul Laity**, in *Kernow*, Aug-Sept, 1989

**1053** The battle to keep the invader at bay and preserve intact the County of Cornwall has been waged since the Second World War.

    **A. L. Dennis** (ed), *Cornwall County Council 1889-1989*, 1989

**1054** Everyone in Britain knows that the Cornish see themselves as a race apart but only those who have lived in Cornwall can feel how deep that conviction goes …

    **Annette Penhaligon**, *Penhalligon*, 1989

**1055** David [Penhaligon] never had to say that he was sympathetic to Cornish nationalism, or power for Cornwall. His voice said it for him.

    **Malcolm Brown**, in Annette Penhaligon, *Penhaligon, 1989*

## 1990

**1056** An attempt has been made to separate the Duchy of Cornwall, which is not subject to English tax legislation, from the territory of Cornwall, the argument being that the Duchy has a separate existence to the geographical area of Cornwall and holds property outside the area. The argument is spurious and flies in the face of the Duchy case of 1856.

    **Kit Hawkins**, in *Kernow*, April-May, 1990

**1057** No Poll Tax 1497. 1497   +   1990
                       An Gof.

    Anti-poll tax graffiti in Liskeard, 1990 [Deacon, Cole and Tregidga, 2003]

**1058** There are the [Cornish] towns, too, where multiple stores make extravagant offers to long-established local shops, then pull them down, and erect in their place shopfronts which are equally recognisable in Wigan, Manchester or Milton Keynes; or create superstores outside the towns and, instead of profits circulating in the area, they are taken away across the Tamar to city-controlled balance sheets.

    **Derek Tangye**, *The Evening Gull*, 1990

**1059** Millionaire entrepreneurs have descended upon Cornwall, attracted by the commercial possibilities of exploiting its mystery, its away-from-the-rat race atmosphere; and they fly in their privately owned helicopters, glancing down at the landscape and seashore, calculating where development would be most profitable.

**Derek Tangye,** *The Evening Gull,* 1990

**1060** Many areas formerly occupied by mines now make up the designated areas of Derelict Land in Cornwall, which covers some 12,000 acres. Cornwall, with 11.6% of the national total, contains more Derelict Land than any other county in Britain.

**Adam Sharpe, John Smith, Lyn Jenkins,** *Mineral Tramways Project,* 1990

**1061** The majority of Cornwall's historic industrial buildings have been abandoned for over a century, and have become, quite literally, a part of the landscape. Derelict engine houses have for so long been a part of the Cornish skyline that they have locally been adopted as potent symbols of pride in the past.

**Adam Sharpe, John Smith, Lyn Jenkins,** *Mineral Tramways Project,* 1990

**1062** Smaller minorities also have equally proud visions of themselves as irreducibly Welsh, Irish, Manx or Cornish. These identities are distinctly national in ways which proud people from Yorkshire, much less proud people from Berkshire, will never know. Any new constitutional settlement which ignores these factors will be built on uneven ground.

Editorial in **The Guardian,** 8 May 1990

**1063** The decision to drop Cornish as a GCSE subject is a lesson for Britain's Celtic fringe. Only six examination candidates on the far side of the Tamar came forward in two years. Clearly once a language has died a natural death, more than good intentions will be needed to revive it.

**The Times,** 21 July 1990

**1064** The Cornish are fortunate to be able to paint their regional discontents in the attractive colours of their Celtic tradition … Merseyside cannot blow a national trumpet. Cornwall can.

**Eric Hobsbawm,** *Nations and Nationalism since 1870,* 1990

# 1991

**1065** We are probably now discussing the end, at least for the foreseeable future, of tin mining in Cornwall, purely as a result of a Government decision. It is a tragedy for those who will lose their jobs and for the surrounding communities and it is an untimely death blow to a tradition of mining in our county which goes back 2,500 years. I have no hesitation in blaming the Government for that.

**Matthew Taylor, MP**, in House of Commons Tin Mining (Cornwall) Adjournment Debate, 6 March 1991

**1066** Now I believe in reincarnation.

**John May**, Cornish loose-head prop, after Cornwall's victory against Yorkshire, 20 April 1991

**1067** It might not have been a classic text book game of rugby, but Cornwall will tell you what you can do with your text book. You really would have to be dead from the neck up not to have recognised yesterday as one of the most fervent and astonishing rugby occasions ever staged at Twickenham, or anywhere else for that matter ...

**Stephen Jones**, in *The Sunday Times*, 21 April 1991

**1068** The most intriguing statistic in the 1991 census might be the fact that 35,000 Cornish rugby fans who headed to Twickenham for the big match register their night abode as a train or hotel.

**Western Morning News**, 22 April 1991

**1069** Something happened on 20 April 1991 that united the people of Cornwall in a way nothing has done since the days of Bishop Trelawny, hundreds of years before.

**Colin Gregory**, *Cornwall: Rugby Champions*, 1991

**1070** ... Cornwall's condition [in 1851] was far enough from the norms of southern England to place it firmly in the 'Celtic fringe' of religious practice.

**Bruce Colman**, 'The Nineteenth Century: Nonconformity', in *Unity and Variety: A History of the Church in Devon and Cornwall*, ed. Nicholas Orme, 1991

**1071** One third of Cornish Methodism today is of Bible Christian origin ...

**Thomas Shaw**, A *Methodist Guide to Cornwall*, 1991

**1072** Cornwall does not wish to be ignored and does not wish to be hyphenated to Devon ... Cornwall is fed up with border blurring, with having more and more decisions that affect daily life decided on the other side of the Tamar.

**Linda Christmas**, *Chopping Down the Cherry Trees: A portrait of Britain in the Eighties*, 1991

**1073** Choughs were once a great deal more widespread, and probably a great deal more numerous. They are part of Cornish tradition – some old books even call them "Cornish chough".

**Simon Barnes**, 'Right choughed', in *The Times*, 2 November 1991

**1074** People must remember that we Cornish are full of the spirit of a peninsula which does not march in line with the rest of the world.

**Joy Stevenson**, in letter to the *Western Morning News*, November 1991

## 1992

**1075** It is fair to alert you to the fact that there is a substantial number of indigenous Cornish people who feel themselves disadvantaged, compared with 'incomers', in relation to class, income, housing, employment and various other aspects of daily living.

**Anonymous**, quoted in Eric Jay, *Keep Them in Birmingham: Challenging racism in south-west England*, 1992

**1076** The ability to be Cornish in Cornwall cannot be taken for granted... There is a feeling of being the last Cornish generation which cannot easily be dismissed as paranoia.

**Neil Kennedy**, 'Racial equality in Cornwall', in *Keep Them in Birmingham ... , 1992*

**1077** It is my custom to quote Cornwall with its English speech and Cornish accent and corrupted Cornish place-names as a warning of what could happen to us [the Welsh].

**R. S. Thomas**, *Cymru or Wales?* 1992

**1078** ... we don't like foreigners telling us what to do, but it's a sad day for the Cornish when the foreigners are the only ones on the [north Cornwall District] council who want to preserve this Celtic land of ours.

**Andrew Hawke**, in *Cornish Guardian*, 16 January 1992

**1079** ... in the reorganisation of power in Britain that must surely come, Cornwall must keep its own identity and should have enhanced power.

**Western Morning News**, 13 April 1992

**1080** ... burly Cornish fishermen waved placards against new European Community regulations and demonstrated the granite independence for which Cornishmen are famous throughout the land. There is a different country across the Tamar.

'England's Edge', in *The Times*, 18 July 1992

**1081** … a thought crossed my mind, with all these thousands of Cornish people wouldn't it be a good opportunity to rouse them to action. If I had a soapbox and a few beers aboard, couldn't I rally them to take the Tower of London or the Houses of Parliament. 40,000 Cornishmen would know the reason why. But what if we achieved our objectives, what then? Anyway, unlike John Major I did not have a soapbox and moreover I had not had any beer – so that was the end of that fancy.

> **James Whetter**, 'Twickenham 1992', in *An Baner Kernewek* 69, August 1992

**1082** 'The Cornish Movement', after a century of re-birth pangs, early childhood uncertainties and enthusiastic but disparate teenage problems, has evolved around it a widely-felt spirit of Cornishness in the Cornwall of the '90s… We are now in a position to adopt a programme of mature, responsible action. This would embrace cultural achievements, political recognition, our economic future, and, most importantly, a popular acceptance by the man in the street of what it is to be Cornish AND/OR to be living in Cornwall.

> **Howard Curnow**, in letter to *An Baner Kernewek* 69, August 1992

**1083** The Cornish may not like it, but … they are no different from the Devonians on the other side of the Tamar.

> **Anonymous**, reported in *Western Morning News*, 29 August 1992

**1084** Athelstan first broke the Cornish mirror eleven hundred years ago, though by then it was itself but a fragment of the Celtic civilisation which once embraced the whole of Western Europe. Cornwall, like Wales, is an English definition. It is the land of the western foreigners, the 'filthy race' of the Anglo-Saxon chronicles. Although the mirror crack'd, it remained serviceable for several centuries as a glass in which Cornish people could see themselves.

> **Brendan McMahon**, 'The Mirror Crack'd: Cultural Breakdown in Cornwall', in *An Baner Kernewek* 69, August 1992

**1085** Having discovered Cornwall, they [the Victorian bourgeoisie] had to change it because they couldn't understand it, and this made them uncomfortable. This process continues, though it has provoked resistance in the form of the language revival and the national movement.

> **Brendan McMahon**, 'The Theft of the Past: Cornwall's Historical Identity', in *An Baner Kernewek* 70, November 1992

1086 I feel Cornish people should make a stand. I declined to put anything on the [census] form because I was unable to do so. At this third appearance in court, the charges against me have been withdrawn. I therefore conclude that it has been decided that to try and force a Cornishman to renounce his nationality is not a viable proposition.

**Rodney Nute**, 1992 [John Angarrack, *Breaking the Chains*, 1999]

## 1993

1087 The future of the Cornish language Revival appears to rest on recognising that the unanimity of the 1950s and 60s will not easily be recovered.

**Philip Payton and Bernard Deacon**, 'The Ideology of Language Revival', in *Cornwall Since the War*, ed. Payton, 1993

1088 In a general political sense, the status of Cornwall as a social and economic periphery of the United Kingdom is by now well established and widely accepted.

**Adrian Lee**, 'Political Parties and Elections', in *Cornwall Since the War*. *1993*

1089 What is now popularly called 'Cornish' culture is the product of three waves of cultural production, which all added aspects to the symbolic repertoire that identity draws on. These three waves can be classified as industrial culture, guide book service culture and Revivalist culture …

**Bernard Deacon**, 'And Shall Trelawny Die?' in *Cornwall Since the War*, *1993*

1090 Its [the Cornish language] ghost walks uneasily among the modern Cornish, present in place and personal names but nevertheless elusive.

**Bernard Deacon**, 'And Shall Trelawny Die?' in *Cornwall Since the War*, *1993*

1091 Cornish Associations world-wide bear witness that Cornish consciousness is not dependent on Cornish births in a geographical sense.

**Peter Mitchell**, 'The Demographic Revolution', in *Cornwall Since the War*, *1993*

1092 … the full accommodation of contemporary Cornwall within the compass of Cornish Studies was not achieved until the establishment in 1970 of the Institute of Cornish Studies …

**Philip Payton,** 'Post-War Cornwall …', in *Cornwall Since the War*, 1993

**1093** ... chronic ill health is linked closely with poverty ... in the North, inner cities and Cornwall, over a quarter of households contain at least one person suffering from long term illness.

**The Times**, August 1993 [*Cornwall Since the War ed. Payton, 1993*]

**1094** It may be called the county [rugby] championship, but when the boys in black and gold trot out the fans are cheering on a national side.

**West Briton**, 14 October 1993

**1095** What I am offering here is a better way to consider our culture as we move into the next century; one in which Cornish politics, society and literature have a higher degree of collaboration, and more importantly, correlation ... Thus, a combination of historical context, theoretical method, political commitment and textual analysis offers any person thinking about Cornish literature and culture the best way forward.

**Alan M. Kent**, 'Cornish Politics, Society and Literature: a plea for correlation', in *An Baner Kernewek* 72, May 1993

**1096** Cornwall's peripherality, geographic isolation and culture maintain a strong awareness of difference amongst the people of Cornwall of which they are fiercely proud. It is this difference which helps to preserve the Cornish identity and sense of community.

**Cornwall County Council**, *Cornwall – One and All: Submission to the Local Government Commission*, 1993

**1097** Geographically Cornwall is distinct from every other English county. It is surrounded on three sides by sea and separated from its only neighbour, Devon, by the River Tamar, still a significant physical and cultural divide.

**Cornwall County Council**, *Cornwall – One and All: Submission to the Local Government Commission*, 1993

**1098** Our future is being hi-jacked by a business led agenda that refuses to recognise Cornwall's territorial integrity.

**Anonymous**, 'The Insidious Background to 'Devonwall'', in *An Baner Kernewek* 72, May 1993

**1099** I'm not anti-Cornish, and it would be foolish to expect that if a Cornish writer travels about England and visits Italy he will not write poems about the places that give him new thrills.

**Jack Clemo**, 19 August 1993 [Andrew C. Symons, 'Clemo's Clay Inferno', *An Baner Kernewek* 104, May 2001]

1100 ... the Cornish are too generous and open-hearted for their own good. They put up no barriers against the people who come in to ruin them and their land.

**Jeremy Jacobson and Annabel Barber**, 'Touring in Cornwall', in *An Baner Kernewek* 73, August 1993

1101 You can't fish in Cornwall and be too much a stranger to modern day smuggling, it's such a popular area for it.

**Roger Nowell**, *The Skipper*, 1993

1102 Thousands, if not millions, of people know our roads, but how many know our Cornish lanes? Yet they are far more in character and hold our secrets.

**A. L. Rowse**, 'Cornish Lanes', in *An Baner Kernewek* 72, May 1993

1103 Cornwall can, and many Cornishmen do, argue that Cornwall is 'a land', a member of the 'Celtic family of nations', a territory distinguished by statute, boundary, culture, history, language and identity. 'Regional arrangements', such as 'west country', be they cultural, administrative, economic or political, are designed to solve other people's problems, but not Cornwall's ... At a time when economic and political structures of Cornwall are threatened with integration into 'Devonwall' by forces seemingly beyond our control, why should the Cornish people, or their Devonshire neighbours, be forced to swallow homogenization? Stop this cultural theft. Let Cornwall breathe. Dump 'west country'! And, remember your alphabet ... C before D!

**Bert Biscoe**, in letter to *An Baner Kernewek* 73, August 1993

1104 It is under Athelstan... that we see the conscious and "official" creation of modern Cornwall, clearly delineated by its eastern border which set the limits of the "West Welsh" as clearly as did the Wye for the "North Welsh".

**Philip Payton**, *The Making of Modern Cornwall*, 1993

## 1994

1105 Mr. Friggans, Portreath, a dear old figure with a nice turn of phrase, was particularly popular. I see plenty of visitors; welcome on your holidays. I expect a lot of you aren't Cornish, are you? – he hastened to add – 'that's not your fault. You can't help that, can you?'

**Charles Thomas**, 'Memories of a Village Chapel (Gwithian)', in *Book of Memories of Cornish Methodism Pt. 2*, comp. Thomas Shaw, 1994

1106 Of the tens of thousands engaged in winning Cornwall's immense wealth of metals only three small groups benefited richly: the lawyers who battened on the disputes arising in a complex industry, the mineral landlords

and the smelters – Carlyle's 'Aristocracy of the Moneybag'.
**A. Guthrie**, *Cornwall in the Age of Steam*, 1994

**1107** Like all the other journeys being made that day [20 April 1991], and those already made, by car, coach, rail, and even by sea and air, this was more than a mere trip to Twickenham, more even than a game of rugby, it was a pilgrimage – a Celtic Nation on the move.
**Frank Ruhrmund**, in *Cornwall's Rugby Challenge: the glory years*, 1994

**1108** We went up "Camborne Hill" and "Way down to Lamorna" a thousand times or more, serenaded "Little Lize" so often and so passionately we must have convinced half of southern England of our love for her, and even, albeit reluctantly at first, went into the garden to pluck "The White Rose", a near act of treason excused by "Their White Rose i'dn the same as ours".
**Frank Ruhrmund**, in *Cornwall's Rugby Challenge: the glory years*, 1994

**1109** It is ironic that at a time when such strong arguments are being made for the strength and persistence of a distinctive Cornish identity, Cornwall's territorial status is under attack from several directions.
**Alys Thomas**, 'Cornwall's Territorial Dilemma …', in *Cornish Studies: Two*, ed. Philip Payton, 1994

**1110** In the spectrum of modern Celticism, Cornwall has come almost to represent a British Tibet; distant, valued by outsiders, and threatened by an occupying power.
**John Lowerson**, 'Celtic Tourism – some recent magnets', in *Cornish Studies: Two*, 1994

**1111** People move out of the naivety stage when they discover their Cornish roots or when they encounter discrimination, especially when they encounter the 'Cornish paradox' – the insistence that Cornwall is part of England but the belief that the Cornish are 'not really English'.
**Allen E. Ivey and Philip Payton**, 'Towards a Cornish Identity Theory', in *Cornish Studies: Two*, 1994

**1112** The course adopted by the [Cornish Language] Board may have been very different had it been generally realised that Modern Cornish was in reality a flexible, varied and distinctly Cornish vernacular, far less influenced by English borrowing than Middle Cornish.
**Charles Penglase**, 'Authenticity in the Revival of Cornish', in *Cornish Studies: Two*, 1994

**1113** ... an entity does not prove to be a Cornish nation, it seems to me, if one has to go to Twickenham, or Tottenham, or somewhere else to assert this
**Ken Phillipps**, *Catching Cornwall in Flight*, 1994

**1114** The [Cornish] Banner is in some respects a strange animal, parochial but global, traditional but radical, a tribute to the past, a challenge to the present, an attempt to shape a more human future in an increasingly objectified world.
**Brendan McMahon**, 'The Role of An Baner Kernewek', in *An Baner Kernewek 75*, February 1994

**1115** Brenda [Wootton] was a multi-faceted character. She was Gwylan Gwavas, Seagull of Newlyn, the Cornish Bard; to the Bretons, La Grande Cornouaillaise; to the French, Mama Cornwall, to the Lorient Festival, Godmother of the Celts; to the Irish, Herself, the Cornishwoman; to most of Cornwall, simply the Brenda of her *Sunday Best* radio programme.
**Sue Luscombe**, 'Introduction', in *Pantomime Stew*, November 1994

**1116** ... it is too often forgotten that Devon was a marcher (or border) county, the River Tamar forming a racial frontier between Anglo-Saxon England and Celtic Cornwall.
**Mark Stoyle**, *Loyalty and Locality: Popular Allegiance in Devon during the English Civil War*, 1994

**1117** Cornwall's Celtic roots create a strong sense of identity within the county ... Some suggest that Cornwall has never legally been incorporated into shire England and the continued existence of the Stannary Parliament for Cornwall encourages this thought, particularly within a Europe of regions.
**Local Government Commission for England**, *The Future Local Government of Cornwall – Draft Recommendations*, 1994

## 1995

**1118** The in-migrants [into Cornwall] have been characterized as middle class, middle-aged, middle-browed city dwellers with integration and assimilation being a one way process of urbanisation rather then ruralisation.
**Dept. of Sociology, Plymouth University**, *Movers and Stayers 1971/91*, 1995

**1119** ... Cornish rubbishspeak ... that concoction of a few computer fanatics, who among [other] things devised the form "Kammbronn" for the old Cornish town of Camborne ...

**James Whetter**, book review of *Out of the Ordinalia*, in *An Baner Kernewek* 81, August 1995

**1120** Had the revivalists of the 1920s decided to continue with Jenner's spelling, we should probably by now had been using something very like Kernuak [Modern Cornish].

**P. A. S. Pool**, *The Second Death of Cornish*, 1995

**1121** ... it is sometimes claimed that revived Middle Cornish is mediaeval, Catholic, pre-industrial and backward-looking, whereas Late Cornish is Protestant, industrial and modern. The argument is invalid. From the ideological point of view languages are completely neutral.

**Nicholas Williams**, *Cornish Today: An Examination of the Revived Language*, 1995

**1122** Those responsible for [National] Trust policy in this area [Mawnan Smith] seem to have forgotten its aims in the pursuit of making money. Thus they have betrayed its original ideals and harmed Cornwall and the Cornish people.

**Jeremy Jacobson**, 'Cornish Drives', in *An Baner Kernewek* 81, August 1995

**1123** Cornwall will be a wisht poorer place with his [Ken Phillipps'] passing.

**Simon Parker**, in *Western Morning News*, July 1995

**1124** If Cornwall wants to be heard in boardrooms around the world, we must do better. Without an effective single voice, Cornwall will continue to be short-changed in London and Brussels.

**Sir John Banham**, reported in *Western Morning News*, 5 October 1995

**1125** Throughout the media, whereas an Irish accent denotes struggle, origin and status in a U2/Bob Geldof sort of way, why doesn't the Cornish dialect give the same? ... There are plenty of 'Paddy Doyles' in Cornwall, but would Alan Parker make a film about their fiction?

**Alan M. Kent**, 'Realism in contemporary Cornish fiction', in *Peripheral Visions*, ed. Ian A. Bell, 1995

**1126** The Cornish conundrum poses a particular problem for regionalists. It is generally assumed that the Cornish would not wish to be part of any region other than Cornwall, which has a population of just 481,000 (including the Isles of Scilly). However, this is larger than the population of Corsica, Valle D'Aosta and other European regions ... Regionalism, whatever its form, is not the neat solution to problems of territorial administration... Cornwall should therefore be offered the option of becoming a county council with regional status.

    **Stephen Tindale**, *Devolution on Demand: Options for the English Regions and London*, 1995

1127    There must be some actual devolution
         for the Cornish to continue their evolution.
**Alan M. Kent**, *Out of the Ordinalia*, 1995

1128 A civilised society should be judged on the way it treats its minorities – whether Cornish or someone else.

    **Ranjit Sondhi**, at the Conference on Cornwall, 1995

# 1996

1129 In 1997 perhaps, another great army from Cornwall will assemble here [Greenwich], perhaps that event will be recorded for posterity, the names of heroes, not "traitors" will be proclaimed?

    **Bill Headdon**, 'Letter from Greenwich', in *An Baner Kernewek* 84, May 1996

1130 We feel that the Commission [for Racial Equality in Cornwall] should take into account all colours of racism in Cornwall, not merely black; there is blatant discrimination against Cornish people.

    **Ray Pascoe**, reported in *West Briton*, 11 July 1996

1131 So what are we, English or British? Or, to an Englishman, are both concepts one and the same thing? It's a terrible arrogance, but I suspect so. The Scots, Welsh, and Irish, even the Cornish, I suppose, have a narrower sense of cultural identity arising out of the ghosts of their vanquished pasts.

    **Ray Connolly**, 'State of the Nations', in *European*, 15-21 August 1996

1132 Those who insist on tinkering with Cornish language spellings really ought to leave place names alone; to respell them merely leads to outlandish versions which are unhistorical, unpoetic, and likely to alienate large sections of the reading public.

    **Donald R. Rawe**, in review of *Berdh Arnowyth Kernewek: Modern Cornish Poets*, An Baner Kernewek 83, February 1996

1133 The elevation [of Cornwall] from earldom to dukedom, and the gift of it to his [Edward III's] son, might appeal to Cornish pride and give the illusion that they were being granted some semblance of autonomy from direct

English rule.

**David Burnett**, A *Royal Duchy: A Portrait of the Duchy of Cornwall*, 1996

**1134** What is very clear in even a brief study of place names in Cornwall is that the vast majority are of Cornish, Celtic stock. Cornish is the predominant language in place names throughout Cornwall from the Land's End to the Tamar. Indeed, the Tamar makes a near perfect linguistic boundary.

**Graham Sandercock and Wella Brown**, *The Formation of Cornish Place Names*, 1996

**1135** As I headed for Cornwall I recalled Heather, at the café in Brixton, telling me, 'It's like another bloody country.'

**Nick Danziger**, *Danziger's Britain: a journey to the edge*, 1996

**1136** It has from time to time been the practice of the monarch to make grants of franchises of treasure troves to various individuals and bodies ... The principal bodies that are believed to hold valid treasure trove franchises are the Duchy of Lancaster, the Duchy of Cornwall and the Cities of London and Bristol.

***The Treasure Act 1996 Draft Code of Practice***, 1996

**1137** ... the Cornish Language is not just a question of phonemes and graphemes; it is part of a wider society, a society that is changing rapidly. It is because of this that the future of Cornish is far too important to be left entirely to the linguists.

**Bernard Deacon**, 'Language Revival and Language Debate: Modernity and Post modernity', in *Cornish Studies: Four*, ed. Philip Payton, 1996

**1138** The future of Cornwall must be based on the prescriptive and constitutional rights of the Cornish people to their own recognised and legitimate Parliament which has never been surrendered.

**Colin Murley, Ray Pascoe and Rod Nute** (eds.), *Cornwall: One of the Four Nations of Britain ...*, 1996

**1139** It is no coincidence that most European languages have their own word for Cornwall (but never for Hampshire or Rutland), as though it were a Scotland or a Wales, so that Cornwall's status is not merely of British but rather wider European significance.

**Philip Payton**, *Cornwall*, 1996

**1140** For outsiders, Cornwall is peace and tranquility, a haven to which one might retire from the mad rush of modern life; for insiders Cornwall is often poverty and

poor housing and a struggle to make ends meet in a low-wage economy.
**Philip Payton**, *Cornwall*, 1996

**1141** ... Cornwall has remained historiographically invisible, the National Curriculum affording Cornish schoolchildren few opportunities to learn about their own land, and with the local media seemingly unable to respond to all the possibilities that present themselves.
**Philip Payton**, *Cornwall*, 1996

**1142** Cornwall always was, and still is, a window to a wider world – something to be experienced profoundly at Ballowall on a fine clear summer's evening, standing on that ancient cairn and gazing westwards into the setting sun, with a hint of the Scillies on the horizon and the wide, calm blue sea beckoning enticingly towards Ireland and to Spain.
**Philip Payton**, *Cornwall*, 1996

**1143** ... there will always be debate as to the authenticity of modern Cornish, for whatever basis it takes, it is a revived language. No one can justifiably claim an unbroken link with the traditional Cornish which died around 1800 and which had been lingering for some time before that. The distinction between traditional Cornish and revived Cornish must always be stressed ... However, as we approach the millennium, the remarkable advance of modern, revived Cornish reaches maturity; one hundred years of progress building on the work of Jenner, Nance, Smith, Gendall, Retallack Hooper, Saunders, Brown and George puts Cornish on a footing comparable in vitality with the other Celtic languages and places Cornish in its rightful position amongst the languages of modern Europe.
**Graham Sandercock**, *A very brief history of the Cornish language*, 1996

**1144** It [St. Ives] was shaped for a way of life. For fishing, for people who lived cheek by jowl and worked together closely. Like a shell that's shaped round a living creature, and left empty when it dies.
**Jill Paton Walsh**, *The Serpentine Cave*, 1996

## 1997

**1145** The Cornish dialect is different from dialects of English because of the influence of Kernewek. It is this influence that Kernewek speakers and academics should tease out and use to make a bridge between the English speaking and Kernewek speaking communities in Cornwall.
**Pol Hodge**, *The Cornish Dialect and the Cornish Language*, 1997

**1146** Probably the greatest contribution to be made to Kernewek by the Cornish dialect is the wealth of phrases that reflect the wisdom and humour of our forefathers.

**Pol Hodge**, *The Cornish Dialect and the Cornish Language*, 1997

**1147** The C[ornish] N[ationalist] P[arty] is the sensible voice of the Cornish people. Of the sensible people. We recognise our geographical, cultural, historical position. We are a small nation in a peninsula of Great Britain. We do not seek our own parliament. An upgrading of our status within Great Britain, yes. County Council can be renamed Regional Council. We should be recognised as one of the constituent nations of the United Kingdom.

**James Whetter**, 'CNP Belongs to the 21ˢᵗ Century', in *An Baner Kernewek* 87, February 1997

**1148** ... often they [Cornish place names] have become so rubbed down, rubbing shoulders with English over the centuries, that some have become difficult.

**A. L. Rowse**, *Cornish Place Rhymes*, 1997

**1149** ... if Cornishness is important it is because it influences those who are not separatists.

**Jeffrey Stanyer**, 'The Janus-faced periphery: Cornwall and Devon in the twentieth century', in *Policy and Politics* 25, 1997

**1150** The Marchers from Cornwall of all ages and from all walks of life, arriving at Blackheath Saturday 21ˢᵗ June 1997

Remembering that our ancestors marched here 500 years ago both to protect their distinctive way of life and to challenge economic injustice

Conscious that in recent years Cornwall has once again not been treated fairly in proportion to our needs – particularly in comparison with the assistance rendered to our Celtic cousins in Wales, Northern Ireland and Scotland

Call upon our Members of Parliament to:
1. Press for the earliest possible establishment of a regional economic development agency devoted exclusively to tackling the economic problems of Cornwall and attracting inward investment. This agency to have its own dedicated budget and personnel and not to be controlled by any wider regional body embracing the more prosperous counties east of the Tamar.
2. Ensure the creation, as a result of the current Boundary Commission review, of a European Parliamentary constituency for the people of Cornwall alone.
3. Support the location of a new university campus in Cornwall.
4. Find means of making space available in the curriculum in State Schools in

Cornwall for the teaching of Cornish history, culture and the Cornish language.
**The Blackheath Declaration**, 1997

1151 Keskerdh Kernow 500 has had its effect; Cornwall has been affirmed to the outside world, but even more importantly we have affirmed it to ourselves.
**Brian Coombes**, 'Keskerdh Kernow 500: A Grand Bard's View', in *An Baner Kernewek* 89, August 1997

1152 Cornish Rebellion Traditional Bitter.
Brewed by **Redruth Brewery** to coincide with the Keskerdh Kernow march

1153    There'll always be voices around South Crofty
       And summer will come and go
       And the gorse will be hiding the Cornish heart
       'Neath a light that will always glow.
**Katie Williams**, 'South Crofty', in *An Baner Kernewek* 90, November 1997

# 1998

1154 The owners of South Crofty … have reached a point beyond which they are not prepared to go in terms of further investment in what they clearly see as a loss-making situation. It is with deep regret that the government is unable to commit public resources.
**Barbara Roche**, Industry minister, in House of Commons, 5 February 1998

1155 Cornish lads are fishermen and Cornish lads are miners too. But when the fish and tin are gone, what are the Cornish boys to do?
**Graffiti on wall outside South Crofty Mine**, c1998

1156 … if the young people go away, Cornwall will just become a place where people come to retire and die – England's burial ground.
**Mark Kaczmarek**, reported in *Cornwall Today*, April 1998

1157 Reality has to be suspended when the Cornish come to town. Instead, emotion takes over.
**David Hands**, in *The Times*, 20 April 1998

1158 … if you want to talk about regional rugby, try Cornwall: there is tradition, geographical identity, social expression. Would 35,000 follow an amorphous Wessex Warriors?
**David Hands**, in *The Times*, 20 April 1998

**1159** At any point in its [the twentieth century's] generally horrifying course Rowse can be found, articulate, vivid, controversial, sometimes brilliant, but never, never inert.

**Richard Ollard**, 'Memorial Address for Dr. Rowse', in *An Baner Kernewek* 92, May 1998

**1160** During the Middle Ages Cornwall had belonged to an international trading, linguistic and religious community, which the Reformation in England progressively severed it from. Anglicization narrowed the parameters of Cornish consciousness.

**Andrew C. Symons**, 'Two Smugglers and the Word', in *An Baner Kernewek* 92, May 1998

**1161** Crossing the border to Cornwall threatens to unpick not just English history, but British history as well.

**James Vernon**, 'Border Crossings: Cornwall and the English (imagi)nation', in *Imagining Nations*, ed. Geoffrey Cubitt, 1998

**1162** ... the Prince Albert Bridge stands as a steel monument to the indeterminate nature of the Cornish-English border, dramatically illustrating the impossibility of imagining where England ends and Cornwall begins.

**James Vernon**, 'Border Crossings: Cornwall and the English (imagi)nation', in *Imagining Nations*, ed. Geoffrey Cubitt, 1998

**1163** Cornwall is closed

Banner used by **Cornish Solidarity** in briefly closing the Tamar Bridge to press home Cornwall's need for Objective 1 status, 26 July 1998

**1164** Cornwall has a long and proud history of industry, innovation and enterprise. Its people are noted for their culture, identity, self-reliance and reliability. However, traditional skills have become obsolete, and there has been a loss of morale and a failure to utilise the full talents of the workforce. In many ... communities there is real poverty and desperation. Cornwall today is poorer than many inner city areas.

**Cornwall Health Authority Report**, 1998

**1165** No one locally has done more [than Ken Phillipps] to keep a knowledge of dialect alive and provide it with academic respectability.

**Andrew C. Symons**, 'She, 'Er and 'Un', in *An Baner Kernewek* 94, November 1998

# 1999

**1166** Convince yourselves you love tourism because it is the future of Cornwall.

**Cairns Boston,** in *Observer Supplement,* 1 January 1999

**1167** The Cornish are a nation because of Blackheath and Hingston Down and the Prayer Book uprising of 1549, because of the Stannary Parliament, because of the Cornish in Moonta and Montana, because of Richard Trevithick and Humphrey Davy. The Cornish are a nation ... by reason of the River Tamar, by recollection of battles long ago and pride in the present valour of their rugby team, because of religious dissent, because of fortitude in the face of economic adversity.

*The Cornish and the Council of Europe Framework Convention for the Protection of National Minorities,* 1999

**1168** Cornwall remains as distinct from the South West of England in terms of religious attendance as it does from England in general.

*The Cornish and the Council of Europe Framework Convention for he Protection of National Minorities,* 1999

**1169** This scattering [of Cornish men and women] has produced a Cornish Diaspora which is unequalled by any county in England.

*The Cornish and the Council of Europe Framework Convention for the Protection of National Minorities,* 1999

**1170** ... we do not consider that the people of Cornwall constitute a 'national minority'.

**Home Office,** *U.K. Report on the Council of Europe Framework Convention for the Protection of National Minorities,* 1999

**1171** Where once the Cornish could flee the invader's fire and sword, now there is no hiding place from his chequebook and pen.

**John Angarrack,** *Breaking the Chains,* 1999

**1172** ... large council estates... intended for Londoners ... have now become colonized by young Cornish families who have been forced out of their village and coastal communities by wealthy incomers. These large estates, which mushroomed all over Cornwall in the 70s and 80s, have become the Cornish equivalent of American ghettos or South African shanty towns, places where low paid locals are shut away out of sight.

**John Angarrack,** *Breaking the Chains,* 1999

**1173** In Cornwall, to look upon yourself as Cornish is to accept a certain way of life. It is not possible to be both Cornish and English for they are two different ethnicities with different national origins. It is possible to be born in Cornwall and be ethnic English; if this is the case then one forms part of the majority. Conversely, it is possible to be born elsewhere and be accepted as Cornish; if this is so then that person forms part of the minority.

**John Angarrack**, *Breaking the Chains*, 1999

**1174** His ['Q"s] flow of rhythm and rhyme is impeccable; in our own day perhaps only Charles Causley has matched it.

**Donald R. Rawe**, "Famous Cornish Poems 4 – The Harbour of Fowey by 'Q' ", in *An Baner Kernewek* 95, February 1999

**1175** On the basis of the evidence presented in this study it appears that most of Cornwall retained until 1500 a secure Celtic culture comprising language, oral and written literature, and Catholic Christianity. English pressure from the towns, the Reformation, and social disruption following the military activities of 1479, 1549 and the 1640s caused a collapse of that unity.

**Andrew C. Symons**, 'Models of Language Transfer: Pt. 2', in *An Baner Kernewek* 97, August 1999

**1176** I hate the Cornish … I hate their poxy language which they make such a fuss about … their fancy foreign food – like clotted cream – which makes the place stink, and I hate their fatuous demands to be treated as a nation.

**Giles Coren**, 'A Truro lass can eclipse me any day', in *The Times*, 13 August 1999

**1177** For many, Cornwall at the end of the Millennium is emerging from a long paralysis, a paralysis born of the swift, utterly traumatic collapse of the Cornish mining economy in the last century but also a loss of much longer historical duration in which Cornish people have been estranged from their linguistic, literary, even constitutional roots.

**Philip Payton**, *1649–1751 The Cornish Eclipse*, 1999

### Early 21st Century

**1178** Assembly Now!

**Graffiti on the former Aver's Garage at Redruth**, early 21st century

# 2000

**1179** We, the People of Cornwall, must have a greater say in how we are governed. We need a Cornish Assembly that can set the right democratic priorities for Cornwall and provide a stronger voice for our communities in Britain, in Europe and throughout the wider world.

**Declaration for a Cornish Assembly**, 2000

**1180** It is intrinsic in the nature of the Union [the United Kingdom] that we have multiple political allegiances: we can comfortably be Scottish and British or Cornish and British or Geordie and British or Pakistani and British.

**Tony Blair**, 'Pakistani or Cornish, we're [the] same at heart', in *The Times*, 12 February 2000

**1181** For its relatively small size, Cornwall has been imagined and written about perhaps more than any other equivalent territory within Western Europe.

**Alan M. Kent**, *The Literature of Cornwall*, 2000

**1182** 'Q' opened a wound through which has seeped a plethora of writers who have viewed the archetypal wisdom of Cornwall as inconvenient and have superseded it with a romantic escapism tailored to the shallow sophistication of the urban market.

**Andrew C. Symons**, 'Writings of War and Revolution', in *An Baner Kernewek* 99, February 2000

**1183**     A hundred Banners waving over Kernow,
A hundred quarterlies, spanning these twenty-five years…
It is not only those gigantic names,
Great heroes of their times and ours as well –
Trevithick, Davy, Borlase and Carew,
Jenner, Nance and Rowse – who built the tower
Of Cornwall's recognition and her pride:
We too in all our quiet persistent ways
Contribute, brick by brick and block by patient block,
To raise that edifice, upon which we proclaim,
Waving our host of banners, Kernow's name and fame.

**Donald R. Rawe**, 'An Baner Kernwek 100', in *An Baner Kernewek* 100, May 2000

**1184** The varieties of present-day revived Cornish may be likened to dialects, interestingly formed not on geographical or social bases, but upon learners' preferences, needs and loyalties.

**Kenneth MacKinnon**, *An Independent Academic Study on Cornish…*, 2000

**1185** A vision of Cornwall tomorrow is of a land of sustained and sustainable prosperity, of an enviable environment in which to live, learn, work and play, of a proud people who know that their identity is their greatest strength and who are never afraid to shout: Cornwall For Ever! Kernow Bys Vyken!

**Philip Payton** (ed), *Cornwall For Ever! Kernow Bys Vyken!* 2000

**1186** If Cornwall is to be successful in times to come, and if Cornwall and its people are to keep their Cornishness, it will need all the optimism, confidence, determination and skill that you – our next generation – can muster. You will all come to carry an important responsibility for preserving the Cornish way of looking at life, the Cornish language and dialect, the Cornish culture and identity, and the very appearance of Cornwall.

**HRH The Prince of Wales, Duke of Cornwall**, in *Cornwall For Ever! Kernow Bys Vyken!*

**1187** Beyond the familiar Scotland-Ireland-Wales triad there now lies the question of Cornwall, and of the very small territories, the Isle of Man, Jersey and Guernsey, which were simply ignored by traditional all-British political reflection ... No one ignores them now.

**Tom Nairn**, *After Britain: New Labour and the Return of Scotland*, 2000

**1188** Cornwall was the automatic choice. There was never any question of creating Eden anywhere else, for an arms-length list of historic, symbolic, economic and practical reasons.

**Tim Smit**, in Martin Jackson, *Eden: The First Book*, 2000

**1189** The Cornish have no desire to work, possessing less ambition to better themselves than a rich woman's poodle, the rich woman being the EU which keeps them raking in the soggy chips by way of outrageous farm subsidies.

**Petronella Wyatt**, 'Cornish loathing', in *The Spectator*, 24 June 2000

**1190** Cornwall is a unique part of Britain with its own history, geography and culture. I hope this book [*Cornwall For Ever! Kernow Bys Vyken!*] will give all of you a little extra pride and encourage your interest in your country.

**Charles, Duke of Cornwall**, Truro, 29 June 2000, reported in *West Briton* 6 July

**1191** If the future King of England can think of Cornwall as a country (and we apologise for misquoting him last week) why do so many others feel able to

dismiss us with a wave of an accountant's scalpel.
Editorial, in **West Briton**, 13 July 2000

**1192** Cornish people are quite used to being on the receiving end of those who wish to unburden their prejudices. Most sensible Cornish people have learnt to humour these people and calmly to suggest medical attention and therapy.
**Andrew George MP**, in press release, 12 July 2000

**1193** Cornwall is a distinct nation and region of Britain and Europe. It has a unique Celtic cultural heritage and language which has been misrepresented to the world as English by English organisations funded by the British government. We declare that, in order to survive as an indigenous national minority, the Cornish people will be best served in the future by developing their tradition of an independent, national parliament based on the existing constitutional position of the Duchy of Cornwall and the Stannaries as is their right under international human rights law.
**Cornish Stannary Parliament**, *Declaration for negotiation with the British government*, July 2000

**1194** Leslie Rowse got it absolutely spot-on in the preface to his *Poems of Cornwall and America* in 1967: 'in the secrecy of poetry it is possible to write one's innermost autobiography, as Hardy found'.
**Charles Causley**, in letter to *An Baner Kernewek* 101, August 2000

**1195** Always remember, Cornwall is a nation, with or without outside recognition. I see nothing wrong in the existence of two Cornish parties which may express different approaches to policies ...
**Brian Coombes**, 'The Cornish Banner/C.N.P.', in *An Baner Kernewek* 101, August 2000

**1196** Cornwall's cultural continuity has received scant recognition from historians or students of literature, yet is one of the most significant in Britain.
**Andrew Symons**, 'The Poetic Vision 1549-1980', in *An Baner Kernewek* 101, August 2000

**1197** If it wishes to gain maximum access to resources, Cornwall needs to insist that it is perfectly possible to be a proudly independent 'region within a region' (with its own unique cultural heritage) while remaining part of the wider South-West.
**Cornwall County Council**, *Cornwall Heritage and Culture Strategy*, 2000

**1198** Those who love Cornwall, whether Cornish by ancestry or not, appear to value Cornish distinctiveness more than was the case fifty years ago.

**Sebastian Halliday**, 'Epilogue', in F. E. Halliday, *A History of Cornwall*, 2000

**1199** The Reformation in Cornwall, issuing forth from London, was not just an attack upon a defenceless people, but a determined destruction of a Euro-Celtic religious and cultural community.

**Andrew Symons**, 'Aspects of the Mermaid', in *An Baner Kernewek* 102, November 2000

## 2001

**1200** Cornwall had the highest proportion of widows to its total female population of any county in 1851.

**John Rule**, 'The Misfortunes of the Mine ...', in *Cornish Studies* 9, ed. Philip Payton, 2001

**1201** Hallelujah – Camborne and Redruth are saved at a stroke, our devastated post-industrial wasteland instantly transformed into a do-it-yourself Milton Keynes kit.

'Forget that scruffy old mine, boy ... it'll spoil the view! Hurry up, there's a traffic jam of carpetbaggers at Pool crossroads.

**Kevin Bennetts** of Cornish Solidarity on the South West Regional Development Authority's proposals for Camborne-Redruth, in *West Briton*, 11 January 2001

**1202** It's cool to be Cornish – it's cool to be counted.

**Bert Biscoe**, in *Western Morning News*, 17 April 2001

**1203** A baker's shop is not an obvious place to find an understanding of Celtic culture, yet food and the ways in which it is prepared and eaten often has much to say about the history of a people. The Cornish pasty is more eloquent than most.

**Alistair Moffat**, *The Sea Kingdoms*, 2001

**1204** It is a sad truth that divisions amongst Cornish speakers do discourage individuals and councils... from using Cornish.

**Brian Coombes**, 'Aberfal and Falmouth: some thoughts on names in Cornish', in *An Baner Kernewek* 104, May 2001

**1205** The formation of the Stannaries, followed by the creation of the Duchy, helped to give identity to the Cornish, and to mark them out as different, not just in character and background, but legally, through a recognised status enshrined in the laws and constitution of the English nation, of which the county became, perhaps reluctantly, a part.

**J. A. Buckley**, *Medieval Cornish Stannary Charters*, 2001

**1206** Cornwall is a different case. It has the characteristics typical of peripheral areas: a feeling of neglect and an experience of deprivation recognised by EU Objective 1 status – as well as by aspirations to nationhood.

**Mark Sandford and Paul McQuail**, *Unexplored Territory: Elected Regional Assemblies in England*, 2001

**1207** The Prime Minister has committed the Government to 'doing devolution where people want it'. Cornwall has given voice to its desire, with 50,000 people signing the Assembly Declaration, seeking a referendum.

**Bert Biscoe**, 'Devolution will make Cornwall richer for all', in *Western Morning News*, 17 October 2001

**1208** We overwhelmingly rejected the idea of a Cornish assembly. We feel that Cornwall has a distinctive nature but because of its distinctive nature we felt Cornwall could contribute to a wider region, not cut itself off by going for a nationalistic Cornish assembly.

**Fiona Bruce**, secretary of the Labour Party of Cornwall, reported in *West Briton* 15 November 2001

**1209** It is a great petition, but for many who signed it, it is an indication of the support they feel for devolving power rather than necessarily saying they want a Cornish Assembly.

**Candy Atherton MP**, in parliamentary debate 12 December, reported in *West Briton*, 20 December 2001

**1210** Cornwall's case is founded upon what Mr. Prescott has described as 'the strongest regional identity in the UK'.

**Bert Biscoe**, 'Time to devolve, say the people', in *Western Daily Press*, 17 December 2001

**1211** The Government in London is raping the county fiscally.
**Kevin Cahill**, 2001

**1212** In his [one correspondent's] view Eden would attract so many wealthy visitors in Cornwall that they would buy up all the houses and raise prices to a level unaffordable on Cornish wages, which are among the lowest in Britain and indeed in much of Europe. This is a difficult argument because it is in essence true; but then it always has been.

**Tim Smit**, *Eden*, 2001

**1213** They [a Breton couple] assumed we were from Cornwall. Why else would we be there [at a Pardon near Plogoff]? He stressed the connections with the Cornish saints ... I think they wanted us to be Cornish, or Welsh, so that they wouldn't feel we were the enemy, the imperialist equivalent to the French.

**Helen Drysdale**, *Mother Tongues: Travels through Tribal Europe*, 2001

**1214**    English Heritage are not so "Choughed",
        Having been "Stuffed" by Operation Chough!
Headline on **Cornish Stannary Parliament** website, accessed April 2001

# 2002

**1215** In present day Cornwall it is easier to self-deceive than absorb the fact that the authorities have systematically lied and cheated in order to articulate circumstances which create the impression that the Cornish nation has only ever been an insignificant sub-division of some awe-inspiring, all-powerful, fully homogenous, fixed and eternal England.

**John Angarrack**, *Our Future is History*, 2002

**1216** Asking London to solve Cornish problems is like relying on an arsonist to put out his own fire.

**John Angarrack**, *Our Future is History*, 2002

**1217** Winning a Cornish Assembly is about 'cutting Cornwall in' to a partnership of the nations and regions of the British Isles, Europe and the wider world.

**Dick Cole**, at the launch of *Devolution for One and All*, March 2002

**1218** There is a new confidence in Cornwall; a hunger for success; a desire to see Cornwall take her place in the world. It is inspiring to be in Cornwall at the moment, and the Cornish Assembly is an essential ingredient in the formula that will attract our young people to stay and build their lives here.

**Bert Biscoe**, at the launchof *Devolution for One and All*, March 2002

**1219** Although today the abandoned mines are not icons of the Celtic revival in Cornwall in the same way that the Cornish language and the annual gathering of Cornish bards ... may be, there is no doubt that the remains of native industry are embraced by revivalists, and underscore a Cornish sense of

ethnic difference …
> **Amy Hale**, 'Whose Celtic Cornwall?', in *Celtic Geographies*, ed. David C. Harvey, 2002

**1220** The spreading use of Cornish on business signs, house names and tourist attractions shows the parallel nature of private enthusiasm and business engagement with an identity widely endorsed beyond the numerically tiny language revival movements.
> **John G. Robb**, 'Geography of Celtic appropriations', in *Celtic Geographies*, 2002

**1221** The Cornish are different. Their language is different and so is their dialect, and some things peculiar to the Cornish psyche – the idiosyncratic humour, the pride, the in-your-face irreverence – simply cannot be expressed in standard English.
> **Simon Parker**, 'Charles Lee – A Critical View', in *Chasing Tales*, 2002

**1222** If this [government proposals to expand devolution to the English regions] is about democracy – which it is – the Government has an obligation to allow everyone in Cornwall to fully consider the arguments for and against a Cornish Assembly, and then vote in a properly constituted referendum.
> **Dick Cole**, in *West Briton*, 16 May 2002

**1223** When the chough returns, it shows that Cornwall is resurgent.
> **Les Merton**, in *Independent*, 22 May 2002

**1224** Dehwelans 2002 emphasized that distinctiveness in culture, language, history and identity which makes us what we are and will be, and gives us growing confidence in ourselves.
> **Ann Trevenen Jenkin**, in *West Briton*, 30 May 2002

**1225** The Cornish voice is still not being heard, Cornishness is not being recognised, and despite lip service being paid to our cause, there is still much with which Michael Joseph and Thomas Flamank could readily identify themselves, were they alive today.
> **Nigel Hicks**, at St. Keverne, June 2002

**1226** Which is best for Cornwall? Is it Senedh Kernow of 40 to 50 members representing 500,000 people in Cornwall, or a South West Assembly with just 25 to 35 members representing five million in the South West, with perhaps two or three members for Cornwall?
> **Phil Rendle**, in *West Briton*, 27 June 2002

**1227** Kernuak becomes Britain's latest official language.

Headline in *The Times*, 10 August 2002

**1228** Cornwall's new confidence is about success ... and, for Cornwall today, failure is not an option – we've been there, done that and worn the tee-shirt out polishing our melancholy!

**Bert Biscoe**, in speech to the Plenary of the Cornish Constitutional Convention, 17 August 2002

**1229** After careful consideration and with the help of the results of an independent academic study on the language commissioned by the government, we have decided to recognise Cornish as falling under Part II of the European Charter for Regional or Minority Languages.

**Nick Raynsford**, Local Government and Regions Minister, in answer to a Parliamentary Question, 5 November 2002 [Answers.com]

**1230** Part of the explanation for the 'Trelawny's Army' phenomenon, the passionate and sustained support for the Cornish team in the county championship, was that there were in fact few institutional opportunities for the collective expression of Cornishness.

**Philip Payton**, ... *a vision of Cornwall*, 2002

**1231** ... whatever their particular interpretations, all [the organisations sharing the Celtic Revivalist vision] insist that Cornwall is at root a Celtic nation, that this Celticity has been denied or obscured as a result of external influences, and that it is the duty of contemporary Revivalists to restore, foster, cherish and proclaim Celtic nationhood.

**Philip Payton**, ... *a vision of Cornwall*, 2002

**1232** ... Caliban – together with his enchanted isle – is a metaphor for Cornwall.

**Philip Payton**, ... *a vision of Cornwall*, 2002

**1233** ... Rowse was an individual of multiple and sometimes conflicting identities. He was Cornish by birth... English by conviction... Celtic by temperament... Transatlantic by accident.

**Philip Payton**, ... *a vision of Cornwall*, 2002

**1234** ... the decision of most Cornish people to back the King in 1642 ...

should be viewed within the context of [an] ancient pattern of ethnic antagonism.
**Mark Stoyle**, *West Britons*, 2002

**1235** Of all the Celtic peoples of the British Isles, the Cornish are those whose voices have been most effectively drowned out by traditional, Anglocentric historiography. For centuries speakers and writers of English have gone out of their way to pour cold water on the suggestion that Cornwall might be anything other than an integral part of England.
**Mark Stoyle**, *West Britons*, 2002

**1236** It is important to recognize that [the] army [that conquered most of South-west England for the King in 1642-43] was composed almost exclusively of Cornishmen and was frequently referred to, by observers on both sides, as 'the Cornish Army'.
**Mark Stoyle**, *West Britons*, 2002

**1237** Rowse was the intellectual and spiritual heir of Richard Carew.
**Mark Stoyle**, *West Britons*, 2002

**1238** There is a strong case to be made that a distinctive Cornish identity exists. The levels of self-identity ... described, plus the distinctive features outlined, suggest a regional identity that may be qualitatively different from any other in England. If 'depth of identity' were to automatically map directly on to strength of political devolution, it is likely that a Cornish Assembly could expect fewer powers than Wales or Scotland, but a South-West regional assembly would have very thin powers indeed.
**Mark Sandford**, *The Cornish Question*, 2002

**1239** People don't take it [Cornish identity] seriously. People think it's a joke, and being Irish, I'm sensitive to that ... In Bristol there's no anti-Irish prejudice because they reserve all their hatred for the Welsh, often on the basis of total ignorance of the culture ... And something similar probably happens towards Cornwall.
**Anonymous**, quoted in *The Cornish Question*, 2002

**1240** ... it [Mebyon Kernow] is a serious and committed presence on the Cornish scene with potential for growth.
**Simon Henig and Lewis Baston**, *The Political Map of Britain*, 2002

# 2003

**1241** England's far southwestern corner, Cornwall is as Celtic as Britanny [sic] … [and] today still possesses a proudly independent spirit, a significant and surprisingly serious separatist movement mustering under its black and white banner and nurturing the Cornish language.

> **Charlie Godfrey-Faussett**, *Footprint England Handbook*, 2003

**1242** The campaign for a Cornish Assembly is the irresistible force of the early 21st century.

> **Dick Cole**, at the Mebyon Kernow Annual Conference, 27 September 2003

# 2004

**1243** They [Cornish hard-rock miners in the first half of the 19th century] became a corps of international tramping artisans, playing a central role in the exploitation of mineral deposits around the world.

> **Eric Richards**, *Britannia's Children: emigration from England, Scotland, Wales and Ireland since 1600*, 2004

**1244** Breton and Cornish were closely related and remained mutually comprehensible languages until the 18th century; and it was surely a homesick Cornishman who found a new home in the south-west of Brittany and decided to call it 'Cornouaille'.

> **Robert Winder**, *Bloody Foreigners: the story of immigration to Britain*, 2004

**1245** … Cornish … died a couple of hundred years ago; efforts to rekindle it have been damaged by infighting among the kindlers.

> **Mark Abley**, *Spoken Here: travels among threatened languages*, 2004

**1246** The [Cornish] language is an integral part of the rich culture of Cornwall which is at the heart of its regional distinctiveness.

> ***Strategy for the Cornish Language***, 2004

**1247** … the Cornish family is believed to be 'special', closer, more kin-orientated. The truth of this is less important than the stubborn belief that it is so.

> **Bernard Deacon**, *The Cornish Family*, 2004

**1248** Although Cornish associations are not meant to be political organisations, by educating their members to acknowledge their ancestry as 'Cornish' and not 'English' they are nonetheless strengthening the case for the

Cornish to be recognised as a national minority within the United Kingdom.
**Bernard Deacon**, *The Cornish Family*, 2004

**1249** ... partly in response to the everyday deluge of Anglicisation, Cornwall and its people, despite the fears of observers in the 1970s, became more 'Celtic' as the millennium reached its end.
**Bernard Deacon**, *The Cornish Family*, 2004

**1250** If your family name is Williams, Richards or Thomas, then the likelihood that your ancestors were Cornish-speaking is as high as, if not higher than, if you have a Cornish locational name of the Tre, Pol and Pen variety.
**Bernard Deacon**, *The Cornish Family*, 2004

**1251** [Charles] Henderson battled to capture the human story of Cornwall. [J.C.] Tregarthen fought to secure the dignity and freedom of nature, whether on the moors and cliff tops or in the hearts of his people. Both battles continue.
**Bert Biscoe**, introduction to new edition of J. C. Tregarthen's, *John Penrose*, 2004

**1252** The Manx face the same dilemma as the communities on the Outer Hebrides, in the Galway Gaeltacht, in west Wales and Cornwall. How far can they go, and how far will they be allowed to go, towards resisting the flow of English immigrants, second-home owners and pensioners without slipping into outright racism?
**Marcus Tanner**, *The Last of the Celts*, 2004

**1253** With their dingy cafés, cheap, 'pound-stretcher' stores and signal lack of shops selling luxuries or Cornish cream teas, these towns [Redruth and Camborne] provide a more accurate portrait of Cornish life today than the 'typically Cornish' seaside villages with their New Age bookshops full of literature on Cornwall's Arthurian legends.
**Marcus Tanner**, *The Last of the Celts*, 2004

**1254** Anglicanism in Cornwall became simply a vehicle for anglicisation. All that Protestantism achieved in cultural terms was the closure of the old springs of Cornish culture.
**Marcus Tanner**, *The Last of the Celts*, 2004

**1255** [In Brittany], as in Cornwall and Wales, the effects of the English invasion are mostly negative.

Marcus Tanner, *The Last of the Celts*, 2004

**1256** Irish, Welsh and Cornish lived on in ghost form among many of the anglophones who did not know those older languages but whose English was certainly shaped by them.
Marcus Tanner, *The Last of the Celts*, 2004

**1257** There are other ways of protecting the identity of Cornwall and the Isle of Man that do not require... linguistic necromancy.
Marcus Tanner, *The Last of the Celts*, 2004

**1258** There is a sense that the Methodist Church is the Church of Cornwall, because it's a rebellion against the Church of England, which was of course imposed upon us as an alien Church ... and ... is still fulfilling that function.
Andrew Phillips, in a CAVA interview, January 2004 [Kayleigh Milden, 'Are You Church Or Chapel?', in *Cornish Studies Twelve*, ed. Philip Payton, 2004]

**1259** ... there's a plague of Methodist buildings all over Cornwall.
Julyan Drew, in a CAVA interview, March 2004 [Kayleigh Milden, 'Are You Church Or Chapel?', in *Cornish Studies Twelve*, ed. Philip Payton, 2004]

**1260** Chapel was something I had to get through, yet the hymnsinging was sweet and harmonious... I'm eternally grateful to those rather boring services; they grounded me in the poetry of the Authorised Version, Wesleyan hymns, and lilting Cornish speech.
D. M. Thomas, author's note in programme for *Hell Fire Corner*, April 2004

**1261** Locals only!
Graffiti on Portreath harbour wall, October 2004

**1262** Is Cornwall the new Soho?
*Media Week*, 23 November 2004

**1263** Cornwall's past is its future.
Sir Neil Cossons, in *West Briton*, 2 December 2004

**1264** The Cornish flag is an important part of people's identity, and we would welcome any government directive to treat it the same way as national flags.

**Karl Roberts**, Carrick District Council, reported in *West Briton*, 9 December 2004

**1265** It is … entirely a matter for the relevant local planning authority to determine whether St. Piran's flag should be permitted or whether they consider it is necessary to take enforcement action.

**Keith Hill**, week ending 25 December 2004, in *Cornish Nation*, January 2005

**1266** The occupants of the carriage fell silent in sympathy as the train rumbled on. Conversation didn't begin again until they were crossing the Tamar, when someone drawled, "'Ere, got your passports 'ave 'ee?" The light-hearted remark relieved the tension and soon there was an animated buzz of conversation as passengers began questioning one another about their destinations. Cornwall was working its old magic. Before long people were swapping life histories and discovering they had something in common. The frosty English reserve which had prevailed as far as Plymouth melted away and Cornish curiosity took over.

**Cyril Hart**, *Sam's War*, 2004

**1267**    Freedom for Cornwall now!
United Kingdom out of Cornwall!

**Lisa Simpson**, The Simpsons' Christmas Message, Channel 4 Television, 25 December 2004

# AUTHOR INDEX

## (references are to quotation numbers)

# SUBJECT INDEX

## (references are to quotation numbers)

Eadulf 8

economy (*see also* regeneration) 388, 570, 838, 876, 938, 1022, 1031, 1033, 1140,1150, 1164

Eden Project 1188, 1212

education 284, 585, 637, 699, 771, 781, 787, 813, 889, 902, 1092, 1141, 1150

Edward, Duke of Cornwall 35

Egbert 2, 4, 8

Eisteddfod 543

Elizabeth I 81

emigration (*see also* diaspora) 281, 340, 355, 370–372, 375, 407, 420, 431, 434, 585, 725, 799, 834, 892, 966, 994, 1004, 1156, 1243

'emmets' (*see also* 'foreigners', in-migration, strangers, tourism and tourists) 957, 1013

employment 845, 876

engine-houses 434, 439, 528, 633, 710, 803, 1061, 1219

England & the English (*see also* Saxons) 13, 24–25, 30, 39–52, 58–59, 65–66, 77, 81, 88, 123, 133, 191, 237, 294, 325, 338, 414, 417, 455, 479, 491, 509, 542, 556, 558, 560, 603, 606, 619, 630, 632, 662, 668, 678–679, 684, 686, 692, 725–726, 733–734, 742, 760, 762, 766, 786, 793, 795, 800–803, 805, 810, 813, 816, 819, 823, 827–828, 833, 836–838, 842, 848–849, 856, 858, 860, 872, 876, 878, 896–897, 900, 909, 914, 924, 929, 936–937, 943, 945, 961, 963–964, 978, 987, 990, 992, 1002–1004, 1011, 1024, 1036–1037, 1045, 1052, 1070, 1097, 1111, 1116, 1131, 1156, 1160–1162, 1168–1169, 1173, 1191, 1193, 1205, 1213, 1215, 1233, 1235, 1238, 1248–1249, 1252, 1254–1255, 1266

English Civil War 97–98, 101–118, 120, 129, 137, 528, 588, 671, 752,1234, 1236

English Heritage 1214

English language 34, 46, 49, 54, 58, 60, 62, 64, 67, 69, 75, 88, 100, 130, 134–135, 146–147, 152, 177, 188, 191, 202, 208, 237, 356, 393, 478, 574, 622, 708, 740, 852, 970, 1077, 1112, 1145–1146, 1148, 1256

ethnicity (see also difference, national identity, territorial status) 489, 861, 1029, 1054, 1128, 1173, 1219, 1234

European Charter for Regional or Minority Languages 1229

European Union/Parliament 962, 1023, 1080, 1150, 1189

Exeter 13, 302

Fal 744

Falmouth 147, 239

Feock 177

ferries 221

fishermen and fishing 29, 56, 68, 71, 172, 277, 291, 346, 385, 428, 460, 502, 564, 584, 719, 883, 1080, 1101, 1155

Flamank, Thomas 809, 1225

flora 836

folklore 532, 689

'foreigners'/'up country' folk (*see also* 'emmets', in-migration, strangers, tourism and tourists) 327, 368, 685, 693–694, 704–705, 742, 776, 791, 851, 901, 909, 978, 991, 996, 1078, 1084

Gendall, Richard 1143

George, Ken 1143

Glasney College 781, 970

Goldsithney 170

Gorran 723

Gorsedd 546, 558, 625, 634, 643, 656, 664, 680, 746, 770, 782, 785, 932, 940, 1219

graffiti 1037, 1057, 1155, 1178, 1261

Grampound 259

granite 570

Great Western Railway 493

Grigson, Geoffrey 731

Gulval 152

Gwavas, William 352

Gweek 354

Gwennap Pit 200, 204, 296, 318, 395

Gwithian 189, 465, 617